The American Highway

The American Highway

THE HISTORY AND CULTURE OF ROADS IN THE UNITED STATES

by William Kaszynski

McFarland & Company, Inc., Publishers
Jefferson, North Carolina, and London

Library of Congress Cataloguing-in-Publication Data

Kaszynski, William, 1953–
    The American highway : the history and culture of roads in the
United States / by William Kaszynski.
       p.   cm.
    Includes index.
    ISBN 0-7864-0822-7 (illustrated case binding : 50# alkaline paper)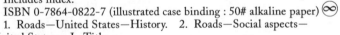
    1. Roads—United States—History.   2. Roads—Social aspects—
United States.   I. Title.
HE355.K33   2000
388.1'0973—dc21   00-56060
                                                       CIP

British Library cataloguing data are available

Cover images ©2000 Digital Vision

Manufactured in the United States of America

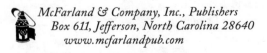

McFarland & Company, Inc., Publishers
   Box 611, Jefferson, North Carolina 28640
    www.mcfarlandpub.com

To my parents,
whose many family vacations
sparked my interest in highway travel,

and Yvonne,
for her support
during the writing of *The American Highway*

Contents

Preface

For most Americans commuting on our nation's high-speed corridors, there is little to remind of us of how arduous overland travel must have been for our forebears a century or so ago. The highway of today dominates the landscape, seeming to tame nature itself as ribbons of concrete scale mountain ranges and cross miles of waterways. On occasion, one might find a rare picture of an early motorist trapped on a muddy country road in order to begin to appreciate how far human ground transportation has progressed since the days of the horse and carriage.

More than two millennia ago, the ancient Romans were master architects of roads, aqueducts, and other monuments of scale. With the exception of the Incas' extensive system of roads, road building was virtually abandoned after the fall of the Roman Empire until approximately 1800, as travel by water remained the most available and economical means of transportation. The young American republic made some early attempts at establishing a navigable system of roads, but the rail and ships using steam power and sail postponed again the development of roads. By the late 1800s, however, streets in major cities were improved with paving using cobblestones, wooden blocks, and brick. Serious efforts at road construction coincided with the discovery of oil and its byproducts and the invention of the internal combustion engine-on-wheels. The French, already the world leader in production by the late 1890s, dubbed the strange new contraption the "automobile," and the word itself quickly spread to the United States and elsewhere.

The American experience in the development of modern roads is an exciting yet little-known story. First, there were the planners, engineers, and countless laborers who scraped paths through farmers' fields and over inhospitable terrain. Groups of ordinary citizens and local, state and federal officials coordinated the planning and location of highway routes, establishing a nationwide system of highway numbering, marking and road signs. Political and social factors, including wars and economic depression, also influenced the vast network of the roads and highways of today. Finally, there are the many businesses started by enterprising entrepreneurs with nothing more than a vision and a few dollars in their pockets that provided fuel, food, and lodging for the weary traveler, some faithfully serving motorists through several generations.

This work is a history of the evolvement of our nation's system of roads and superhighways during the past 100 or so years. The first decades of the 20th century saw the infant automobile and tourism industry take hold. Following World War I, the rapid proliferation of the auto forced the federal government to plan the first national network of hard-surfaced roads since the early 1800s, called "federal-aid" highways, with help from the states. As America's love affair with the auto continued through the Roaring Twenties and the Great Depression, these highways quickly became outdated. After the Second World War, pleasure travel and

1

auto production made a quantum leap, renewing pre-war calls for a modern system to meet the growing army of cars and trucks crowding America's highways. In the 1950s, President Dwight Eisenhower, along with other politicians and business leaders, enacted legislation establishing an interstate freeway system which has become the backbone of the nation's ground transportation.

Today, highway planners are designing safer highways that complement the natural surroundings with minimal impact on wildlife habitat. Historic highways and bridges are being saved and restored to original condition thanks to the efforts of preservation groups as the public becomes more aware of their unique role in our nation's social and transportation history. Highways will no doubt continue to serve as well as entertain the American motorist, well into the future.

This book contains a visual record of over 300 rare photographs and charts, drawn from the National Archives, the Federal Highway Administration, corporate and other sources, and the author's own collection. The author would like to give special thanks to the following individuals and corporations who have contributed materials that have made this book possible:

• Richard F. Weingroff, George Hay, Anne Barsanti, and Kandace Studzinski, Federal Highway Administration.

• David J. Hensing, American Association of State Highway and Transportation Officials.

• Barbara Crystal, American Automobile Association.

• Jovietta Mecenas, Julia Konstantinovsky, and D. Maia Huang, Chevron Corporation.

• Kathy Triebel, Phillips Petroleum Company.

• Mona Kowalczyk and Mike Miotski, Mobil Corporation.

• H. R. Hutchins, Shell Oil Company.

• Walter H. Williams, Texaco, Inc.

• Kirk Dougherty, Greyhound Lines, Inc.

• Jack Graham, Ethyl Corporation.

• Lisa G. Domene, KFC Corporation.

• Tonya Lind, Dairy Queen Restaurants, Inc.

• Charles "Chip" Rosencrans, Stuckey's Corporation.

• Ted H. Hustead and Bill Hustead, Wall Drug Store.

• Bill Chapin, Rock City, Inc.

• Meramec Caverns.

• John J. Wallace, Connecticut DOT.

• Christine J. Baker, Pennsylvania Turnpike Commission.

• Joanne Domka, General Motors Media Archives.

• Ford Motor Company and Henry Ford Museum.

• Cynthia Munk, New York State Thruway Authority.

• JoAnn Martin, New Jersey Turnpike Authority.

• Nancy E. Vaughan, Best Western International, Inc.

• Kerry L. Wightman, Holiday Inn/Bass Resorts.

• Barbara Leveroni, Franchise Associates, Inc.

• Marla Cimini, Howard Johnson International, Inc.

• Douglas Anderson, Ramada Franchising Systems, Inc.

• Mary Jo Conway and Lydia Kiefer, McDonald's Corporation.

• Stewart Williams, Citgo, Inc.

• Celeste Speier, National Automobile Highway System Consortium.

• Jeffrey L. Durbin, Society for Commercial Archeology.

• Candace Neal, Motel 6.

• Utah State Historical Society.

• Robin Milligan, *Baltimore Sun/ SunSource*.

• Kim Oster, *Washington Post*.

• Pat Dyer, Portland Cement Association.

• Jim Coleman, Missouri DOT.

• Leslie Fowler and Ed Lebeouf, Kansas DOT.

• Chris Miller, *Popular Science* magazine.

Table of Illustrations

The First Generation (1920–1945)

The Golden Age (1946–1969)

The Interstate Era (1970–2000)

The Future

A Brief History of Roads

The development of roads for human transportation has a rather uneven history. Historical records document several roads constructed by the Assyrians to aid troop movements at approximately 700 B.C., and there have been other minor accounts of paved city streets in Egypt and elsewhere. The system of roads built during the Roman Empire is the first recorded account of the construction of a network of roadways. Rome was the first major civilization to develop a system of passable roads that would link even distant corners of the Empire.

During its peak, the Roman system consisted of 11,000 miles of 29 separate roads throughout the Mediterranean region, some even reaching the Middle East and Great Britain. Although Roman roads were built primarily to move armies quickly and keep law and order throughout the Empire (not to mention speeding tax collection), there were some unintended benefits. The roads helped expand trade and improved communication, melding even remote regions into a single political entity, providing what westerners commonly refer to as the "known world" with a rare sense of community. One of Rome's most vital links, the Appian Way (named for Appius Claudius Caecus, a Roman consul responsible for its construction), was started in 312 B.C., and measured 350 miles between Rome and present-day Brindisi in southern Italy.

The Roman road was usually 13 to 17 feet in width, and approximately 4 feet thick. The Romans started with a layer of small broken stones, followed by several inches of larger stones cemented with lime mortar. Next, a layer of fragments of brick and pottery mixed with clay and lime was added to give support to the roadway, and finally, flat stones (either rectangular or irregular in shape) were fitted together and cemented with a mix of gravel and lime to finish the road. While there was no standard blueprint for the configuration of Roman roads, it was learned that several layers of materials were necessary for a road's longevity. Workers were often employed to make bricks by hand for road surfaces, particularly in cities. The Roman roads nearest to Rome, such as the Appian Way, were constructed more elaborately than in the more far-flung regions of the Empire, with road width measuring up to 35 feet in some places. Some 800 years after its construction, one historian wrote that the Appian Way was wide enough for two carriages to pass each other. The "Via Appia" included separated shoulder roads for pedestrians and slower traffic, while the middle lane was reserved mainly for the military and wheeled vehicles. The roadway was finished with a layer of six-inch-thick, polygonal blocks of "silex" (a lava-based stone similar to quartz or silica). The Roman road was crowned at the center, allowing drainage to ditches on the sides of the roadway. In addition to being master road builders, the Romans are credited with excellent architecture, bridge construction, and a system of aqueducts using the arch design. In A.D. 100, the Emperor Trajan erected a large column in the heart of Rome, carved with a map of the Roman roads in the Italian peninsula,

probably the world's first road map. The Romans also placed stone pillars at regular intervals to mark each mile. Roman roads have withstood over 2,000 years of use, and portions of the Appian Way and other Roman roads are still being used today.[1]

Road building ceased for almost 2,000 years following the construction of the Roman roads. The Inca civilization built an impressive system of roads during its height in the 1400s. Like the Romans, the Incas built roads for chiefly military purposes; later, the roads served to speed communication. The main Inca road followed the Pacific coastline from Tumbes (near the border of Peru and Ecuador) to Talca, a distance of over 2,000 miles, while a second road of over 3,000 miles traveled from Quito to Cuzco, through Bolivia and Argentina, and back to Peru. Minor roads branched off from the main system. In desert regions, stone walls were built along roads to block drifting sand; in mountainous areas, "switchbacks" were used and stairs were carved into rock to climb higher elevations. The Incas used suspension bridges made of vegetable-fiber cables to cross rivers; one of these bridges was reputedly still in existence in the 19th century. Although the Incas had not invented the wheel, its roads were wide enough for carts or carriages.[2]

Following the collapse of the Roman Empire, Europe spent many centuries fighting invading barbarians, plagues, famines, and political upheaval. The Roman Catholic Church commissioned the construction of a few stone arch bridges during the 11th century. The original London Bridge was built between A.D. 1176 and 1209.[3] Roads, or "ways," were merely dirt paths, and travelers were at the mercy of the elements. The French developed a national system in the Middle Ages, linking their major cities. In medieval England, the King needed to maintain a reliable system of roads so that his army could move quickly to quell any challenge to his rule. Townspeople naturally maintained roads only within their own village, neglecting the roads connecting other cities and towns. The main routes became known as the "King's Highways," while local roads were called "by ways." The early English roads were built by digging two parallel trenches and depositing the leftover earth between the trenches, building a roadbed. The resulting roadway was higher than the surrounding landscape, hence, a *high way*. Other historical spellings of the word, such as "hyway" or "high-way," are found. One advantage of this simple design was that runoff during rainy weather could drain toward the ditches, keeping the roadway in dry condition.

The English kings found it necessary to maintain its highways, as inclement weather frequently washed out roads. They also cleared bush from the roadsides, which concealed highway robbers who plagued travelers of the day. Laws were passed that required all able-bodied men from the ages of 16 to 60 to work one day per year to repair town streets, and one day per year working on the King's Highways. The Crown later charged a fee, or "toll," on some highways. The earliest recorded toll road in England dates to 1663, a road from Huntington to Ware.[4]

As Europeans emigrated to North America, they found a vast, sparsely-populated wilderness. From the Appalachians to the Rockies, the first roads were bison paths, which were useful since they connected water sources and followed the most level routes. Early settlers encountered a network of Indian trails, which also used lines of least

Opposite, Top: Original section of the Appian Way on the outskirts of Rome. Ancient civilizations often buried their dead within the city walls. The Romans, however, constructed burial tombs on the outskirts of the city along the Appian Way on the road to Pompeii, away from habitable areas. Some Roman roads are still being used throughout the Mediterranean region, including this section just outside of modern Rome. Much of the roadway has been covered with asphalt, except this rare piece of the original "Via Appia." Some remnants of the burial tombs can be seen in the distance (courtesy Albert Z. Kaszynski).

Bottom: Roman bridge in Cordoba, Spain. A fine example of excellent engineering by Roman bridge builders, this stone bridge leading into Cordoba, Spain, dates to the 1st century B.C. Originally constructed of granite, it has been rebuilt several times during its 2,000-year history. Still in good condition, this typical arch-style bridge still supports local traffic as it crosses the Guadalquivir River on the approach to the city (courtesy Albert Z. Kaszynski).

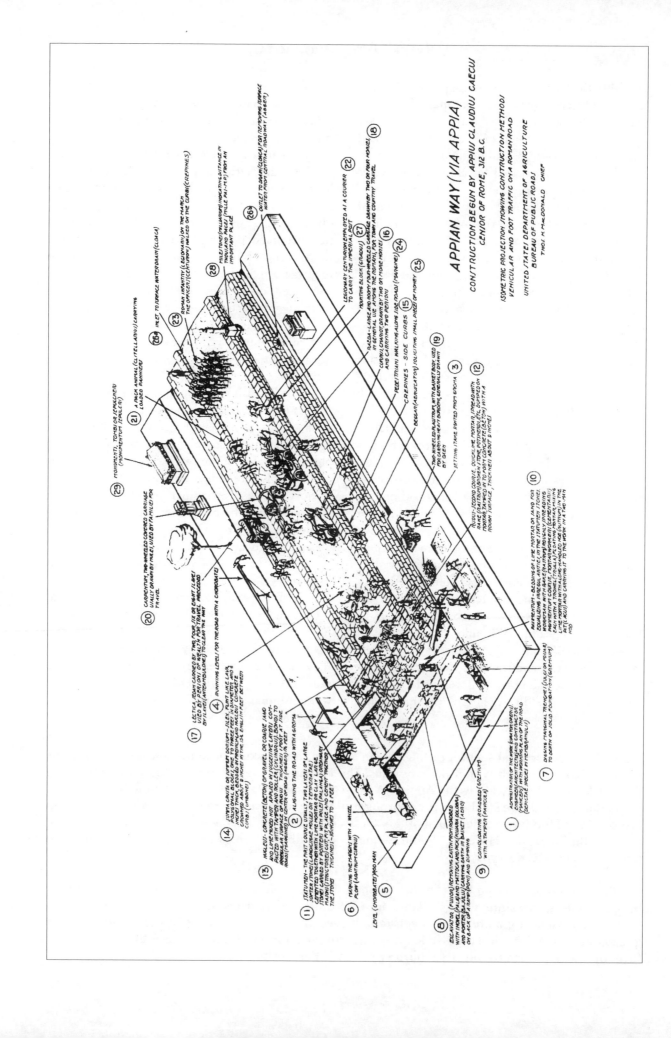

APPIAN WAY (VIA APPIA)

CONSTRUCTION BEGUN BY APPIUS CLAUDIUS CAECUS
CENSOR OF ROME, 312 B.C.

ISOMETRIC PROJECTION SHOWING CONSTRUCTION METHODS,
VEHICULAR AND FOOT TRAFFIC ON A ROMAN ROAD

UNITED STATES DEPARTMENT OF AGRICULTURE
BUREAU OF PUBLIC ROADS
THOS. H. MACDONALD   CHIEF

resistance, following mountain passes and short-cuts when necessary. Early colonists referred to these trails as "trodden paths." Indians helped the American colonists blaze trails, which gradually were widened to accommodate wagons.

The oldest highway in America dates to 1673, when a post rider delivered mail from New York City to Boston. The trip took two weeks, but the route was improved and eventually became the Boston Post Road. Benjamin Franklin, then deputy postmaster, established a system of postal roads, as mail service was an extremely important means of communication in those days. Franklin personally toured the 500 miles of the upper, middle, and lower Boston Post Road to mark the route with milestones. Eventually, a system of post roads connected the major cities in the thirteen colonies.[5]

The inauguration of stagecoach passenger and mail service in the late 1700s necessitated improvements. By the Revolutionary War, larger colonies such as New York and Pennsylvania were at the forefront of road building. Wood was used, particularly across marshy areas, by laying planks or logs crosswise across the roadway, the latter commonly referred to "corduroy" roads. Some rare portions of these early roads can still be found in a few isolated places.

After the war, the federal and state governments did not fund road construction, so private enterprise took over. Land companies purchased

Above: Model of laborers building the Appian Way. This model was constructed by the Bureau of Public Roads in 1933 and displayed at the National Museum in Washington, D.C., for an exhibition on the history of road building. Skilled laborers and conscripted slaves alike were employed to build a vast network of roads that far outlived the Roman Empire. Roman roads, bridges, and aqueducts served as models for further generations of civil engineers and architects (National Archives [33-334-A]).

Opposite: Cross-section of roadway of Appian Way. This drawing demonstrates the complexity of the Appian Way and other Roman roads, showing the layers of road materials used and different avenues of the roadway used by various types of traffic. Through patient trial-and-error, Roman road builders discovered many of the basic principles of road making, such as proper drainage and use of multilayer subbases. Also displayed by the Bureau of Public Roads at the National Museum in 1933 (National Archives [33-460-A]).

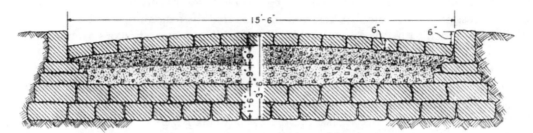

ANCIENT ROMAN 2-LANE MILITARY ROAD.

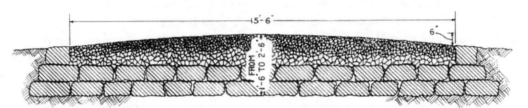

FRENCH ROAD (ROMAN METHOD) PREVIOUS TO 1775.

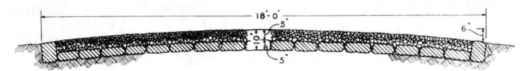

TRÉSAGUET ROAD, FRANCE, 1775 TO 1830.

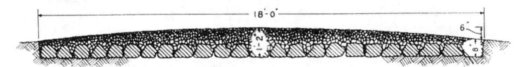

TELFORD ROAD, ENGLAND, 1820.

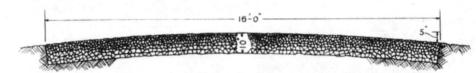

ORIGINAL MACADAM ROAD, ENGLAND, 1816.

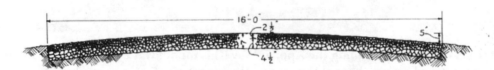

MACADAM ROAD, UNITED STATES, 1900.

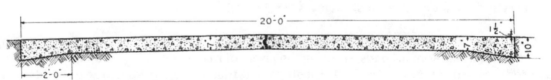

HEAVY-DUTY 2-LANE CONCRETE PAVEMENT, UNITED STATES, 1934.

right-of-ways and cleared the land. In 1775, the Ohio and Transylvania Company, with the help of Daniel Boone, built a wagon trail called the "Wilderness Road" through a pass at Cumberland Gap and across Kentucky to the Northwest Territories. In one month, Boone's party of 30 ax men cleared a 209-mile path through Kentucky. Other roads were built during this period. The Philadelphia and Lancaster Turn Pike Company built the first hard-surface road in 1794, a 62-mile macadam toll road from Philadelphia to Lancaster, Pennsylvania, using hand-broken stones, covered by a layer of gravel, which made travel easier in poor weather conditions. In the next 40 years, many "turn pikes," as they were called, appeared. To cover the costs of maintaining these early roads, early travelers stopped at gates made of logs or spears

Stage stop at Eagle Hotel on Lancaster Pike, Pennsylvania. A stagecoach leaves the Eagle Hotel, located 17 miles outside of Philadelphia on the Lancaster Pike. The Lancaster Pike was an improved colonial road that charged travelers a toll to defray the costs of building and maintaining the road. Inns and stage stops with overnight accommodations were a welcome respite throughout the former Thirteen Colonies during the early days of overland travel. An etching by Isaac Weld during his travels in North America, 1795–1797 (National Archives [32-238]).

called "pikes," which were opened after a toll was paid. The practice of charging a toll originated in England and quickly spread in the northeastern United States. Over 175 turnpike companies were formed, constructing approximately 3,000 miles of roads in the early 1800s. One notable main highway, the "National Road," also known as the "Great National Turnpike," was approved by an act of Congress providing for an east-west road from Cumberland, Maryland, through the Midwest, and ultimately to St. Louis. The road started prior to the Revolutionary War, and was later improved and lengthened from the original "Braddock's Road" in southern Pennsylvania through Wheeling, West Virginia, then further west to Columbus,

Indianapolis, and ending at Vandalia, Illinois. The tide of westward migration prompted Congress to appropriate funds in 1806 to level hills and clear trees, purchase land, and widen the road to 60 feet. Due to politics and other factors, progress was slow and construction halted in 1852. However, for almost 50 years, the National Road was the busiest thoroughfare in America.

Interest in road building waned as the 19th century progressed. Travel by water remained the cheapest and most common means of transporting men and material to build the new nation. A system of canals was built, mainly to facilitate east-west traffic. By the 1840s, the steamboat and fast clipper ships made their appearance, although only briefly.

Opposite: Cross-sections of roads from ancient Rome to modern U.S. highways. From the Smithsonian Report for 1936 entitled "Via Appia in the Days when All Roads led to Rome," by Albert C. Rose. These cross-sectional drawings show how the thickness of roads has gradually decreased due to improvements in materials and engineering over the past 2,000 years (National Archives [36-40]).

Waterloo Inn on the road between Baltimore and Washington. Taken from the personal narrative of Fred F. DeRoos during his journeys throughout the United States and Canada in 1826, this early lithograph depicts the first stage stop on the road from Baltimore to Washington, D.C., an important route connecting the nation's capital with cities in the northeast. Present-day U.S. 1 now passes near this site (National Archives [32-367]).

Technological advances caused road building to fall out of favor, as newer and more efficient ways to travel were developed. By 1825, toll fees on turnpikes could not cover the cost of road repairs, and road building was abandoned. Travel for most settlers going overland meant negotiating crude pathways that ranged from dust to mud, depending on the weather, until reaching the nearest railhead, which could be many miles.

America's westward expansion followed several main routes, which allowed easier travel for horse-drawn wagon trains. In 1825, the U.S. government surveyed a new pioneer trail from Missouri to Santa Fe, New Mexico, and paid the Osage Indians for the right to cross their land. However, the Pawnees and Comanches had claims to the same land, and west-bound migrants routinely came under attack. Legendary frontiersman Kit Carson traveled what became known as the "Santa Fe Trail," helping protect wagon trains from Indian raids with his ingenious defensive strategies. In 1841, fur traders and missionaries marked out the famous "Oregon Trail" from St. Joseph, Missouri, to Oregon's Will amette Valley. By 1843, over 1,000 settlers had traveled the Oregon Trail on their way to the northwestern U.S. territories. The "Southern Route" and "California Trail" branched off from the Oregon Trail, headed for Los Angeles and Sacramento, respectively. The California Trail was blazed across Nevada by prospectors following the Gold Rush of 1848.

There were other important pioneer trails. After Ponce de León's discovery of Florida in 1513, Hernando de Soto and 600 Spaniards cut a trail across Florida through Mobile, Alabama, all the way to the Texas border in 1539. De Soto's remarkable trail came to be known as the "Trail of the Conquistadors." Another road of Spanish origin is the "El Camino Real" (meaning "The Royal Highway of the King of Spain"), or, the "Spanish Mission Trail," which was built during the time of the Revolutionary War. The El Camino Real connected the 21 Franciscan missions located along the California coast on its 530-mile route from San Diego to San Francisco. Stagecoach robberies and other criminal activity flourished along the road in the 1850s, and much of the route was in poor condition. The road itself claimed the lives of some travelers, with some dangerous portions perched precariously above ocean cliffs. Local vigilantes had to be formed to discourage the rash of robberies. The notorious Black Bart alone was responsible for 28 stages hold-ups during his eight-year crime spree.[6]

Travel by stagecoach became commonplace for many travelers by the mid–1800s, and several companies developed their own chosen routes to the West Coast. In 1849, service was established between St. Joseph, Missouri, and Santa Fe, New Mexico. The public clamored for mail service throughout the West, but disputes over routing delayed congressional action until 1857, when Congress passed the Post Office Appropriations Act,

Top: A wagon train on the Oregon Trail in western Nebraska. A painting by well-known pioneer artist William H. Jackson, this view shows a wagon train heading west near present-day Scottsbluff, Nebraska. On the horizon is the thin rock spire called Chimney Rock, a strange formation that guided pioneers on their way west on the Oregon Trail. This view is looking west from Court House Rock (courtesy Utah State Historical Society).

Bottom: Three Crossings Station on the Sweetwater River. An illustration by William H. Jackson for "The Pony Express Goes Through" by Howard R. Driggs, with a pony express rider leaving the Three Crossings station in southern Wyoming. During the Pony Express' brief two-year history, the system of riders spaced at 15-mile intervals carried the U.S. Mail from St. Joseph, Missouri, to Sacramento, with a second route from St. Louis to Los Angeles and San Francisco. The best recorded time brought news of Lincoln's election to the West Coast in November 1860 in just six days (courtesy Utah State Historical Society).

offering subsidies to anyone who could deliver mail from the Mississippi to San Francisco within 25 days. The first contract went to John Butterfield, William G. Fargo, William B. Dinsmore and their associates. Butterfield and his partners chose the "oxbow route" from St. Louis to San Francisco via Fort Smith, Arkansas, and San Diego, a distance of 2,795 miles. Stagecoach stations were placed at 10-mile intervals, with the inaugural run leaving St. Louis on September 15, 1858. The journey took 24 days, 18 hours, 35 minutes, and was so successful that additional routes were soon established.[7]

With the success of Butterfield's Southern Overland Mail and always striving for improved efficiency, Americans soon demanded even faster mail service to California. A new company developed a system of relay riders and fast horses. A central route from St. Joseph, Missouri, along the Oregon and California trails to Sacramento, California, was chosen, with a second route (The Butterfield Route) from St. Louis through Little Rock, El Paso, Yuma, Arizona, to Los Angeles and on to San Francisco. Approximately 75 lightweight riders, specially clothed to reduce wind resistance, were stationed at 15-mile intervals and given two minutes to change saddlebags and horses. Called the "Pony Express," its best recorded time was in November 1860, when news of Lincoln's election took just six days to make the journey from Fort Kearney, Nebraska, to Fort Churchill, California.

Velocipede riding school, New York City, 1869. The year 1869 is important for the inception of two of the country's late 19th century recreational sports: bicycling and the greatest of all American pastimes, baseball. This lithograph from the February 13, 1869, issue of *Harper's Weekly* is a comical view of amateur riders trying to learn the art of bicycling (early models were called "velocipedes") (National Archives [40-3431]).

However, when the first telegraph lines linked California to the East the following year, the Pony Express quickly became obsolete, making its final run in 1861.[8]

Following the Civil War, the nation resumed its migration toward the Rockies and the Pacific. The railroads, aided by generous grants for right-of-ways by Congress, spread further west, spurring a competition between two railroads giants. The historic meeting of the eastbound Union Pacific and the westbound Central Pacific railroads at Promontory Point, Utah, on May 10, 1869, ushered in a new era in travel and communication. For the remainder of the century, the railroads dominated domestic land travel in America. The railroad could cross most types of terrain, and its importance in speeding the economic and cultural union of the new nation as it expanded west cannot be underscored.

In the 1890s, the country got caught up in the new bicycle craze, and "bone-shakers" became a common sight on city streets across the country. Bicyclists in urban areas crowded onto the few paved streets and paths that existed, especially on Sundays, since many worked six-day work weeks. They formed clubs and urged local officials to improve roads to support their leisure activity. However, government, both state and local, was slow to act on the wishes of a few weekend hobbyists. In 1891, New Jersey was first to give state moneys to the counties for road improvements. Other states slowly followed with their own state-aid road programs. Seeking better roads, many bicyclists started the "Good Roads" movement, and thousands of bike enthusiasts began petitioning state and local governments for all-weather hard-surfaced streets and roads.

The United States Supreme Court's landmark decision of *Monongahela Navigation Company v. United States* paved the way for federal involve-

"The right of way." A drawing by A.B. Frost for *Harper's Weekly* in 1896. As the number of bicycles began to crowd urban and rural thoroughfares, the clash between two-wheelers and existing modes of transportation was inevitable. Although a few major cities, mostly in the East, had acceptable roads and pathways for bicycle usage, dirt roads were the norm. Here, a narrow country lane causes a debate between a group of bicycle riders and a farmer on a horse-drawn wagon over who should have the right of way (National Archives [37-388]).

ment in roads. The majority justices wrote that "the power of Congress to regulate commerce carries with it power over all means and instrumentalities by which commerce is carried on."[9] Up until this time, many scholars and others believed that the federal government did not have the power under the Constitution to regulate or construct highways. There was no federal income tax at the time, and many advocates of states' rights were suspicious of any expansion of federal power.

The federal government acknowledged the necessity of road improvements as the 19th century was about to end. The railroads had already reached most areas of the country, but could only serve people living nearby the rail line. This left many, particularly rural residents, stranded many miles except by horse or on foot. The United State Post Office was in dire need of better roads along its postal routes. This became even more necessary when the post office instituted rural free postal delivery. In 1892, Senator Charles R. Manderson of Nebraska introduced a bill calling for a National Highway Commission to study future road improvements. The measure was an idea proposed by General Roy Stone, who saw the need for construction of more reliable roads for both military and civilian purposes. A similar bill was introduced in the House of Representatives by Rep. Philip S. Post of Illinois. The final bill ultimately became the Agriculture Appropriations Act of 1894, which President Benjamin Harrison signed into law just prior to leaving office in March 1893. The act appropriated only $10,000 and authorized the Department of Agriculture to study the feasibility of better roads. In October 1893, Agriculture Secretary J. Sterling Morton established the Office of Road Inquiry, the first federal agency responsible for highway improvement. Secretary Morton appointed General Roy Stone as its first special agent and engineer of road inquiry. A firm believer in a major federal effort to upgrade the nation's roads, General Stone announced to Secretary Morton in an ORI bulletin in 1894, "The quagmires, ruts, and wrecked wagons that mark our common highways, the reckless waste of the old road system, the social and commercial isolation that is imposed upon our people, and especially our farmers, assuring a large part of winter and spring months must

"Somebody blundered." So reads the caption from another issue of *Harper's Weekly* in 1896, this one showing a mishap between two bicyclists. As the 19th century drew to a close, the United States lagged behind Europe in improved urban roads. Competition for road space by bicycles and the emerging automobile became acute by 1900, causing a nationwide demand for improved roads. Bicycle clubs and others who stood to benefit from road improvements were a main force behind the "Good Roads" movement in the 1890s, which helped pave the way for a national effort in road construction to accommodate a new invention in transportation, the "horse-less carriage" (National Archives [37-787]).

sooner or later convince us that bad roads cost more than good ones."[10]

As its title suggests, little more than "inquiry" was accomplished by the Office of Road Inquiry. Although limited by its tiny budget, the ORI did construct the nation's first "object lesson" road in New Brunswick, New Jersey, a 660-foot long, 8-footwide rock macadam road at the New Jersey Agricultural College in 1897. Besides attending meetings and giving advice to state officials, ORI did increase public awareness of the need for better roads. Although its impact was limited, the Office of Road Inquiry was an important first step towards a concerted federal effort to improve the nation's roads.[11]

City streets in the late 1800s were either dusty or a morass of mud and animal waste. Navigating the narrow urban corridors was a nuisance for both driver and pedestrian, and the sophisticated urbanite in high-fashion Victorian dress had to endure a disgusting mix of foul odors, smoke from burning wood or coal, and noisy horse-driven vehicles. As 1900 approached, American cities became an urban logjam of horses, wagons, and carriages. The nation's first transportation crisis was looming. The country's population was increasing rapidly due to steady European immigration in the latter part of the 19th century. Some of the newcomers migrated west to homestead farms, while many congregated in the major urban centers of the East and Midwest, providing labor for the Industrial Revolution that was sweeping America and Europe. Even the introduction of electric street cars did not alleviate the increasing urban congestion. The efforts of urban transportation officials could not keep up with the population surge.

The movement for better roads in the late 1800s was mainly an urban phenomenon, started by bicyclists searching for weekend escapes. Meanwhile, rural America had to make due with earth paths. A typical horse and buggy could travel only 5 miles per hour in favorable weather. Travel time to transport ripened crops and livestock to the nearest city or railhead was often critical for farmers. The focus on improved roads gradually turned to a new invention that was emerging. While the public's attention was focused on bicycles, a unnoticed assortment of bicycle makers, inventors, blacksmiths, and backyard mechanics were tinkering with the new internal combustion engine, little knowing that they would be instrumental in starting a revolution in transportation and communication in the coming century.

There are several historical accounts of the invention of a forerunner of the modern-day automobile. The earliest recorded effort can be traced to the 2nd century B.C., where a Greek in Alexandria, Egypt, built an engine run by steam power. No one could think of a practical use for the invention, so it faded into obscurity. The steam engine was revived in the late 1600s, and crude steam engines were used for pumping water and hoisting coal out of mines. An Englishman, James Watt (1736–1819), worked to correct many of the defects of the steam engine and produced a reliable version. Watt collaborated with Matthew Boulton (1728–1809) to form Watt & Boulton, and together the two went into the steam engine business. They hired an able mechanic, James Murdoch (1754–1839), as one of their assistants. While working in his spare time, Murdoch mounted a small steam engine on a wagon and called his vehicle a "road carriage." The steam engine turned the wagon's wheels, and the vehicle ran continuously in a circle in his empty storeroom. Murdoch was about to travel to London to patent his invention, but was dissuaded by Boulton, who thought that a patent would depress the sale of steam engines. Boulton wrote to Watt in 1786 about Murdoch's creation, but the idea went no further.[12] However, the invention was reborn in 1813 when another Briton, George Stephenson, improved Murdoch's design and built the world's first steam-driven locomotive, called the "Locomotion," which could travel on iron rails at speeds of up to 20 miles per hour. Further work on Stephenson's invention yielded more speed. In 1829, a winner in a competition held on a short stretch of track between Manchester and Leeds, England, appropriately named the "Rocket," was clocked at an amazing 30 miles per hour. Soon, the new technological sensation was used to transport more and larger cargo, and the railroad soon became one of the most important components of the Industrial Revolution. Only sailing ships could move more goods faster, but they were limited to ocean travel. Besides, Stephenson's locomotive could travel anywhere a rail line could be laid, and the railroads were heralded as one of the most important scientific advances of 19th century.[13]

The steam engine was adapted further for a variety of industrial and transportation uses, such as steam-operated water craft and farm machinery.

For a time, a new generation of fast sailing ships took over ocean travel, peaking in the 1840s. However, wind power depended on unpredictable weather conditions and could not match the reliability of steam power. In America, river boats and ocean-going vessels increasingly adopted steam power, and the sail was slowly replaced as the 1800s progressed. Without steam-driven river craft and railroads, the American West would not have been settled until sometime in the early 20th century. Basic supplies, as well as the latest European luxuries and furnishings, could now be delivered to virtually any segment of the continental United States.

While steam power dominated transportation during most of the 1800s, others in the United States and the Old World worked on alternative sources of power-driven machines. Inventors started experimenting with various gases, first heating turpentine and other oils to create "inflammable air" that could replace steam to drive engines. In the late 1800s, gasoline refined from crude oil or coal looked promising. A French engineer, Jean Joseph Lenoir (1822–1900), patented a one-cylinder gasoline engine. The small engine used a mixture of vaporized air and gasoline that was injected into a carburetor and when ignited by a spark, burned the gasoline and air mixture to move a piston two revolutions, hence, a two-cycle engine. However, Lenoir's engine had a few drawbacks. The gasoline merely burned in the cylinder, resulting in a fairly low-power engine. A compressed gas-air mixture would create an explosion and therefore more power, but the engine was not designed to handle the force. There was no way for the burned gas to escape, although Lenoir partially solved the problem by placing an outlet valve in the cylinder to allow gas to escape. In 1862, after some further improvements, he built a four-wheel vehicle outfitted with one of his gas engines. Lenoir left Paris and drove into the countryside, making a 15-mile round trip in approximately three hours. However, nobody paid much attention to Lenoir's experiment, and the idea was soon forgotten.[14]

In the early 1870s, German inventors Nikolaus August Otto and Eugene Langen developed a single-cylinder, four-cycle gasoline engine. Both men lacked technical knowledge to design an engine or to make necessary improvements, so they employed engineer Gottlieb Daimler (1834–1900). After several years of hard work, Daimler perfected the engine. While the German effort was in progress, an Austrian named Siegfried Marcus had already built a complete motor vehicle in 1875. Marcus' motor carriage was years ahead of its time, using a four-cycle, water-cooled gas engine with electric ignition, intake and exhaust valves. However, Marcus could not secure financial backing, and due to lack of interest on the part of the public and industry, the project was abandoned. Once again, the opportunity for a quantum advance in technology was passed up.[15]

There were other experiments in Europe and in the United States. George B. Brayton attempted to built a usable vehicle with a two-cycle motor, but failed like many other inventors. Gottlieb Daimler left Otto & Langen in 1882 and went out on his own. He decided that the Otto engine was too heavy for practical use as a motor vehicle, so he designed a lighter engine that was faster and more powerful, turning 900 revolutions per minute as opposed to 200 rpm. Daimler improved the carburetor and ignition and tried it on a bicycle and a boat. Both worked well, and he patented both inventions. Meanwhile, another German, Karl Benz (1844–1929), was competing with Daimler to become the first to produce a self-propelled motorized vehicle. Benz's first attempt was a three-wheeled model, but Daimler one-upped him and unveiled a four-wheel, gasoline-driven carriage that would distinguish him as being the first to invent the automobile as we know it today. Benz's vehicle could only drive forward, while Daimler's could also go in reverse. Both men produced a small number of their motorized carriages during the ensuing years, and Daimler even convinced some cities to use his engines for its streetcars.[16]

In France, the firm of Pahhard & Levassor designed a motorcar using Daimler's engine to produce a superior vehicle in 1890. At first, only a few dozen were sold, but soon they were selling hundreds of units. The French called their car an "automobile" (self-moving), and by 1898 the word became commonplace even in the United States. France quickly led the world in automobile production, although most were luxury models appealing mainly to wealthy buyers.[17]

Following the successes of German and French inventors, it was America's turn to join the international fervor over the automobile. Two brothers in Springfield, Massachusetts, Charles Duryea, a skilled mechanic, and Frank, a toolmaker, pooled their talents and $1,000 to build the nation's first motorcar. For his part, Charles designed a two-cycle gasoline engine, while Frank concentrated on the remainder of the vehicle. Their first prototype was modestly successful, but a few glitches had to be worked out before it could be commercially viable. Frank Duryea left Springfield and returned to work at his Illinois bicycle shop. Frank completely redesigned the engine, making it a four-cycle, water-cooled engine and adding a carburetor, which Charles' two-cycle model lacked. The big day arrived on September 20, 1893, when Frank Duryea test drove his new invention on Springfield's city streets. Onlookers were mesmerized by the strange, noisy contraption. Frank made further improvements, such as electric ignition and a belt-driven transmission, which featured two forward gears and a neutral position. He unveiled his new model the following year. The new Duryea car looked like any ordinary horse-drawn carriage, except for its rear-mounted engine, and was vastly superior to his first model or anything made in Europe. The car had a top speed of 18 miles per hour, faster than horse-driven transportation.[18]

The Duryea brothers next decided to put their invention to a new test. In the late 1890s, the infant automobile industry was already involved in auto racing both here and abroad. *The Chicago Times-Herald* sponsored a 52-mile automobile race, offering a $2,000 prize to the first-place finisher. The latest automobiles from the United States and Europe entered, as did the Duryeas. The race started on a cold Thanksgiving Day in 1895, amid snow, slush and mud roads. Frank Duryea came in first, with a Benz coming second, an hour and a half later. Just to show that their victory was not just beginner's luck, they entered another race in New York City the following year and again, Frank claimed first place, with brother Charles placing second. Later in 1896, they took their car to England for the London-to-Brighton Race and repeated their success, beating out a class of able competitors. Despite their impressive string of victories on the auto racing circuit, the Duryeas could not mass-market their car. They built 13 models in 1897, but the brothers had disagreements on everything from financial matters to design decisions, so the Duryea Motor Wagon Company was disbanded.[19]

The budding automobile industry was composed generally of two groups: carriage makers, like Studebaker and Buick, and bicycle manufacturers, like Duryea. After a few years of experimenting, the consensus was that features of both bicycles and carriages should be included. Eventually, the automobile evolved into a hybrid of the two. A further controversy was choosing from several available power plants, since steam and electric engines were in competition with gasoline-powered versions. Great improvements had been made in steam and electric power, and it looked for a time that the gasoline internal combustion engine might be scrapped altogether. However, makers of gas-driven vehicles designed lighter models, while the weight of the steam boiler and limited range of battery-driven cars eventually made the gasoline engine the logical choice.[20]

While Frank and Charles Duryea were involved in auto racing, other amateur American inventors were working on improved versions of the motor car. In 1897, Ransom Eli Olds founded his own company, the Olds Motor Works, headquartered in Detroit. In contrast to the expensive models the Europeans were producing at the time, Olds thought that the public needed a reliable, yet affordable, car. Another inventor, Henry Ford, had been building automobiles since 1896, mainly while working for the Detroit Automobile Company. Other entrepreneurs with names that are still household names today (as well as those long-forgotten) were about to join enter the exciting new age of the motor car.[21]

The Early Days (1900–1919)

History will no doubt record that the majority of man's greatest achievements in technological progress occurred in the 20th century. Industry and science have experienced giant advances in the field of medicine, not to mention aviation and space travel, entertainment (movies, radio, television), and nuclear energy, just to name a few. All things considered, the internal combustion engine on wheels has made the greatest impact, transforming the earth's landscape and starting new industries now employing one in ten Americans. Other spin-offs from the automobile come to mind, including a new brand of auto based pop culture. The 20th century easily earns the title "The Century of the Motorcar."

Despite early public resistance to the so-called "horse-less carriage," Americans quickly embraced the new invention and started purchasing them in ever-increasing numbers. In 1900, Ransom Eli Olds (1874–1950) promised to manufacture a "small runabout" costing only $650. Ransom Olds simply named it the "Oldsmobile." Such an idea seemed like a pipe dream, since no one could build a motor car for anything under $1,000. Early automaking was crude and each unit handmade. Tool-and-die making, while adequate at the time, was not up to the close tolerances necessary for efficient mass production. Parts frequently were not interchangeable and had to be finished by hand, causing costly delays. But this did not deter others from pursuing their vision of the ultimate motorcar. Henry Leland (1843–1932), who had

been supplying transmissions for Olds, teamed up with Detroit financiers William H. Murphy and Lem W. Bower to form the Cadillac Auto Company in 1902. Leland's insistence on quality workmanship resulted in a superior car which was much faster than the Oldsmobile and at a comparable price. The Model A sold for $750 and the two-seater Model B was priced at $900. The success of the two models made Cadillac a top seller by 1905.[22]

After the demise of the Detroit Automobile Company, Henry Ford (1863–1947) continued working solo, developing several models, including a racer. On October 10, 1900, Ford entered his racing version in a Detroit automobile race and came in first, beating out Alexander Winton. Winton and Ford started the Henry Ford Company, but disbanded the business two years later. This second business setback didn't discourage Ford, and as he secured some financial backing to form the Ford Motor Company in 1903. The new company produced its first models for public sale that year, and sales went well. Another key player in the turn-of-the-century automobile manufacturing industry was David Dunbar Buick, president of the Buick Manufacturing Company, a manufacturer of carriages and plumbing supplies. In 1902, Buick entered the business of automaking, producing 16 cars in 1903, and only 37 units the following year. A wealthy businessman, William Crapo Durant (1860–1947), bought enough stock in Buick to take over the company in 1904. Durant was worth

several million dollars, having achieved considerable success as a manufacturer of road carts. As the quality of workmanship of automaking improved markedly each year, and with the public's appetite for cars steadily growing, Durant could foresee that the horse and buggy days were over. Under Durant's leadership, Buick made great strides in manufacturing and sales of its newest models. The result was the Model F, which featured a two-cylinder engine with superior horsepower. The new Model F competed well against the models that Olds, Ford and Cadillac were offering.[23]

By 1905, Olds, Ford, Cadillac, and Buick were squeezing out the competition. Hundreds of small makes, unable to match the mass production of the larger companies, were forced to close their doors. Newcomers such as the Winton, Pierce-Arrow, Franklin, and Peerless, to name a few, hung on for a few years, then either went out of business or were merged into their competitors. The process of elimination of the smaller car makers accelerated when Durant formed the General Motors Corporation in 1908. That same year, Ford's Model T hit the market. The car earned its nickname "Tin Lizzy" due in part to its simple, homely appearance. The car was nothing fancy and the body had a higher than normal road clearance that distinguished it from the others on the market. However, Ford's design proved to be its major selling point, as the car could travel over deep ruts and muddy terrain. Farmers in particular loved the "T," since they encountered the country's worst roads. The first Model T had an in-line four-cylinder engine capable of speeds of up to 35 miles per hour, and was such a good buy at $875 that Ford temporar-

1908 Ford Model "T" Touring Sedan. This is the first of 15 million "Tin Lizzies" built by the Ford Motor Company through the late 1920s. First priced at $875, Ford's introduction of the moving assembly line in 1913 revolutionized the automobile industry, reducing the price of the Model T to just $345 by 1916. By World War I, Ford's new $5 a day wage allowed Ford employees to afford the very product they were producing (From the Collections of the Henry Ford Museum and Greenfield Village).

ily stopping taking new orders during the 1908 model year due to the volume of orders.[24]

As automobile production increased steadily, buyers now had an excellent array of makes and models to choose from, but there was still one major problem facing motorists: no roads. While America was still preoccupied with completing the settlement of the West, Europe had been building roads for over a decade. British engineers McAdams and Telford developed a hard road surface called "macadam," consisting of a stone or rock foundation topped by a layer of brick or broken stones. The roadbed drained runoff efficiently and

Opposite, Top: A view of Fifth Avenue, New York City, circa 1900. A photograph taken on Easter Sunday morning in 1900 of New York City's Fifth Avenue shows a crowded procession of horse-drawn vehicles on one of the city's major arteries. In the midst of this busy thoroughfare is one lone automobile, attesting to the fact that the horseless carriage was still a novelty at the turn of the century (National Archives [46-767]).

Bottom: Automobiles and horses at the Mount Washington Hotel, Bretton Woods, New Hampshire. The first models of the new internal combustion engine vehicles were noisy contraptions that routinely frightened horses, much to the chagrin of city and rural folk alike who still relied on horsepower for transportation. This 1904 photograph records an early attempt to accustom horses to automobiles by placing horse-drawn surreys between cars (National Archives [6529]).

was able to withstand the heavy pounding of wagon wheels and steel horseshoes as compared to ordinary dirt. In the U.S., state and local governments started experimenting with various road surfaces. In 1898, Los Angeles County was the first locale to use oil on an earth road (a short six-mile piece) to keep down choking dust. By 1901, no concrete roadway existed in the United States and there were only 650 miles of macadam roads. Unlike the European roads, American macadam roads often used only the natural soil for the foundation layer, and muddy potholes quickly developed. By 1904, the U.S. had 108,283 miles of gravel roads, 38,622 miles composed of various materials (stone, shell, or sand), and 1,997,908 miles of dirt roads.[25]

City streets were often paved with cobblestone, bricks, or wooden blocks, if they were paved at all. Brick paving was favored in cities, as it outlasted other materials. The first use of brick beyond a corporate limit was an 8-foot wide portion on South Woodland Avenue and Wooster Pike in Cuyahoga County (Cleveland), Ohio. Macadam roads were few and rarely in good condition, so other road paving materials were explored. In 1879, a new material called "portland cement" was invented in Scotland. The process required heating a mixture of limestone and clay, combined with rocks (aggregate) for strength, which hardens when added to water. A single city block in the town of Bellefontaine, Ohio, was paved with portland cement (also called "concrete") in 1891, the first such project in the United States. Two years later, Rochester, New York, paved a portion of South Fitzhugh Street with portland cement, but the pavement quickly crumbled and was resurfaced several years with "asphalt" or "bituminous," a mixture of refined petroleum, sand and gravel. Another material called "bituminous cement" was

Top: Michigan Boulevard, Chicago, circa 1910. A view looking north shows a wide street treated with a surface using an asphalt combination. Asphalt, or "bituminous," was developed at the turn of the century and patented by Fred J. Warren. The process involves heating a combination of refined petroleum, sand and gravel. This photograph demonstrates that autos were beginning to outnumber horses in the years just prior to World War I (National Archives [3905]).

Bottom: Dirt main street, Checotah, Oklahoma. This photo shows a typical unimproved street in small town America, a stark contrast to paved streets in the nation's major cities. In the early years of the new century, highway improvements were so slow that many believed that it would take at least 50 years before rural areas would see modern roads. Taken on January 27, 1912, by B. H. Burrell (National Archives [7267]).

Top: **First portland cement pavement, Bellefontaine, Ohio. In 1879, this new material (a mixture of limestone, clay, and rock fragments to add strength) was invented in Scotland. In 1891, the town of Bellefontaine, Ohio, paved a one-block, 8-foot section of Main Street with portland cement, the earliest known usage in the United States. This photograph shows an original street along the county courthouse as it appears today. The location is marked by a several historic plaques, one crediting this early paved road with starting the Good Roads Movement (Author's collection).**

Bottom: **U.S. Mail carriage on Tennessee postal road, 1904. Mail service in rural regions was slow and dependent on good weather conditions at the turn of the century. The Post Office Department and the Office of Road Inquiry instituted Rural Free Delivery in 1896, and modest improvements "to postal roads" were made to speed mail service to isolated rural areas. Farmers joined the Good Roads Movement and others in petitioning local and state governments to increase expenditures for better roads. Eventually, citizens looked to the federal government for a solution to the nation's transportation problem. This postal carriage is shown making a delivery on Chester's Road, south of Jackson, Tennessee (Courtesy, FHWA, USDOT).**

patented by Fred J. Warren. The first known use of bituminous concrete was a project in Pawtucket, Rhode Island, in 1901, with the state later using bituminous concrete for its rural roads by 1905. Portland cement produced around 1900 was laid in 6–8" sections, usually 6" thick. The size of the sections gradually increased as methods improved. Unjointed, continuous concrete was tried, but expansion and contraction from temperature changes caused transverse cracking.[26]

The Office of Road Inquiry began studying different types of road surfaces early on, and established a road materials laboratory in 1900. After the turn of the century, General Roy Stone left the ORI and was replaced by Martin Dodge. More states were starting their own state aid road programs, while the U.S. Post Office was soliciting congressional support for better postal roads. In 1901, Dodge was involved in the first "Good Roads Train," a successful public-relations effort sponsored by the National Good Roads Association. A group of road boosters and others boarded a train from Chicago to New Orleans, giving lectures along the way to increase public awareness of the need for better roads. Dodge believed in a coordinated federal-state effort and with his assistant, M.O. Eldridge, proposed legislation to Congress in 1902 to provide federal funds to the states. In December of the same year, Rep. Walter P. Brownlow of Tennessee introduced a bill creating a Bureau of Public Roads to administer federal aid to the states. Brownlow's proposal would have required the federal government to pay 50 percent of state or county roads, but federal grants were limited to only $20 million per year. In the end, objections by opponents quickly killed the Brownlow bill. Some members feared that a federal road program would tie up federal dollars for decades in the future, while others doubted that Congress had the power under the Constitution to appropriate funds for national roads. The latter objection, however, was removed in 1907 when the U.S. Supreme ruled in *Wilson v. Shaw* that the commerce clause of the Constitution does grant Congress the authority to construct interstate roads.[27]

The Office of Public Road Inquiry continued despite the lack of federal support. In August 1902, OPRI helped build an object-lesson

Top: "Where the mule has the advantage." Many a farmer got the last laugh when called upon to rescue unfortunate motorists stuck on muddy rural roads. When this photograph was taken in 1914, many still believed that the automobile would be a passing fad, impracticable in navigating the country's dirt roads and trails (National Archives [10752]).

Bottom: Earth Road repaired with pine logs, 1912. A typical example of one of the rudimentary road repair techniques used during the early decades of the 20th century. Here, a rainstorm washed out a ditch and a section of a dirt road in a rural area. Pine logs 2 to 3 feet in length make a hasty repair. Wooden logs, planks and crushed rock were used in all parts of the country prior to 1900 for road building before the availability of concrete and asphalt surfacing materials. Near Stafford, Virginia (National Archives [7364]).

road on the Old National Turnpike (later U.S. 40) between Frostburg and Cumberland, Maryland. With $5,000 in funds provided by Allegany County, the road bypassed some of the steepest hills which bedeviled travelers for over 100 years. President Theodore Roosevelt expressed his support for the Good Roads Movement when he addressed the National Good Roads Convention in 1903. Roosevelt advocated American expansionism during the nation's empire-building days of the early 20th century, and declared, "When we wish to use descriptive adjectives, fit to characterize great empires, ... invariably one of those adjectives used is to signify that that empire built good roads.... The facility, the art, the habit of road building marks in a nation those solid, stable qualities, which tell for permanent greatness." [28]

President Roosevelt got his opportunity to make his permanent contribution to the American highway when he signed the Agriculture Appropriations Act of 1905, which terminated the OPRI and created the Office of Public Roads (OPR). On July 1, 1905, the OPR became the first permanent federal road agency, with an annual budget of $50,000. The Act required that the OPR's director had to be a "scientist and

Top: A mud road near Meridian, Mississippi, 1912. Photo is taken on Bonita Road in front of C. J. Odum's homestead, a farmer and merchant living four miles from town who had to pay extra to haul supplies through this nearly impassable morass. Local post office authorities also paid $12.50 for a horse team to pull one day's mail over this road. Improved mail delivery was a major impetus to the passage of highway legislation in the early decades of the 20th century (National Archives [7043]).

Bottom: A good road in Mecklenburg County, North Carolina. Southern states in particular had few reliable roads, hampered by heavy seasonal rainfalls and lack of funding for road projects. This photo shows a rare improved road with wagons loaded with wood and cotton bound for city markets. The band of prison convicts in the center of the picture are probably working on improving the road (National Archives [1794]).

have charge of all scientific and technical work." Logan Waller Page, who was already serving as OPRI's chief of tests, was selected as OPR's first director. Educated at the Virginia Polytechnic Institute and Harvard University, Page's technical background made him an excellent choice for the job, which paid just $2,500 per year. The progressive movement of the late 1800s and early decades of the 20th century advocated clean government and abolition of the patronage or "spoils system," resulting in the passage of the nation's first labor and antitrust legislation. Progressive ideals also embraced the notion that scientific expertise should supersede political considerations in governmental decision making. Page, like others at the time, believed that the planning and con-

Top: Horse-drawn "drag" on rural road near Arlington Farm, Virginia, 1907. A grizzled man poses next to a "drag," or "road scraper", a device commonly used to grade dirt roads in the early days of road building. The unidentified worker could have been a farmer improving a road in near his farmstead. However, individuals and local governments alone could not build and maintain enough roads to benefit the country's ground transportation needs, particularly in rural America (National Archives [396]).

Bottom: Logan Waller Page, Director of Office of Public Roads, 1905–1918. Logan Page was a major figure in the development of the American highway system during the early decades of the 20th century. Page first worked as a geologist and testing engineer for the Massachusetts Highway Commission before starting with the Office of Road Inquiry as chief of testing in 1900. During his tenure with the Office of Public Roads, Page used his post to promote better roads and advocate a larger federal role in road construction. Logan Page lobbied Congress as it considered the Federal-Aid Road Act of 1916 and helped found the American Association of State Highway Officials (AASHO). He died on December 9, 1918, in Chicago while attending an AASHO meeting. From "AASHO: The First Fifty Years, 1914–1964" (Copyright 1965 by AASHO, Washington D. C.; used by permission).

struction of highways should be the purview of the technical expert, free of partisan politics. Using his post at OPR until his death in 1918, Page spearheaded a new initiative to involve the federal government in roads programs.[29]

Under Director Page's leadership, the OPR immediately started several new object lesson road projects. One was in Jacksonville, Florida, a 15-foot wide brick road approximately one mile in length, completed in 1905. Also finished the same year was a 2,047-foot macadam road built on the grounds of the United States Weather Bureau at Mount Weather, Virginia. The innovative road, 15 to 18 feet in width and six inches in depth, used concrete curbs, catch basins and cross drains. The following year, OPR started an experimental highway project at the U.S. Naval Station in New Orleans using a seven-inch subbase of oyster shells, covered by a four-inch layer of clam shells. The total cost for this shell road was $14,569.23. Experiments continued, and on January 3, 1908, the Office of Public Roads completed a 2,945-foot asphalt road on the Missouri State Fairgrounds in Sedalia. The road ran from the edge of town to the state fairgrounds and was 24 feet wide, four inches in depth at the edge and six inches deep in the center.[30]

The sluggishness of federal action prompted local officials to press forward with their own road programs. Macon County, Missouri, started a limestone macadam road in December 1905. The road's dimensions were 2,700 feet in length, 14 feet in width and a depth of eight inches. The road was completed at a cost of $3,229.16, $1,478.39 of which was for 2,217 tons of stone at 66 2/3 cents per ton. Manual laborers were paid $1.50 per day, while teamsters garnered $3 a day. Another project was the Tri-State Road, a 12,300-foot object lesson road at Cumberland Gap, Tennessee, completed in October 1908 at a cost of $2,875.00.[31]

In 1909, Wayne County (Detroit), Michigan, ran an experiment using brick, granite, wood block, and portland cement surfaces. A device using an iron-rimmed wheel and a second wheel with horseshoes revolved around a circular track lined with each type of road surface to test for durability. The cement surface proved superior, as the others surface types rapidly deteriorated. That same year, Wayne County used cement to pave a one-mile stretch of Woodward Avenue outside of Detroit. The Wayne County road was 18 feet wide and 6½ inches thick, making it the longest cement

road at that time. By 1912, the country had a total of 250 miles of concrete roads.[32] However, federal and state governments were slow to meet the growing demand for better roads. By 1910, each state was in the process of establishing their own highway departments to build roads to be funded by toll taxes, general property taxes, and bond issues. Auto license fees covered only the cost of vehicle registration. By 1919, at least four states started a national trend in funding highway construction by levying the first state gasoline taxes.[33]

Road building after the turn of the century, although primitive, was a laborious, multi-step process. Improving an existing road or pathway meant clearing the shoulder area of vegetation before new fill could be added to widen the roadway. In the case of building a new road, plows and other farm machinery using horse-power (or mule-power) were used to clear the way. Steam shovels were used to move earth to fill in rough areas or holes in the roadway. The initial road surface was prepared by a horse-drawn road scraper or "drag" to level the roadway. On the bigger road projects, a grading crew using horses or machine equipment were used instead of dragging. The roadbed was then "rolled," using a vehicle with heavy steel-drum wheels, much like those used today to compress and smoothen asphalt roads. The sequence of the subsequent layers depended on the type of the road that is being built. For macadam roads, a sublayer of clay and sand followed by broken stones formed the top layer. In some cases, oil was spread over the top surface to "glue" the loose material together. New machinery such as the pressure oil spreader speeded the process. The early macadam roads did not hold up very well to weather and traffic, and they needed frequent repair, so road builders turned to brick, concrete and asphalt surfaces, again using several layers of subgrade. A road's life span is very much dependent on the quality of subsurface materials, and technology was constantly being improved. In many areas, the absence of state or federal funding forced local governments to levy property taxes to pay for road construction. Most rural areas could not afford hard-surface roads, so oiled dirt roads were a often a cheap alternative.

Private citizens began to take matters into their own hands and started forming organizations to improve automobile travel. Bicycle clubs were early advocates for highway improvements, but they were soon replaced by automobile clubs as the motor car became more common. In 1902, with

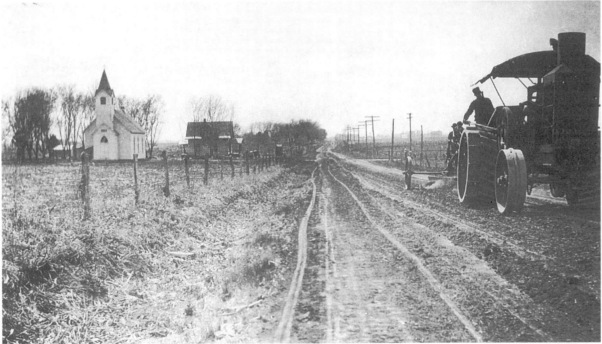

Top: Steam shovel loading earth into wagon. An early steam power shovel and horse-drawn wagons are pictured clearing the way for a new road near Linnville, Ohio. After the diesel-powered shovel was introduced in the late 1920s, steam shovels soon disappeared. This photograph was taken by W. E. Rosengarten in 1914 for the Bureau of Public Roads (National Archives [12345]).

Bottom: Tractor grading roadbed for Lincoln Highway, Boone County, Iowa. A tractor and road grader gives a section of the Lincoln Highway two miles east of Ogden, Iowa, a "spring redressing." Although the route for the Lincoln Highway was first announced in 1913, it took years before any real improvements were made to hard-top the highway. In most instances, the route was maintained by county and occasionally, state governments. Photo taken by W. E. Rosengarten in May 1916 (National Archives [14311]).

Top: Typical grading crew, Michigan, 1911. A crew of road "graders" pose for a photo on a dirt road with teams of horses. Horses, mules, and man-power were the mainstay of early road building, with motorized equipment still in scarce supply. Construction crews often recruited local farmers to help build roads for modest pay. Rural residents badly needed better farm-to-market roads and many were eager to help out when new routes ran through their locales (National Archives [39-3789]).

Bottom: Rolling a layer of marble rock near Rogersville, Tennessee. Early highways, particularly in rural areas, were usually surfaced with materials found locally. Rock and other minerals adjacent to new highways were used for gravel or macadam, or for mixing cement and asphalt. This photo shows a steam roller leveling a layer of broken marble taken from a nearby quarry. Photo by L. E. Boykin, July 7, 1911 (National Archives [5614]).

Spreading tar over macadam road, Westminster, Maryland, September 1910. A road crew coats a macadam road with tar using two-inch steam hoses from a tank car. The 275-degree Fahrenheit bituminous dried to make a hardened surface, making a somewhat waterproof roadway. Macadam roads had to be resurfaced frequently, as the roadway quickly disintegrated under the weight of traffic. Taken by C. C. Ahles (National Archives [4171]).

only 23,000 registered cars in the United States (compared to 17 million horses), at least 50 auto clubs already existed nationwide, each with its own purpose and agenda. That year, nine clubs met in Chicago to form the American Automobile Association (AAA), an organization dedicated to the furtherance and improvement of automotive travel. Since its founding, the American Automobile Association has provided automobile travelers with up-to-date tourist information, road maps, and other services. The AAA was a major supporter of the Good Roads Bill of 1903 and later highway-related legislation.[34]

In 1912, Congress considered legislation introduced by Rep. Dorsey W. Shakelford of Missouri to upgrade and improve rural roads. Under the Shakelford proposal, the federal government would pay a rental fee to counties for use of local roads for mail delivery. The revenue from the rental fees could then be used for road construction and upkeep. In the early days of highway construction in America, farmers and other landowners who benefited from road improvements paid for them through their local property taxes. The property taxation approach was burdensome on taxpayers and was far short of the amount of funding needed to build hard-surfaced roads. The Shakelford bill encountered opposition in the Senate from AAA and other road boosters who favored interstate roads instead of local or rural roads. This group also believed that the first roads built under a federal road program should follow the most important routes as the railroads did as they spanned the West. As usual, infighting and rival interests killed the Shakelford bill in the Senate.[35]

However, the Good Roads Movement refused to go away. On November 22, 1910, 30 state and national organizations met in Washington, D. C., to form the American Association for Highway Improvement (renamed the American Highway Association in 1912). Logan Page was invited to the conference, which unified various good roads associations, railroads, and highway agencies into one potent lobbying group. The slogan "Get the Farmers Out of the Mud" began to resonate in the nation's capital once again, and Congress responded

Top: Spraying oil over resurfaced macadam road, Rockville, Maryland, October 1913. A more efficient method of surfacing roads with oil was the introduction of the pressure road oiler, shown here behind a team of horses. Modern versions of the pressure road oiler are still being used for spraying oil on bituminous roads to bond new asphalt to old roadbeds and for other purposes (National Archives [10161]).

Bottom: Girls working on Rockville Pike, Montgomery County, Maryland. America's entry into World War I in 1917 created labor shortages in many industries as millions of men joined the armed forces. Women were often employed to replace lost workers. A crew of girls are spreading rocks over a newly-oiled rural road in Maryland in 1918. Taken by J. K. Hillers (National Archives [16675]).

Top: AAA LOGOS, 1906, 1915, 1922, 1983, 1997 (courtesy, AAA).

Bottom: AAA roadside service vehicle aiding motorist. In 1902, approximately 1,000 delegates from nine auto clubs met in Chicago to form the American Automobile Association, an organization dedicated to improving roads and travel for the American motorist. From its inception, "AAA" (as it is commonly called) has been an ardent supporter of highway legislation such as the Good Roads Bill of 1903, as well as opposing anti-automobile laws and ordinances. The organization's members enjoyed benefits such as free road maps, available as early as 1905, and roadside emergency service, starting in 1915. This AAA publicity photograph shows a AAA man with a three-wheeled motorcycle helping a stranded motorist (Courtesy, AAA, 1997).

by enacting the Post Office Department Appropriations Act for 1913. The act established a joint congressional committee to report to Congress on federal aid for highways and appropriated $500,000 to improve postal routes. During the next several years, the federal government conditioned funds by limiting the workday to eight hours, and a 1915 executive order banned use of convict labor on federally-funded projects. County officials objected to federal requirements, especially

A. L. Westgard expedition crossing the Rio Puerco, Bernalillo County, New Mexico, 1911. A group of early tourists fording the Rio Puerco approximately 21 miles west of Albuquerque, New Mexico, on one of A. L. Westgard's cross-country motor tours. Often referred to as "The Pathfinder," Westgard traveled thousands of miles over difficult terrain throughout the continental United States, charting the best routes for future generations of motorists. Pioneer travelers encountered bad weather and unexpected hazards, such as faulty bridges, loose soil and mud roads. In this photo, taken in November 1911, Westgard's group is pulling vehicles stuck in a quicksand river bottom (National Archives [7092]).

the Office of Public Roads' role in setting standards, and did not give their full support to the program. However, 456 miles of postal roads in 28 counties in 17 states were ultimately improved. One lesson that was learned from the 1913 Act was that aid should go directly to the states instead of to the over 3,000 county governments.[36]

The AAA and other organizations, which included automobile enthusiasts and businesses hoping to profit by improved roads, began charting interstate auto routes. Auto club members and other early trailblazers embarked on rigorous cross-country junkets following known Indian and pioneer trails, while exploring new routes. In those days, roads were identified by names chosen by some of these early "pathfinders." There was very little to guide them and trips were often prematurely ended by a host of possible highway fiascoes. One early pathfinder, A. L. Westgard, gained a national reputation for his many cross-country auto treks. Westgard kept a journal of his travels and drew his own road maps along the way. Westgard formed the "Touring Club of America" and in 1910 announced his "Trail to Sunset" route from Chicago to Los Angeles. The OPR even made Westgard a Special Agent in recognition of his expertise in charting new routes. On March 4, 1911, Westgard set out with his 37-horsepower truck dubbed the "Pioneer Freighter" in search of new long-distance routes which were also of interest to the OPR. That same year, the OPR published a map with 12 proposed transcontinental routes totaling 15,000 miles, using ideas submitted by highway organizations and auto clubs, local communities, and others. Included were the Pacific Highway, the Montreal-to-Miami Highway, and the Ocean-to-Ocean Highway. Other highway pioneers followed Westgard's example. The Quebec-Miami-International Highway was drawn in 1911; the name was changed to Atlantic Highway in 1915. Even Carl G. Fisher, a wealthy automobile manufacturer, plotted his own transcontinental route from Times Square in New York City to Lincoln Park in San Francisco.[37]

In 1913, the Lincoln Highway Association was officially formed to build the country's first east-west, coast-to-coast highway. The project was a purely private initiative and depended on donations from the public and the auto industry. The route was called the "Lincoln Highway" in honor of the late president (Abe Lincoln's birth centennial was in 1909) and started at Jersey City, New Jersey, and traveled through Philadelphia, Pittsburgh, Fort Wayne, Indiana, past the south end of Chicago, across Iowa, and then following pioneer trails such as the Overland Trail and the Pony Express route via Cheyenne, Salt Lake City, and ending in San Francisco. Private contributions alone were inadequate, and progress of the ambitious project proceeded slowly. However, the Lincoln Highway's boosters developed an ingenious scheme to fund the highway, called the "seedling mile." The Association chose a stretch of rural road between two towns along the route and with the financial backing of local concrete companies, graded and paved a hard surfaced highway. The quality of the new road was startling to people living adjacent to the new highway, who were used to swampy roads, and excited drivers eagerly sped along the short pieces of new road. As the word about the new Lincoln Highway spread, cities and towns further along the planned route donated funds for the project. The eventual length of the Lincoln Highway came to 3,385 miles and

Top: A. L. Westgard's contingent stops during a cross-country junket to chat with travelers in a covered wagon driven by jack rabbit mules, Nevada, 1912. The scene symbolizes the end of one era and the ushering in of a new one, as the new motor car quickly proved its superiority over horse-drawn travel, a mainstay of transportation for thousands of years of human history (National Archives [6866]).

Bottom: Racers on Washington Post Truck Run, May 1913. Almost as soon as the automobile came into use, racing competitions formed, pitting driver and vehicle against each other. Henry Ford himself entered several such races early in his career, winning his first race in Detroit in October 1900. Pictured here are contestants in the Washington Post Truck Run, competing on a course between Washington, D. C., and Fredericksburg, Virginia, May 5–8, 1913 (National Archives [9495]).

Trail markings. These drawings of markings for several of the over 250 trails that criss-crossed the United States in the early 20th century is taken from an early road map. Trail organizations adopted their own system of colored stripes and symbols, often painted on trees, fence posts, and other objects on the roadside to guide motorists. However, the sheer number of trail routes made this method of highway marking confusing to travelers by the 1920s (Courtesy, Society for Commercial Archeology).

remains America's longest highway. The project took over two decades to complete, and was not completely paved until 1935. However, the Lincoln Highway did become the nation's first hard-surface transcontinental highway, and was often called the "Main Street of America." Encouraged by the success of the Lincoln Highway, other trail organizations started charting their own routes. The Ozark Trails Association held a convention in 1913 and started a road traveling southwest from St. Louis into New Mexico. The main branch of the "Ozark Trail" eventually became part of U.S. Route 66, which runs from Chicago to Los Angeles. The National Old Trails Road Ocean-to-Ocean Association, founded in 1915, proposed routes that followed the nation's historic trails. In 1914, OPR and the American Highway Association collaborated on a highway maintenance experiment along the 893-mile Washington–Atlanta Highway. The route later became part of the Bankhead Highway, which took a swing through the southern states from Washington, D.C., to Los Angeles via Atlanta. The highway was named for Alabama Senator John H. Bankhead's early support in advocating federal aid for national highways while serving as a member of Congress from 1887 until his death in 1920.[38]

Popular Named Trails and Highways

Arrowhead Trail (Salt Lake City–Los Angeles); U.S. 91.

Atlantic Highway (Ft. Kent, ME–Miami); ME-11, U.S. 1

Black and Yellow Trail (Chicago–Yellowstone National Park); U.S. 14.

Blue Ridge Parkway (Great Smoky Mountains National Park–Shenandoah National Park); U.S. 11.

Boone-Wilderness Road (Williamsport, MD–Boonesboro, KY); U.S. 25, U.S. 25E, U.S. 58, U.S. 11.

Boston Post Road (Boston–New York City); U.S. 1.

Cherry Valley Turnpike (Albany–Syracuse, NY); U.S. 20.

Detroit–Lincoln–Denver Highway (Detroit–Denver); U.S. 6.

Dixie Highway (Detroit–Miami); U.S. 25, U.S. 27.

Dixie Beeline (Chicago–Nashville); U.S. 41.

Dixie Overland Highway (Atlanta–San Diego); U.S. 28, U.S. 80.

Lincoln Highway, Pennsylvania. Called the "Main Street of America," the Lincoln Highway was conceived in 1913 as the country's main east-west transcontinental route serving the northern states. Designated as U.S. 30, the Lincoln Highway is the nation's longest highway, measuring 3,385 miles from Atlantic City to Astoria, Oregon. The photo is of a section of the Lincoln Highway in the Pennsylvania Appalachians in the 1930s (National Archives).

Inland Route (San Diego–San Francisco); U.S. 101.

Jackson Highway (Chicago–New Orleans); U.S. 51, U.S. 45.

Jefferson Highway (New Orleans–Texas State Line); U.S. 90.

Jefferson Davis Highway (Washington, D.C.–Mobile, AL); U.S. 29; U.S. 31.

Lancaster Pike (Philadelphia–Chambersburg, PA); U.S. 30.

Lee Highway (New York City–San Francisco); U.S. 11, U.S. 64; U.S. 6.

Lincoln Highway (New York City–San Francisco); U.S. 30.

Lone Star Route (Chicago–Beeville, TX); U.S. 66, U.S. 67, U.S. 59.

Mississippi Valley Highway (Ely, MN–Gulfport, MS); U.S. 61, U.S. 49.

Mohawk Trail (Greenfield, MA–Schenectady, NY); MA-2; NY-2, NY-7.

National Old Trails Road (Baltimore–Los Angeles); U.S. 50, U.S. 66.

Natchez Trace Parkway (Nashville–Port Gibbons, MS); Natchez Trace Pkwy.

Ocean Highway (New York City–Miami); U.S. 13, U.S. 17.

Old National Pike (Cumberland, MD–Vandalia, IL); U.S. 40.

Old Oregon Trail (Independence, MO–Oregon City, OR); U.S. 30, U.S. 26, WY-220, U.S. 287, WY-28, U.S. 30.

Old Spanish Trail (St. Augustine, FL–San Diego); U.S. 70, U.S. 80, U.S. 90.

Ozark Trail (St. Louis–El Paso, TX); U.S. 66, U.S. 277, U.S. 80.

Redwood Highway (Grants Pass, OR–San Francisco); U.S. 99, U.S. 101.

Rocky Mountain Highway (Denver–Yellowstone National Park); U.S. 87, U.S. 20.

Roosevelt Highway (Port Jarvis, NY to Erie, PA); U.S. 6

Santa Fe Trail (Independence, MO–Santa Fe, NM); U.S. 56, U.S. 66.

Susquehanna Trail (Buffalo, NY–Washington, D.C.); U.S. 219, NY-17, U.S. 11, U.S. 111.

Three "C" Highway (Cleveland–Columbus–Cincinnati, OH); U.S. 42.

William Penn Highway (New York City–Pittsburgh); U.S. 22.

Will Rogers Memorial Highway (Chicago–Los Angeles); U.S. 66.

Yellowstone Trail (Boston–Seattle); U.S. 20, U.S. 12, U.S. 10.[39]

In the South, the "Good Roads Movement" was active in pressing state governments for funds for local farm-to-market roads. Eventually, a dozen interstate routes entering the South from the North were developed, boosting commerce and helping to bring the region out of rural isolation. Among these new routes was the "Dixie Highway," formed by a disparate group of citizens in 1915. The original Dixie Highway traveled from Detroit, Michigan, to Miami, Florida, with other routes added later. Carl G. Fisher was the chief inspiration for the Dixie Highway, no doubt due to the fact that he owned extensive land holdings in the Miami area and no roads existed to aid migration to south Florida. Fisher believed that highway routes should include as many large cities and points of interest as possible, while others, such as Dixie Highway Association president Henry Jay, favored the most direct routing to save travel time. Since everyone wanted the new roads to run through their town, competition for route selection was keen, and politics often prevailed over practicality. The resulting route of the original Dixie Highway was, as described by Fisher, was a "four thousand-mile wandering pea-vine." [40]

Other popular routes included the National Old Trails Road (Baltimore to Los Angeles), Ocean Highway (New York to Miami), the Yellowstone Trail (Boston to Seattle), as well as others too numerous to mention. Each route was identified by its own symbol, which were painted on telegraph and telephone poles, or whatever could be found on the roadside. The Lincoln Highway used red, white, and blue stripes with the letter "L," and the Dixie Highway used the letters "D. H.," with red and white stripes. The markers were placed at key intersections and at proper intervals so as to be easily visible to motorists. By 1920, over 250 named trails were designated by various trail organizations. The tangled maze of trails became a nightmare for motorists, particularly when several routes converged or arrived at the same destination.[41]

Besides navigating the country's primitive pathways, the motorist's next task was to locate overnight accommodations. The earliest autos (except luxury models) had no windshield or roof, exposing motorists to the elements. To protect themselves from wind, dust, and rain, men wore goggles and raincoats while women wore veils and long coats called "dusters" for protection. By the end of the day, travelers needed a place to relax and clean up from the long day on the road. By 1900, Amer-

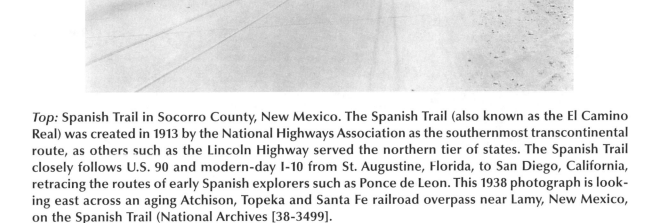

Top: Spanish Trail in Socorro County, New Mexico. The Spanish Trail (also known as the El Camino Real) was created in 1913 by the National Highways Association as the southernmost transcontinental route, as others such as the Lincoln Highway served the northern tier of states. The Spanish Trail closely follows U.S. 90 and modern-day I-10 from St. Augustine, Florida, to San Diego, California, retracing the routes of early Spanish explorers such as Ponce de Leon. This 1938 photograph is looking east across an aging Atchison, Topeka and Santa Fe railroad overpass near Lamy, New Mexico, on the Spanish Trail (National Archives [38-3499].

Bottom: Improved portion of the Boston Post Road in Connecticut, 1926. Improved communication, particularly through better mail service, was a major argument in favor of road construction throughout American history. In 1673, a post rider delivered a packet of mail between Boston and New York City in two weeks. The route became the Boston Post Road (formerly known as the King's Highway), which became the main highway between the two cities and was later designated as a portion of U.S. 1, which runs from Madawaska, Maine, to Key West, Florida (National Archives [35-1157]).

Top: Surviving portion of the Emigration Trail, Utah. The Emigration or Mormon Trail was used by Mormon settlers as they migrated west into the state of Utah in the 1840s. Remnants of the Mormon and other pioneer trials remain today. This photo shows the old trail off to the left, with dirt road for autos on the right to preserve this historic trail (National Archives [46-1493]).

Bottom: Old Cumberland Road (National Pike), one mile east of Polish Mountain, Maryland. The most ambitious early American road project was the Cumberland Road (renamed the National Pike), funded by Congress in 1806, with a proposed route from Cumberland, Maryland, to St. Louis. Originally called "Braddock's Road" (named for the famous English general whose grave lies just off the road in eastern Maryland), this route carried a tide of settlers migrating to the Midwest. However, construction proceeded at a snail's pace, and the project was eventually abandoned in 1852. This 1939 photo is 11 miles east of Cumberland, Maryland, and shows the road in relatively unimproved condition (National Archives [39-3127]).

"Bad roads." Many periodicals appeared in the early 20th century aimed at motorists and promoting better roads, such as *American Motorist* (an AAA publication) and *Good Roads* magazine. This cartoon from the December 1916 issue of *Better Roads and Streets* magazine shows how "bad roads" impede progress and prosperity (Courtesy, US DOT, FHWA). 56.-59.

icans still favored travel by rail to overland stagecoach, and hotels came to be located near the town's rail station. At the turn of the century, virtually all lodging consisted of hotels. In 1910, there were 10,000 hotels operating in the United States, with approximately one million rooms. The first auto tourists typically checked in for the night at

the hotel in the center of the nearest town, some calling themselves "motor hotels." However, as tourism increased, travelers wanted a faster way to stop for the night, which meant bypassing the center of town to avoid city traffic. Occasionally, farmers located just outside of town provided tourists with a crude shack and kerosene lamp for a nominal charge. In 1913, city workers in Douglas, Arizona, built six wooden structures on a vacant lot on the outskirts of town for travelers to stop for the night. Other municipalities followed suit and dozens of "auto camps" started offering a new low-cost alternative to the hotel. The popularity of auto camps continued almost uninterrupted until the Second World War. The land was cheap and many early motorists preferred them to more expensive and formal hotel.[42]

Although travel by rail was at its peak in 1900, some 13 railroads were in bankruptcy by the outbreak of the First World War. By the 1910s, auto production and travel saw a rapid increase. Travelers were either those on business trips or vacationers taking short trips to the seashore or the mountains. With over two million cars on the roads by 1914, the automobile, as well as the American traveler, needed more roadside accommodations.

Fill 'er Up!

By the mid–1800s, the world supply of whale oil for lighting became scarce, with prices approaching $5 a gallon. Crude oil seepage had been known for centuries, but no one had developed any commercial use. In the 1850s, Samuel M. Kier began selling crude oil as a cure-all, then found a way to refine it into kerosene and even invented a lamp. As the demand for kerosene soon outstripped supply, a young Dartmouth graduate dispatched "Colonel" E. L. Drake to Titusville, Pennsylvania, to drill for new sources. In August 1859, at a depth of only 69.5 feet, Drake struck oil, and an oil rush ensued.[43] The new "black gold" was initially used as a lubricant, but the invention of the internal combustion engine created for a new use for "gasoline," a derivative of the petroleum refining process. At first, gasoline could be found at industrial depots, where it was stored in large drums with a spigot at the bottom. The early motorist, particularly farmers, sometimes had to journey considerable distances to fuel sources. At the turn of the century, the hardy consumer had to provide their own containers and transport the volatile product home for storage and later transfer it into the car's gas tank. For more convenience and safety, blacksmith shops, carriage and bicycle shops, hardware and grocery stores started selling gasoline, along with kerosene.

In 1885, a Fort Wayne, Indiana, entrepreneur named Sylvanus F. Bowser modified a water pump into a "self-measuring gasoline tank" that pumped fuel from a barrel. His first customer was local grocery store owner Jake Gumper, who was so impressed with the invention that he quit his business and started to work for Bowser. The Bowser pump was first used for oil, then adapted to pump gasoline from a 50-gallon tank enclosed in a wooden cabinet. Mr. Gumper painted the words "filling station" on the outside of the cabinet. In 1905, the owners of the Laessig & Grenner Gasoline Company in St. Louis improved Bowser's pump further by attaching a rubber hose to an upright storage tank to dispense gasoline into the automobile tank. The result was the forerunner of the gasoline station.[44]

A variety of crude gas pump designs proliferated in those early days, appearing at roadsides everywhere. However, with motorists lining up at curbsides for gas, congestion and accidents resulted. The Standard Oil Company, which monopolized the oil industry at the time, decided that standardized retail outlets would be more efficient. In 1907, station owner John McLean opened up the first filling station for Standard Oil in Seattle, Washington. McLean's idea used a drive-through design, which got drivers off the main thoroughfare and allowed customers to enter and exit the station easily. Inside a small building, McLean placed a tank on a platform with a glass measuring device and a rubber hose.[45]

The methods of delivering gasoline continued to make improvements. In the first decade of the century, the first underground storage tanks appeared. By 1910, a glass spinner with an audible bell (one clang per gallon) was invented, and in 1912, a translucent glass "globe" on the top of the gas pump was added. Gas pump globes were inscribed with each brand's logo and lighted internally so that they can be spotted on dark highways at night. However, some early consumers were suspicious of the quantity of gasoline they were being sold, so taller pumps were introduced, topped by a glass reservoir containing a scale which filled with gasoline. Since consumers could now see the gasoline they were buying, some gas companies decided to get trendy and added a dye to color their gasoline. Texaco used green, Esso was red, Sunoco was blue. This was changed in the 1920s, after it was discovered that sunlight caused the gasoline to form an unpleasant-looking brown film in the glass cylinder. To fix this flaw, the glass was given a blue tint to block out ultraviolet light. The first manual pumps were improved by the introduction of the electric motor-driven pump in 1923. In 1929, the first metered pumps made the sale of gas more precise.[46]

The Standard Oil Company of Ohio, established by John D. and William Rockefeller in 1870, controlled 90 percent of domestic oil refinery capacity and almost all of its pipelines in the early part of the 20th century. In 1906, the U.S. government sued the oil giant, charging it with monopolistic practices in violation of the Sherman Anti-Trust Act. In 1911, the U.S. Supreme Court forced Standard Oil's 34 subsidiaries to become separate companies, with the further provision that they have no business relationship with each other. However, several of the former Standard Oil companies continued to use the familiar "Standard" name for years later. The five largest of the former Standard Oil companies, in order of sales, are: Exxon, Mobil, Chevron, Amoco, and Atlantic Richfield.

With the breakup of Standard Oil, competition was finally possible, and numerous new gasoline companies emerged. During the 1920s, there were over 100 brands and approximately 100,000 filling stations dotting the landscape, with even the smallest hamlet having at least one outlet. Over the decades, the number of name brands has gradually declined, with several dozen remaining today. Some of today's familiar trade names have interesting corporate histories.

Chevron

Following Colonel Drake's discovery of crude oil, profits from oil production slowly increased as new uses for the product were discovered. In California in the 1870s, men searched for oil as their predecessors prospected for gold. Frederick Taylor put his money into an oil rig north of Los Angeles at Pico Canyon and struck oil. With a group of investors, Taylor formed the Pacific Coast Oil Company on September 10, 1879. However, John D. Rockefeller opened a marketing office for his new company in San Francisco the same year, hoping to expand his operations in the west. In 1900, Standard bought the small but oil-rich company and built the largest refinery in California at Richmond. Standard continued to drill in Kern County (near Bakersfield, north of Los Angeles) and struck oil in January 1910. As the Richmond refinery grew to keep up with production, a second refinery at El Segundo, California was built. As auto production continued to soar, a new oil based road paving material called "asphalt" was introduced, increasing demand for oil. The thick California Crude was ideal for asphalt production, and the Richmond refinery added it to their product line.[47]

After the U.S. Supreme Court ordered the break-up of the Standard Oil Company, the former Standard subsidiary became known as "Standard Oil Company (California)." Following World War I, with its West Coast reserves nearly depleted, the company explored for oil throughout the Rockies and ultimately overseas. Spectacular gushers at Montebello, Elk Hills, and Huntington Beach made Standard California the largest producer of crude oil in the United States for a short time. The company merged with another strong producer, Pacific Oil Company, and changed its name to Standard Oil Company of California (Socal). The company pioneered a new aviation fuel, Red Crown Gasoline, which burned well in thin air and cold temperatures. Charles Lindbergh made aviation history on his transatlantic flight using Standard Red Crown fuel. To help guide pilots, the company had its early filling stations paint the name of its city on their rooftops. Several other former Standard Oil subsidiaries continued to include the word "Standard" as a part of their corporate identification for decades after the breakup of John D. Rockefeller's original Standard Oil Company. The Standard name remained in the midwest region until it was changed to "Amoco" in the 1970s. Standard-Chevron continued into the late 1960s, when the company changed its name to simply "Chevron."[48]

Phillips Petroleum Company

By the mid–1870s, the United States was beginning to recover from the tragic aftermath of the Civil War, and the Industrial Revolution that had already swept Europe was gaining momentum in America. The railroads were expanding and demand for oil for industry was rising dramatically, touching off a frenzy of oil prospecting not seen since the gold rush days. Businessmen and wildcatters flocked to the site of each new discovery, hoping to get in on the new wealth. After learning of an oil strike in the Oklahoma Indian Territory, Frank Phillips left his banking position in Iowa and moved to Bartlesville, Oklahoma, an oil boom town, to seek his fortune. With the financial backing of his banker father-in-law, he organized the

Chevron Logos: 1930s; 1940s; Modern (courtesy, Chevron).

Lady posing at Standard station, circa 1922. The Standard Oil Company, founded by John D. Rockefeller, was actually made up of 34 subsidiary companies, as Rockefeller bought out competitors or drove others out of business by ruthless underpricing. In 1911, the U.S. Supreme Court dissolved Standard Oil under the Sherman Anti-Trust Act, resulting in 34 separate companies, among them, familiar names such as Exxon, Mobil, Amoco, and Chevron. However, some former Standard Oil subsidiaries, like this early 1920s outlet, continued to use the Standard name well into the 1960s and 1970s (Courtesy, Chevron Corporation).

came unpredictable during the early 1910s, but quickly returned after the price of oil skyrocketed during World War I. They incorporated in 1917, naming the new oil company the Phillips Petroleum Company, with headquarters in Bartlesville. The new company started with $1 million in assets and acquired new sites in the Texas Panhandle. By 1924, the Phillips Petroleum Company had a net worth of $103 million.[49]

As auto production continued to soar, so did the demand for oil and its by-products. By 1926, nearly 15 million Model T Fords alone plied the nation's roadways, and Phillips' assets now totaled $266 million. On November 19, 1927, the company opened its first filling station in Wichita, Kansas. As the company started to sell its gasoline to the public, it needed a catchy trade symbol. They considered using the numbers "66," since that was the specific gravity number of their new fuel. Advertising marketers of the day used numerals in naming products, and "66" was again suggested after U.S. Highway 66, which ran from Phillips' refinery in Borger, Texas, and near Bartlesville on its way to Chicago. A company official, while road testing the new fuel enroute from Bartlesville to Tulsa, commented "This car goes like 60 on our new gas!" After glancing at the speedometer, the driver exclaimed "Sixty, nothing; we're doing 66!" The official repeated the story at the next company meeting and was asked where the incident took place. Upon learning that they had been traveling on U.S. Highway 66, "Phillips 66" became the obvious choice. In 1930, the company's products were marketed with a new logo using the U.S. Federal-Aid

Anchor Oil and Gas Company in 1903. Frank brought in his brother, E. L., and together they sold enough stock in the company to start drilling in 1905. The first three holes yielded nothing, however, and with just enough money for a fourth well, the Phillips brothers' luck changed and they proceeded to hit 81 consecutive oil strikes. The brothers returned to banking when the oil business be-

Phillips logos: 1928; 1929; 1930; 1959 (courtesy, Phillips Petroleum Company).

Highway System shield and the familiar name, "Phillips 66."[50]

Mobil

Following the Civil War, Matthew Ewing invented a method of distilling crude oil to make kerosene in a vacuum. A by-product of the process was a residue that made a superior lubricant. With the financial backing of Hiram Bond Everest, the process was patented and the Vacuum Oil Company was formed in 1866. Everest bought out Ewing and continued the company's successful line of manufacturing lubricants, harness oil, and other products. In 1869, Everest patented his "Gargoyle 600W Steam Cylinder Oil," which was capable of withstanding high heat and pressure while minimizing friction in steam engines. This oil, still in use today, allowed manufacturers to build larger, faster machines to increase production. In 1879, John D. Rockefeller bought 75 percent of the Vacuum Oil Company. In 1882, Rockefeller organized various companies within the Standard Oil Trust, one being Standard of New York (Socony), which marketed and refined petroleum products in New York and the New England states.[51]

After the Supreme Court dissolved Standard Oil in 1911, both Vacuum Oil and Socony became separate companies. While Vacuum expanded its refining capability, Socony moved into oil production. Vacuum Oil acquired Lubrite Refining Company of St. Louis in 1929, the Wadhams Oil Company of Milwaukee in 1930, and also in 1930, took over White Star Refining Company, with 1,500 filling station outlets in Michigan, Indiana, and Ohio. Meanwhile, Socony purchased the Magnolia Petroleum Company, already established for 20 years in the Southwest, and the General Petroleum Company of California in 1926. Socony's marketing area covered the West Coast, Southwest, and Northeast, but not the Midwest. In 1930, Socony bought out the White Eagle Oil & Refining Company, with stations in eleven Midwestern states.[52]

The modern company known as Mobil was formed when Vacuum and Socony merged in 1931, becoming the Socony-Vacuum Oil Company. The new company now had affiliates in 43 states and interests in overseas markets in 50 countries. The company changed its name to Socony Mobil Oil Company in 1955, and on its 100th anniversary of its founding became the Mobil Oil Company in 1966.[53]

The Mobil name and its "Flying Red Horse" have long played a role in the company's trademark history. Mobil oil was first marketed in New England in 1899 and became a registered trademark in 1920. The origin of the word is uncertain, but may have come from the Latin word "mobilis," meaning "capable of being moved," which seems appropriate for motor vehicles. The company's famous Pegasus symbol appeared in 1911 and was first used by a former Socony company in South Africa. It was Mobil Sehiya of Japan that gave Pegasus its red coloring, and the "Flying Red

Left to right Mobil logos: 1911; 1933; Mobil/Socony-Vacuum 1930s; 1955; 1965 (Courtesy, Mobil Corporation).

Horse" symbol was adopted shortly after Socony and Vacuum's merger in 1931. In 1966, the company changed its name to "Mobil," with its new logo featuring a red "O" in the company name. However, since the company has become so identified with Pegasus, Mobil has retained the flying red steed for marketing purposes. As of the printing of this book, a merger between Mobil and another former Standard Oil Company giant, Exxon, was announced to form a new corporation, "Exxon Mobil."[54]

Shell

A British importer of mother-of-pearl, a popular material for decorative and other uses around the turn of the century, decided in 1907 to expand its product line to include oil products. The Royal Dutch Shell Company was thus formed, appropriately adopting the name "Shell" in deference to the company's original product. The new company embarked on a global search for oil, and with the discovery of oil in the Dutch East Indies, Royal Dutch Shell quickly became a world leader in petroleum refining and exporting.[55]

The company soon eyed the burgeoning American market. In 1912, hoping to make inroads in the U.S., Royal Dutch Shell formed the American Gasoline Company, based in Seattle, Washington. The new company's goal was to sell gasoline to motorists in the Pacific Northwest and San Francisco Bay areas. On September 16, 1912, the oil tanker *S. S. Romany* arrived at the small port of Richmond Beach, just north of Seattle, carrying over a million gallons of gasoline from Sumatra. The new fuel was promptly pumped ashore into the storage tanks at a brand-new water terminal. A few days later, an equally-new Shell tank car delivered 8,000 gallons of gasoline to its first retail outlet in Chehalis, Washington. The new gasoline, called "Shell Motor Spirit," had a

high specific gravity and performed well for hard-to-start engines of the day. Shell soon gained a loyal following in the northwestern United States.[56]

After the discovery of oil in California, American Gasoline purchased the California oil fields in 1913. The company built a state-of-the-art refinery at Martinez, California, which featured the country's first modern continuous process refinery. This was followed by the 1918 completion of a major refinery in Wood River, Illinois, which still serves the midwest region. In 1921, Shell made a spectacular oil discovery at Signal Hill, California, in a newly-developed exclusive residential area near Long Beach. The Signal Hill Field would later prove to be one the top-producing fields in the continental United States. The strike set off a rush of oil drilling and the area was soon covered with make-shift wooden derricks.[57]

In 1922, the various Shell companies around the country merged with the Union Oil Company of Delaware, forming the Shell Union Oil Company, a holding company. The merger created a publicly-held corporation until 1985, when Royal Dutch Shell Group assumed 100 percent ownership of Shell Union Oil. Today, the company's yellow shell emblem remains a familiar roadside symbol to motorists nationwide.[58]

Texaco

The Texas Company was founded in 1902 in Beaumont, Texas, by oil man "Buckskin" Joe Cullinan and New York investor Arnold Schaler. The new company, initially capitalized at $3 million, struck oil at Sour Lake, Texas, in 1903. The company grew rapidly, building a refinery at Port Arthur, Texas, and establishing a retail marketing system. In 1928, the Texas Company became the first U.S. oil company to sell its products in all 48 states.[59]

During the 1930s, the company expanded overseas and entered into joint ventures with Standard of California and oil producers and the company's name was changed to Texaco, Inc. Texaco adopted its red star logo during the Great Depression, and

Shell logos: 1930s; 1960s; Modern (Courtesy, Shell Oil Company).

Top: Shell gas station. This modest 1919 Shell station, located somewhere in California, typifies the humble origins of the American gasoline filling station; a tiny building, a simple carport, and two pumps. Standardized filling stations would come later (Courtesy, Shell Oil Company).

Bottom: Shell gasoline trucks in Ohio, circa 1926. On October 1, 1912, a parent company to Shell Oil, the Roxana Petroleum Company was organized in Oklahoma to develop new reserves and sell to outside buyers. Roxana produced beyond expectations, and it diverted much of its capacity to a new refinery in Wood River, Illinois. Today, Shell's Wood River refinery remains its main source of oil products for the Midwest (Courtesy, Shell Oil Company).

Texaco logos: 1930s; 1950s; 1968, Modern (Courtesy, Texaco, Inc.).

was one of the few companies that marketed throughout the entire country. Texaco also was among the first oil companies to introduce standardized filling station architecture. The company employed a single-building design, which included an attached garage and in some instances, a small cafe. Today, Texaco places in the top five domestic oil giants in sales, and its stations are still found in every state.[60]

The Federal-Aid Road Act of 1916

By 1913, 1.3 million cars were owned by Americans eager to explore the country; by 1920, nearly 10 million autos plodded along on the nation's mud and dirt trails. New Jersey and Massachusetts were the first states to establish their own state highway departments. Government involvement in road building was hampered by the progressive philosophy of industrial efficiency through capitalism and reliance on technological progress. Highway construction was best left to engineers instead of politicians. Office of Public Roads director Logan Page lobbied Congress to expand OPR from merely an advisory agency into a leading national authority on highway construction. Page envisioned a coherent federal highway program that would aid rural mail routes as well as travelers, and coordinate state and federal highway authorities in the planning and construction of roads. Page continued to push for more federal aid, and some meager appropriations did make their way down to states. Due to Page's persistence, Congress steadily increased funding for the Bureau of Public Roads.[61]

In 1914, the American Association of State Highway Officials was formed. The AASHO consisted of state and federal highway officials who wanted to coordinate highway construction and planning on a national level. In September 1915, a small group of AASHO members, headed by Thomas H. MacDonald (chief engineer for the Iowa State Highway Commission) met in Oakland, California, to put together a new federal-aid bill to submit to Congress. The AASHO proposal called for a $75 million appropriation to be spent over five years by the states. Funding would be based on the following formula: one-third based on the state's land area; one-third on state population; and one-third on the state's total mileage of rural free delivery (RFD) and "star routes" (non–U.S. postal routes awarded to private contractors). The federal government would pay half the cost of a project up to a limit of $10,000 per mile. The states would have been required to establish state highway agencies to select rural post roads and obtain approval from the Department of Agriculture. State governments would also be prevented from charging tolls, and each legislature was required to approve the AASHO bill's provisions. At Logan Page's urging, a key provision allowed OPR to approve design and other aspects of state highway plans for any federal aid project to assure quality control and uniformity.[62]

Before AASHO could present its proposed bill to Congress, Rep. Shakelford introduced another bill in early 1916. The new Shakelford bill set aside $25 million for improving rural post roads (RFD routes) and star routes, with the federal government paying for 30–50 percent of the costs using a formula based on a state's population plus the total mileage of all RFD and star routes. The bill overwhelmingly passed the House and went on to the Senate Committee on Post Offices and Post Roads, headed by Sen. John H. Bankhead of Alabama, for approval. In those days, committee chairmen wielded almost dictatorial power and could table or completely redraft legislation at will. Being a strong supporter of a federal role in highway programs, Sen. Bankhead completely rewrote the Shakelford bill, using the AASHO proposal. On May 8, 1916, the Senate passed the Bankhead bill, adding an additional $10 million over a ten-year period for improvements on national forest roads. A joint committee of both houses debated the Shakelford and Bankhead bills. Urban legislators objected because both bills excluded any funds for cities, and some believed the funding to the states were inadequate. Others thought that the bills might not pass constitutional muster, while southerners saw an erosion of states' rights. Still others felt that funds would be distributed based on political favoritism and wasted on unnecessary "pork

barrel" projects. After a day of rancorous debate, a joint Senate-House committee approved the Bankhead version on June 27, 1916. The bill states that the secretary of agriculture and state highway departments shall agree on which routes shall be added or improved, and the character and method of construction. However, the final version related only to rural post roads. The Congress finally passed the bill, later entitled the "Federal-Aid Road Act of 1916." [63]

President Woodrow Wilson signed the bill in an elaborate White House ceremony with members of Congress, AAA, and AASHO on hand July 11, 1916. It should be noted that President Wilson himself was an auto buff who enjoyed daily drives for a reprieve from the pressures of the Oval Office. The Federal-Aid Road Act was a historic landmark in the American highway saga. For the first time in nearly a century, the federal government took an active role in a nationwide system of highways through financial assistance to the states. The

First federal-aid highway, Richmond, California. January 30, 1918, is an important date in highway history, as the Bureau of Public Roads issued a certificate of completion for the first federal-aid highway project under the Federal-Aid Highway Act of 1916, a short 2.55 mile route on the San Francisco Bay. The photo shows some of the first vehicles using the new road, a 20-foot wide bituminous concrete pavement, complete with drain culverts. The road was completed at a total cost of $53,938.85 (Courtesy, U.S. DOT/FHWA).

act authorized the first federal gasoline tax to help pay for highway construction and maintenance. One main objective was to connect main population centers, and not serve as a feeder system to rail and water routes, or for mere pleasure travel. The states were allowed to plan, build and maintain roads under the 1916 federal act. The Office of Public Roads officially became the Office of Public Roads and Rural Engineering on July 1, 1915; exactly three years later, it was renamed the Bureau of Public Roads (BPR). The Bureau of Public Road's authority was limited to inspecting highways and encouraging efficiency. However, a handful of small federal-aid projects did get funded. The first highway project using federal aid under the 1916 act was completed on January 30, 1918, a short 2.5 mile stretch from Richmond, California (near Oakland), to the Alameda County line. This historic highway was 20 feet wide and made of portland cement surfaced with bituminous concrete.[64]

New highway construction was interrupted by World War I, as road projects were delayed due to shortages in manpower and materials. By early 1919, only 13 miles of federal-aid highway were completed. Some shortcomings in the 1916 act became evident, such as the $10,000-per-mile limit on funding. While attending an AASHO meeting in Chicago, Logan Page unexpectedly passed away on December 9, 1918. Thomas H. MacDonald, who was instrumental in drafting the 1916 Federal Aid Highway Act, took over BPR in early 1919. MacDonald and AASHO worked to correct the shortcomings of the Federal-Aid Road Act of 1916. To increase revenue for road projects, Congress passed the Excise Tax Act of 1919, which levied the first federal excise taxes on the sale of automobiles, auto wagons, trucks, and tires, and accessories. The taxes collected were used to build the first federal-aid highways contemplated under the 1916 Act.[65]

Under Thomas H. MacDonald, the Bureau of Public Roads worked closely with AASHO to coordinate the planning of a network of national highways. No one was exactly sure what form such a system would take, but the universal consensus was that interstate highways were necessary for the economic and social growth of a modern nation. One difficulty was reconciling rural concerns for better farm-to-market roads with those favoring long-distance highways. MacDonald advocated using federal-aid funds for a system of primary and secondary roads instead of focusing on rural post roads. The BPR faced a daunting challenge, as many of the few existing hard-surfaced roads had crumbled under the weight of heavy military transportation during World War I and would have to be completely rebuilt. On July 7, 1919, the first U.S. Army transcontinental truck convoy left the zero milestone on the Ellipse south of the White House for a journey on the unfinished Lincoln Highway to San Francisco. The convoy hoped to test the army's ability to travel long distances using motorized transport. Among those present was a young Dwight D. Eisenhower, who accompanied the convoy as an observer. The arduous 62-day journey demonstrated the poor conditions travelers encountered on America's early roads. At the close of the decade, it was clear that a new approach in highway planning was needed to meet the expected crunch of motor vehicle traffic that would come following the end of the First World War.[66]

The First Generation (1920–1945)

The period between the two world wars can be clearly divided between the gaiety and opulence of the 1920s and the drab, hard times of the 1930s. In 1919, the United States became an urban nation for the first time in its history, as the 1920 census showed that a majority of Americans (54,157,973 versus 51,552,657) now lived in cities.[67] The two decades following World War I saw the American Road transformed from dirt and mud to a nation-wide system of reliable, hard-surfaced, all-weather highways.

The automobile and the growing network of roads were causing some subtle social changes in the United States. In rural America, people rarely traveled more than a dozen miles from their farms or towns due to the hardships associated with travel. Farm children attended the local one-room schoolhouse, where all eight grades were taught. The auto industry started building trucks, delivery vehicles, then buses. School bus service was started as early as 1912 in California. The school bus was first used in rural areas to take children to newer "consolidated schools" which contained classrooms for all eight grammar school grades. This spared school children miles of walking, as well as saving time. Other states followed California and there were 12,000 school buses in use nationwide in 1923; by 1926, the number increased nearly three-fold to 32,800.[68]

A new revolution in auto production started in 1913 when Henry Ford introduced the moving assembly line. The idea of "progressive assembly" had been used by the railroad and bicycle indus-tries before 1900. Workers stood stationary and were assigned to a particular task on the line in-stead of carrying parts to the vehicle. The result was a significant increase in production and a great savings in manufacturing costs. Ford next moved its assembly operations to its new Highland Park plant, and output increased from 78,528 cars in 1912 to 168,304 in 1913. By the 1916–17 model year Ford built 730,000 cars, and by 1923, produced an amazing 2,201,000 units. Ford passed on the costs savings to consumers and dropped the price of its inexpensive runabout to only $346 in 1916.[69] The company became so profitable that Ford rewarded its workers by reducing the workday from nine to eight hours per day and announcing an unprece-dented $5 a day wage. For the first time, a factory worker at Ford could not only afford a new car, but had more leisure time to enjoy it. Of course, there was a dark side to production increases, as work-ers were expected to keep up with increasing pro-duction demands of plant foremen. Comedian Charlie Chaplin satirized the plight of the assem-bly-line worker in his classic 1936 film *Modern Times*.

The Roaring Twenties was one of the most

exciting eras in U.S. history. A tide of new inventions and social trends virtually guaranteed that it would not be life as usual after the Great War. Prohibition and the stock market craze contributed to a new "live for the moment" attitude, one of self-indulgence not seen in the nation's previous history of pioneer sacrifice. Prosperity and installment credit allowed consumers to afford new luxuries, from appliances to cars, for the first time. The advent of the radio and the growth of the film industry spawned a new type of pop culture that contrasted sharply with the restrictive Victorian Era. The standard six-day workweek gradually decreased after labor legislation, particularly in the '30s. With the automobile, urbanites could escape the city for weekend excursions in the country, while the farmer could finally travel to the "big city" to get in on all of the latest consumer trends.

The construction of new all-weather roads in the 1920s and '30s gave Americans an exciting alternative to travel by stage, water, or rail. The automobile allowed more individual freedom, at least where roads existed. For those fortunate enough to be able to afford a car, auto travel was still risky, and the early tourists were often met by impassable roads and mechanical breakdowns. Long-distance travel by auto required both skill and brawn and was not meant for amateurs or "Sunday drivers." For the less adventurous, particularly the very young, the elderly, and those with physical handicaps, train travel remained the only option. Millions of rural residents lived miles from the nearest railroad depot and trains did not serve many smaller towns. As the country's ground transportation slowly shifted from horse-power to engine-power, the lack of roads still prevented many in the nation's hinterlands from taking advantage of the automotive revolution.

In Minnesota's northeast corner, iron miners on the Mesabi Iron Range had to walk several miles to work each day. The journey was especially tiresome on the trip home after a hard day's labor at the mines. The Mesabi Range contained one of the richest iron deposits in the world, a virtual underground mountain of high-grade iron ore discovered in the late 19th century. The ore extracted from the area fueled America's industrial revolution and is credited with helping win the First World War. A Swedish immigrant and former miner living in the Mesabi Range town of Hibbing, Carl Eric Wickman, became a typical American Horatio Alger success story, eventually owning his own auto dealership. Being an ex-miner, Wickman appreciated how miners would welcome a system of transportation that could take them to work each day, and he figured that he could probably make a small profit ferrying workers to and from their jobs using some of the vehicles from his car lot. A 1914 Hupmobile touring car, manufactured by the Hupp Motor Company of Detroit, sat unsold on the lot. A truly splendid piece of automotive machinery, the Hupmobile came equipped with many factory extras, such as leather seating and copper and brass accents. Considered a luxury car, the Hupmobile nevertheless was capable of carrying five passengers and a driver comfortably. Wickman spent $600 and converted the Hupmobile into a "bus," then started charging 15 cents one-way or 25 cents for a round trip from the town of Alice to Hibbing. From the start, Wickman's Hupmobile-bus was filled to capacity, with extra passengers hitching a ride on the running boards.[70]

Wickman's venture quickly became more than just a side business from his regular car dealership duties. He needed extra help, so he picked a blacksmith, A. G. "Bus Andy" Anderson, and with several investors formed the Mesabi Transportation Company. By the 1920s, the Mesabi Transportation Company extended service to nearby Duluth, approximately 80 miles away, and expanded its routes further south to Minneapolis. The company gradually bought up smaller bus lines and established a nationwide system. In 1930, the company became the Greyhound Lines, choosing the sleek greyhound for its company symbol. In 1931, the company purchased its first busses from the Mack Truck Company. The 1931 "Mack Bus" was specially designed for comfort, with mohair seating and side curtains to shelter passengers from sunlight and dust. Equipped with a powerful six-cylinder engine and shock absorbers, the new busses ushered in a new era in cross-country travel. With their grey-blue coloration, the company's busses were appropriately referred to as "greyhounds."[71]

In the decades to follow, Greyhound dominated the bus industry, with some competition from rival Trailways. The company was always a step ahead of industry standards, focusing on passenger comfort and faster travel, continuously updating its fleet. After World War II, with passenger cars in short supply, Greyhound introduced brand-new models to attract the public. The 1947 Silversides was the first to offer air-conditioning, while the 1948 ACF Brill model added heating

Top: Greyhound busses, 1931 to 1954. Six vintage Greyhound busses are pictured with drivers wearing period uniforms. From right to left: the 1914 Hupmobile, the 1931 Mack Bus, the 1937 Supercoach, the 1947 Silversides, the 1948 ACF Brill, and the 1954 Scenicruiser (courtesy, Greyhound Lines, Inc.).

Bottom: Map of the Principal Routes of the U.S. Federal Aid Highway (by author).

Greyhound bus, 1930s. Travel by bus increased steadily during the 1920s and '30s, as many people still were not served by railroads or could afford automobiles. During the course of this century, railroads have abandoned unprofitable routes, leaving bus service as the only means of travel in many areas. The Greyhound Bus Company promoted trips to such attractions as the 1939–40 New York World's Fair, noted by the emblem on this vintage bus (courtesy, Greyhound Lines, Inc.).

units under the floor and ergonomically contoured seating. The 1954 Scenicruiser featured a two-tier design, with 10 passengers on the driver level, and 33 seated "up top." New glare-resistant glass and a powerful air-conditioning system changed the air throughout the bus every 40 seconds. A public address system allowed the driver to speak to the passengers, and a three-axle alignment and tension rubber shackles produced a smooth ride. Currently, Greyhound's latest bus, produced by the Eagle Bus Company in Brownsville, Texas, is state-of-the art, with "Forsilastic" suspension and improved air-conditioning.[72]

By 1919, total mileage of all domestic roads exceeded three million miles, but less than 10,000 miles of new construction were hard-surfaced roads. Critics of the Federal–Aid Road Act of 1916 complained about the lack of progress. Thomas MacDonald presented BPR's new proposals to Congress, and the result was the passage of the

Thomas H. MacDonald, chief of Bureau of Public Roads, 1919–1953. Thomas H. MacDonald is the architect of the federal-state relationship that is the foundation of the current federal-aid highway system. While serving as chief engineer on the Iowa Highway Commission, MacDonald worked with AASHO and OPR in getting the Federal-Aid Road Act of 1916 passed. Following Logan Page's untimely death in 1918, MacDonald was appointed to fill Page's post at the renamed Bureau of Public Roads. Under MacDonald's stewardship, the nation built a first-rate national highway system that greatly aided commerce while saving productivity, time, and lives. Before he retired in 1953, MacDonald was instrumental in the transition from the aging federal-aid highways to the new interstate system (From "AASHO: The First Fifty Years, 1914–1964," Copyright 1965, AASHTO, Washington, D. C. Used by permission).

Federal Aid Highway Act of 1921. The 1921 Act expanded further the federal government's role in road planning and fulfilled MacDonald's vision of a national highway system. Under the act, federal aid to the states increased to an average of $75 million per year during the 1920s. The act sought to meet the demands of urban and rural interests by designating up to 60 percent of federal aid funds for interstate highways and limiting interstate roads to three-sevenths of total state highway mileage. Further, federal-aid highways in any state could not exceed 7 percent of all state highway mileage.[73]

The percentage of state road spending for urban versus rural roads was established by many state constitutions in subsequent years. Oregon imposed the first state gasoline tax in February 1919, followed by Colorado and New Mexico. After overcoming legal objections by the oil companies, other states soon imposed their own state gasoline taxes. The combination of federal and state funds stimulated a burst of new road construction. The national average rate of state gas taxes, a mere 3.04 cents per gallon in 1928, raised $490 million in highway revenues by 1930. By 1924, every state had

a highway department, with authority over main routes called "state systems." Total highway expenditures by all levels of government increased from $1 billion in 1924 to $2.4 billion by 1939. The total number of motor vehicles on the roads increased from 9.2 million in 1920 to 26.7 million by 1930.[74]

Besides charting the actual routes of the new federal aid highway system, a more uniform method of highway designation was needed. Routes on rural roads were marked by rocks, sticks, and any other makeshift method of directing travelers to their destination. With new highway routes on the drawing boards, the old haphazard system of named trails was clearly obsolete. In 1917, a plan initiated by Wisconsin State Highway engineer Arthur R. Hirst abandoned the approach using named roads in favor of a numerical system, the first in the country. Showing his distain for the trail organizations, Hirst remarked that "The ordinary trail promoter has seemingly considered that plenty of wind and a few barrels of paint are all that is required to build and maintain a 2,000-mile trail." Wisconsin's state highways were

"Horror sign" on dangerous curve. In the days before uniform state and federal marking of highways, locals used a bit of imagination and occasional humor as they constructed their own homemade road signage. Sometimes words alone were not enough to deter careless or speeding drivers, so more graphic methods such as this "horror" sign were used. This sign was intended to warn drivers of a dangerous curve ahead (From "AASHO: The First Fifty Years," Copyright 1965, AASHTO, Washington, D. C. Used by permission).

marked by an inverted triangle and assigned a numeral, with the words "State Trunk Highway" at the top. Wisconsin also erected standard black-and-white signs warning of railroad crossings, curves, steep hills, and other hazards. In the early 1920s, New York and New Jersey started posting uniform road signs statewide. Some auto clubs even put up their own road signs, such as the Automobile Club of Southern California, which posted signs throughout the state, even marking one route from Los Angeles to Kansas City.[75]

The movement for a nationwide system of highway routes and road signs got some needed direction from the efforts of three state highway officials in 1922. Road marking methods varied widely from state to state, with many locales erecting their own ad hoc signage. While driving through their respective states in search for ideas for a uniform system of road signs, J. T. Donaghey (Wisconsin), A. H. Hinkle (Indiana) and W. F. Rosenwald (Minnesota) decided that the shape of highway signs should be standardized nationwide. Rosenwald of Minnesota concluded that "if each shape had a definite meaning, it would be a great advantage for night driving as undoubtedly the shape could be distinguished long before the words could be." The three men presented their plan to the Mississippi Valley Association of Highway Departments, which agreed on a plan proposing rectangular black-and-white signs for information such as mileage to the next town, a circular-shaped sign to warn of railroad crossings, and octagonal for stop signs. The plan was proposed at the annual meeting of the American Association of State Highway Officials (AASHO) in 1924. A subcommittee on Traffic and Control of Traffic under E. W. James of the Bureau of Public Roads slightly modified the plan, and assigned yellow and black coloration instead of black-and-white. The AASHO meeting concluded by adopting a resolution asking the Secretary of Agriculture to appoint a board made up of BPR and state highway officials to "cooperate in formulating and promulgating a system of numbering and marking highways of interstate character."[76]

In response to AASHO's request, Secretary of Agriculture Howard Gore formed the Joint Board of Interstate Highways on March 2, 1925. The Joint Board included BPR chief Thomas H. MacDonald, E. W. James, and A. B. Fletcher, also of BPR, and 21 state highway officials. On April 20 and 21, 1925, the group met at BPR headquarters,

while James led regional meetings throughout the country during the weeks to follow. Lou A. Boulay, an Ohio highway official, suggested using the United States' federal shield with "U.S.A." and a route number as a design for highway markers. Frank F. Rogers of Michigan hastily drew a rough sketch of a six-pointed shield design, and Rogers' drawing was quickly approved by the joint board. Full approval of the design was delayed because several states argued that the name of the each state should be included in the design. After voting to drop the states' names on August 3, the members reversed themselves after some southern officials opposed signs bearing only "U.S.A." The result was the final approval of the familiar U.S. highway shield marker using the same black-and-white color scheme as the various directional and other road signs.[77]

At group meetings, state highway officials designated an 81,000 mile nationwide system. This was pared down by the joint board to 50,100 miles after eliminating some unnecessary midwestern routes. However, under intense lobbying from states and trail associations, the network was expanded to 75,800 miles. Despite the ambitions of these early highway pioneers, the final mileage for the U.S. system measured just under 40,000 miles when completed in the late 1930s.[78]

A committee assigned to study standardized road signs endorsed the recommendations of the Mississippi Valley Association and AASHO. The ASSHO asked the sectional committee on color code of the American Engineering Standards Committee (AESC) for its input. The Joint Board opted for a yellow-colored stop sign instead of red, since it found that red paint and baked enamel were unavailable.[79]

In August 1925, the joint board appointed a committee of five (composed of Oklahoma's Cyrus Avery, Oregon's Roy Klein, South Carolina's Charles Moorefield, Missouri's B. H. Piepmeier, and Illinois' Frank T. Sheets) to study a system of highway numbering. By the mid–1920s, the country was in the midst of a massive state-by-state road construction effort. While the committee debated the issue, James sent the committee a map of the United States using a "systematic plan for numbering interstate routes." James' plan called for even-numbered east-west routes (using multiples of ten for principal routes) and odd numbered north-south routes (using numbers ending in 1 or 5 for principal routes). As one example, U.S. 1

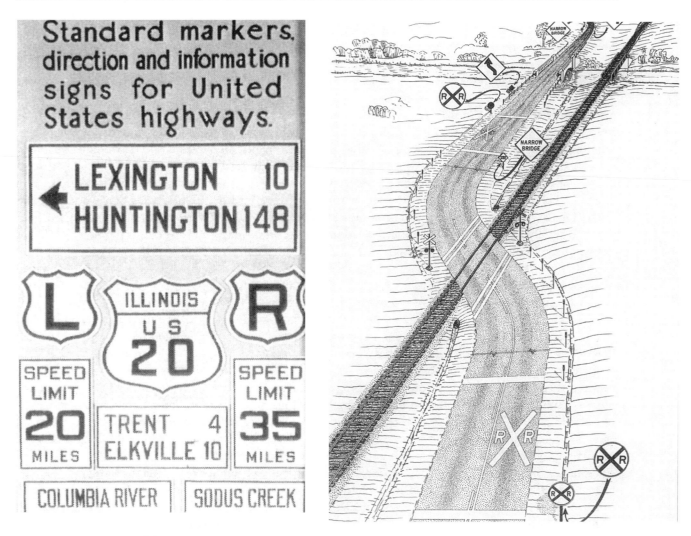

Left: U.S. federal-aid highway signs. In 1925, W. M. Jardine took over as secretary of agriculture and approved the Joint Board of Interstate Highways' numbering plan for the federal highway system on November 18, 1925. Standard black-and-white signs were also approved. The six pointed U.S. highway shield was proposed by Lou A. Boulay, an Ohio highway official, at a regional meeting of the joint board and officials from BPR and 21 states on April 20–21, 1925. Some southern highway officials objected to using "U.S.A." on the proposed signs, but Boulay's shield design was eventually adopted, with each state noted at the top and the letters "U.S." placed in the center (courtesy, U.S. DOT/FHWA).

Right: Diagram of highway using approved standard markings. A page from the Manual of Uniform Traffic Control Devices for 1948 with signs approved by several national highway organizations. The original guidelines were approved in 1929 by the National Conference on Street and Highway Safety and the American Association of State Highway Officials (AASHO) (National Archives).

travels a north-south route along the Atlantic Seaboard, while U.S. 101 on the west coast follows the Pacific Coast. This simple system was flexible, as it allowed for expansion of future routes. The committee agreed on James' map using a system of one-, two- and three-digit routes, and submitted their proposal to the joint board on October 16, 1925.[80]

Reaction to the proposed highway numbering system was mixed at first. The first to object were the organizations for the many named trails. As self-perpetuating entities, the trails boosters saw their own financial future at stake if any new nationwide system were implemented. Many predicted that the named trails would fade into obscurity if a standard highway numbering system was allowed. The AASHO met again on January 14–15, 1926, after receiving a torrent of requests for changes to its routing and numbering plan. Some proposed minor changes; others took months to decide. Several of the most hotly-contested routes were not finalized until nearly the end of 1926. Due to factors such as terrain and politics, the order of the routes in James' plan were not always east-west or north-south. Some routes ran diagonally, such as U.S. 52 from the Canadian border in North Dakota to the Atlantic Coast in South Carolina. There were also a few exceptions to James' numbering scheme, such as a portion of U.S. 30 in Oregon located north instead of south of U.S. 20. Overall, the system was logical and, in the absence of a better proposal, difficult to argue against.[81]

Business interests and trail organizations, the latter trying to preserve their organizations in the face of possible extinction, lobbied strenuously with the AASHO during 1926. Every state wanted a main, or "naught" route (a route number ending in "0") running through their state, not only for prestige purposes but since a major transcontinental highway would bring added business and commerce in areas adjacent to heavily traveled routes. The Lincoln Highway's number "30" was quickly approved, since James had already gained the support of the large Lincoln Highway Association in his efforts to persuade the joint board to adopt his numbering proposal. Proponents for U.S. Route 60 wanted their route to run from the East Coast to Los Angeles through Chicago, on the premise that a northern routing would carry maximum cross-country traffic. However, this proposal violated the AASHO's numbering scheme, since U.S. 60 had to lie between routes 50 and 70, placing it somewhere in North Carolina and Kentucky, much further south than Chicago. Further, routing U.S. 60 through Chicago would leave Kentucky with no major "naught" route, much to the ire of Kentucky governor W. J. Fields, who lobbied hard against the proposal. Fields faced heavy opposition, including three board members from states where the proposed U.S. 60 would cross (Avery, of Oklahoma, Piepmeier of Missouri, and Sheets of Illinois), but the logic of his argument resonated with the joint board. After numerous proposals and counter-proposals, Kentucky got its U.S. Route 60. Opponents secured their chosen route from Chicago to Los Angeles, following historic old trails such as the Federal Wire Road in Missouri and the Osage Trail in Oklahoma. Despite having to settle for a non-

naught numeral, Avery and company's highway would bear the famous double-sixes in one of highway history's ironic twists.[82]

The AASHO continued its work and received final requests until its annual meeting in November 1926. The executive committee expanded the new system to 96,626 miles and included compromises on many routes. On November 11, 1926, AASHO agreed on its final version of the federal highway numbering system. The AASHO plan immediately gained public acceptance, and laid the foundation for America's first system of national highways since the early 1800s.[83]

After adopting its new system of road signage for federal-aid highways, AASHO and the state highway departments worked on a uniform system of highway marking for national use. Rural highways in particular needed a standard system. Center lines where painted with various colors depending on location, and were either black, white, or yellow. In 1929, AASHO published its first "Manual for Highway Signs," incorporating the sign designs already approved. The manual was the "bible" for local and state highway departments and remained the accepted standard nationally for the next several decades. Later that year, the National Conference on Street and Highway Safety (NCHS) approved its own designs for signing highways. Officials at AASHO and the NCHS recognized that there couldn't be two conflicting systems, so in 1931, a joint committee composed of eight AASHO members and seven representatives from the NCHS met to iron out their differences. The group became known as the "National Joint Committee on Uniform Traffic Control Devices" and eventually became a permanent institution, with its chief mission being to maintain a uniform system of highway marking. The joint committee put out its first "Manual of Uniform Traffic Control Devices for Streets and Highways" in 1935, which specifies the recommended "definitions, sizes, shapes, colors, legends, location, and alphabet series," as well as uniform traffic control devices, barricades, and highway striping. The manual was updated in 1937, 1939, 1942 (called the "Wartime Emergency Edition"), 1948, 1954, 1961, and 1962. During the early years, the National Association of County Officials, the American Municipal Association, and the Institute of Traffic Engineers helped revise the manual. At the urging of Congress, the states adopted the Manual of Uniform Traffic Control Devices. The standards set forth

Top: Reflecting stop sign at night. A photograph taken by the Bureau of Public Roads demonstrates the added illumination provided by use of reflectors on a stop sign on a dark rural road. The photograph was taken in the Washington, D. C., area in 1933 (National Archives [33-495]).

Bottom: Neon stop signs on U.S. 206 at junction near Trenton, New Jersey. Although it is difficult to tell from this photo, the lettering on these two stop signs is actually outlined with neon tubing for added visibility at night. These rarities are now gone, as they never made it into widespread usage. The Red Tavern Restaurant and a Tydol gas station lie in the background of this intersection located in a rural area north of Trenton, New Jersey (National Archives).

in the manual are still used today, including the octagonal red stop sign, yellow warning signs, and black-and-white signage for mileage and other purposes.[84]

As Americans raced into the countryside for pleasure travel in ever-increasing numbers, there was little to guide them and few services available. To meet the needs of the motorist, a new industry in lodging, tourism, filling stations and food service sprang up overnight. Henry Ford, always looking for ways to encourage auto purchases, together with Harvey Firestone and his other fellow cronies, promoted camping by documenting their auto trips on film. Countless new jobs were created to cater to the needs of the traveling public, as well as the automobile itself.

The first gas retailers sold more kerosene and motor oil than gasoline. Gradually, gasoline sales accounted for the bulk of filling stations' profits. One problem with the early gasoline was engine "knock" upon acceleration, which was annoying as well as harmful to engines. As auto engines became more sophisticated, the oil companies started experimenting with different fuel blends. The

Top: "Curve—45 mph" sign using reflector buttons. Warning signs using glass (later, plastic) reflector buttons came into use at railroad grade crossings, curves and other hazards in the early 1930s. They were a simple yet effective aid for motorists driving at night. Chemical companies had not yet invented reflective paints which are used currently (National Archives [947-1348]).

Bottom: Manual Stop-Go sign at intersection of 14th and Pennsylvania Avenues, Washington , D.C., 1925. The number of motor vehicles in the United States increased steadily during the 20th century with only a few minor interruptions. This fact remains as long as the nation's population continues to increase and people continue to choose the auto as their primary means of travel. Manual traffic control devices were first used at busy intersections before electronic traffic control systems were developed in the late 1930s (National Archives [31959]).

Ethyl logo (Used by permission, Ethyl Corporation).

choice was always narrowed to just one grade of gas, but competition necessitated ingenuity, and the oil companies started searching for new grades of gas to boost sales. In 1921, Charles F. Kettering, with the aid of a team of chemists, found the solution to engine knock with the discovery of tetraethyl lead (TEL), a chemical compound that provided more power without engine knock when added to gasoline. Two years later, Kettering formed the General Motors Chemical Corporation, a joint venture of General Motor Corporation and the Standard Oil Company of New Jersey. In 1924, the new company became the Ethyl Gasoline Corporation (eventually shortening its name to the Ethyl Corporation in 1942). Gas retailers soon offered a second grade of gasoline with the new additive for an extra charge. Motorists now had two choices; regular and premium, or "ethyl," which contained higher amounts of the ethyl additive. The Ethyl symbol was prominently displayed at filling stations and quickly became the choice of the discriminating driver who demanded superior performance. The trade name "Ethyl" became so widespread that it became synonymous with higher grade gasoline.[85]

The first gas station customers merely had to stop alongside a station's gasoline pumps conveniently located at curbside. However, vehicles stopping for gas created a traffic hazard, so cities and towns passed ordinances regulating placement of gas pumps. Since customers had to drive completely off the roadway for a fill, the first "drive-in"

stations appeared. The early filling stations were little more than a carport overhanging a few gas pumps suspended from a small building. By 1920, numerous national and regional brands were available. With so many brands to choose from, gasoline companies had to find new ways to attract customers. Each company adopted its own company logo to inspire customer loyalty. In the late 1920s, the larger companies went further by introducing the first standardized filling station designs to further familiarize the public with their products. Perhaps the earliest was the "cottage style" gasoline station designed by C. A. Petersen for Pure Oil Company in 1925. A little white building was designed to resemble an English cottage, with a steep blue tile roof and a letter "P" on a false chimney. The design was so successful that Pure kept using this style into the early 1950s. A few years later, Phillips Petroleum and several others copied the design. Soon, gas station buildings resembled a small bungalows, blending in with the surrounding neighborhood. The "City Beautiful" movement during the early decades of the century was particularly effective in convincing local businesses to conform to its vision of urban esthetics, and this included commercial architecture such as gasoline stations. Inspired by the Chicago Columbian Exposition of 1893's "Great White City," activists promoted the first "urban renewal," tearing down old, substandard buildings and replacing them with broad tree-lined boulevards, parks, and other public projects of large scale. Thus, the filling station owner adopted a friendly-looking building to give the customer the feeling of entering a home rather than a gasoline station. Other examples of standardized station designs is Sinclair's Spanish adobe-style, complete with tile roofing. Sinclair and Socony both used the American colonial style for their early standardized station designs.[86]

The more quaint styles of the early days gave way to the "art deco" and "streamline moderne" designs of the 1930s and '40s. Although the term was not coined until 1968, what is referred to as art deco today can be traced from designs suggested at the Exposition Internationale Arts Decoratifs et Industriels Modernes in Paris in 1925. A reaction perhaps to the stodgy Beaux Arts, which was the standard around 1900, art deco emulated the industrialized world's move towards the machine age. The design's motifs are simplified abstractions and include use of geometric forms. The art deco

(continued on page 70)

Top: Ethyl filling station, 1923. The marketing of gasoline products became more sophisticated after Charles F. Kettering and a team of chemists invented tetraethyl lead (TEL) as a gas additive. Kettering sold "ethyl" through its own outlets, like the filling station pictured here, and to oil companies. "Ethyl" reduced engine knock, which was a serious problem for motorists when engine technology was still primitive and the quality of fuels highly variable. Consumers now had two choice of gas: regular, or premium (ethyl). Drivers claimed they got more power on higher-grade ethyl gas, and the Ethyl trade name became synonymous with higher quality gasoline. The station pictured was located at 330 South Fourth Street, Richmond, Virginia (Used by permission, Ethyl Corporation).

Bottom: Chevron filling station, 1930s. A tidy Standard Chevron filling station with an NRA sign on the sign pole, dates this photograph to the mid–1930s, since the National Industrial Recovery Act was declared unconstitutional by the United States Supreme Court on May 27, 1935 (courtesy, Chevron Corporation).

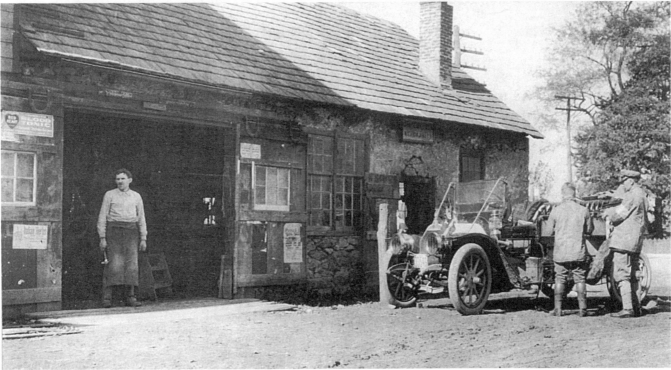

Top: DX Gasoline Pumps. A 1940 photograph of a cottage-style DX gasoline station, located somewhere in Missouri. This station sold products of the D-X Sunray Oil Company, headquartered in Tulsa, Oklahoma. Like numerous other brands, D-X has disappeared from the American highway scene (National Archives [40-189]).

Bottom: "Delayed 10 hours for a 10 cent nut." A blacksmith stands in the entrance to his shop as he works on a disabled vehicle on the Lancaster Pike in Pennsylvania. Blacksmith shops and livery stables were the early forerunners of today's modern auto repair facilities. This photograph records a frustrating delay in the vacation plans of some early travelers, whose trip from New York to Atlanta was marred by a broken nut. Photo taken in November 1909 (National Archives [2376]).

Top: Country store with gasoline pumps, Goldvein, Virginia. As the 20th century began, gasoline was first sold at almost every available roadside stop, including country stores, as pictured here in Goldvein, Virginia, approximately 15 miles north of Fredericksburg on State Route 17. After the first gas pumps were invented, crude models soon sprouted up along every thoroughfare, causing a traffic hazard as lines of cars unexpectedly blocked streets at roadside pumps. Gradually, gasoline filling stations located off the edge of the roadside began to appear (National Archives).

Bottom: Gas and liquor station, Tampa, Florida. Early filling station proprietors used fuel sales as an opportunity to sell an array of products to motorists. This independent gas station advertises an odd combination: gas and liquor. This station was located on U.S. 541 in Tampa, Florida. Photo taken by J. K. Hillers in 1938 (National Archives).

Top: In Washington, D.C., an example of a more traditional style of service station architecture is this handsome Sinclair station with two wings housing six bays for auto repair. Sinclair Oil, based in Salt Lake City, Utah, used colonial and mission-style designs for its filling stations in the 1930s and 1940s (National Archives).

Bottom: Attendants serving customers at Gulf station. This photo captures busy station attendants gassing up two cars at a substantial–looking brick-exterior Gulf station located at Massachusetts Avenue NW and 49th, Washington, D.C. (National Archives).

Iceberg gas station, Albuquerque, New Mexico. This eye-catching mockup of an iceberg must have seemed like an amusing mirage to travelers passing through Albuquerque on a hot day. This Tydol gas station was a landmark on Route 66 during the 1930s and 1940s. An outlet for the Tide Water Associated Oil Company, established in 1878 in Tulsa, Oklahoma, Tydol was the purveyor of automotive products such as Flying A Gasoline and Veedol Motor Oil (National Archives [48-1521]).

style was popular for a wide range of architecture, from skyscrapers (New York City's Chrysler Building) to schools, movie theaters, public buildings, cafes and eventually consumer products.

As "art deco" was being imported from Europe to the United States in the late 1920s, a new group calling themselves "industrial designers"—among them, Norman Bel Geddes, Henry Dreyfus, Raymond Loewy, and Walter Dorwin Teague—were busy at work designing new consumer products. Their new designs were referred to as "streamlining," although they actually bore few similarities to art deco. The new style can best be described as a heavy use of horizontal lines, making automobiles, trains, buildings, even toasters appear to be speeding, or in motion. Streamlining was promoted as the "shape of the future"; buildings featured rounded corners and even bridges were given subtle ornamentation in the

form of a few added horizontal lines. Bel Geddes, Dreyfuss, Loewy, Teague, and others started a design fad that influenced design of restaurants, gas stations, and motels in America for several decades.[87]

A third style adopted by the gasoline filling station during the 1920s through World War II was called simply the "International Style." Originating in Europe, this school of architectural design opted for a plain, smooth structures, devoid of any lines or ornamentation to suggest any style. Businesses, apartment buildings and homes looked like boxes with windows. In the 1930s, Texaco decided to scrap its traditional-style stations for a new look, so they hired designer Walter Dorwin Teague. Teague came up with the famous "Type EM," a square building covered with porcelain-enameled metal units for easy cleaning. Texaco used this simple design well into the 1950s. Mobil

"Art deco" Gulf station, circa 1937. By the 1930s, gasoline filling station architecture evolved from mundane, utilitarian structures to works of art. The streamline moderne and art deco styles gave the average corner station a bold and exciting appearance. This double-wing Gulf station with five bays for repairs typifies the new status the automobile achieved in 20th century American life. New Forbes and Murray Gulf, 1937 (courtesy, Chevron Corporation).

hired the consulting firm of Frederick G. Frost, who designed a square building with a cylinder-shaped addition attached to the main corner, resembling an oil drum.[88]

Many filling stations, particularly those of operated by the independents, used individualized designs to attract customers. Famed architect Frank Lloyd Wright, a critic of the International Style, designed several innovative filling stations of his own during the 1930s. Wright had some unconventional ideas about human society and how it relates to and is influenced by architecture, and he believed that the modern filling station would replace the old general store as the social center of town. One of Wright's original stations can still be found operating in Cloquet, Minnesota. Wright's filling station was a large two-story structure with enough area on the second floor for people to gather and discuss politics or the latest town gossip. The flamboyant designs of this era exemplifies the lofty place that the automobile had now earned in 20th century America, as station design had attained a sort of art-form status.

As competition continued among oil produc-

ers, smaller competitors were slowly being edged out by the larger corporations. The independents and mom-and-pop operations were forced to utilize more creative marketing techniques. As highways improved and speeds increased, new ideas were needed to catch to the attention of the passing motorist. Some filling station buildings took amusing shapes, such as windmills or tea pots, or incorporated leftover airplanes and railroad cars. Surviving examples of these early stations remind us how a small dose of highway humor can sometimes break up the monotony of traveling.

Filling station proprietors continued to search for new ways to cater to the motoring public. In this age of self-service, it is difficult to imagine pulling up to a gas pump and being greeted by not one but several attendants, all eager to clean your windows, check your oil and water, and give directions, not to mention selling auto-related products. The major brands gave away free road maps and small gifts imprinted with their company logo as one marketing gimmick. Others offered free gifts with each gas purchase, sometimes using redeemable gift stamps. The female traveler in

Top: Frank Lloyd Wright gas station, Cloquet, Minnesota. A remaining example of a rare filling station designed by famed architect Frank Lloyd Wright. Wright designed a few homes and commercial buildings late in his career, among them this two-story Phillips 66 station with a large room in the second level for people to gather and socialize. Wright advocated alternative living styles in his elder years and envisioned the gasoline filling station as the logical replacement of the small town country store as the center of village life. This Phillips 66 station, which claims to be the only service station designed by Wright, was actually built in 1957 (photo by author).

Bottom: Phillips attendants polishing gas pumps, 1936. A promotional photograph shows three industrious Phillips attendants at work keeping a typical cottage-style station in top condition. This station was located at 4th and Chestnut streets near the company's headquarters in Bartlesville, Oklahoma (courtesy, Phillips Petroleum Company).

particular demanded clean rest room facilities, so the major brands responded with new advertising campaigns designed to attract the more discriminating customer. The Phillips Petroleum Company was at the forefront of the new "cleanliness" fad, with its "Phillips 66 Highway Hostesses" marketing plan of the late 1930s and early '40s. As the name suggests, a team of female inspectors made routine stops at Phillips 66 service stations to check for cleanliness. The Hostesses, smartly dressed in their blue uniforms and driving the company's fleet of marked cars, offered station owners ways to improve service and "certified" rest rooms that passed their sanitation test. Company literature of the time referred to its Hostesses as "couriers of comfort and protection," and Phillips even hired nurses to ensure that its stations were "hospital clean." The goal of the company's 1940 program was for the Highway Hostesses visit each of its approximately 2,000 service stations once per month. The Hostesses gave motorists free ice water, helped cars in distress and even gave first aid if necessary. Other brands such as Texaco, with its "White Patrol," joined in. Veteran travelers from this era no doubt have fond memories of the good old days of highway travel.[89]

In the early days of highway travel, before autos had heaters and air-conditioning, the roadside filling station was a welcome sight to the tired and thirsty traveler. Filling stations gradually became larger in size, adding garage bays for repairs. Station design became more streamlined, some with new metal/porcelain exteriors popular in the late 1930s and '40s. Back then, cars needed servicing more frequently than today, and highway breakdowns were more frequent. By World War II, synthetic rubber and tubeless-tires replaced the old unreliable tubular tires that stranded many a traveler with frequent blowouts. Autos were not very reliable compared to today's modern vehicles, and a disabled car on the roadside with a boiling-over radiator was not an infrequent sight. The gasoline filling station was a modern-day oasis for the 20th century traveler.

Just as the motor vehicle itself needed proper care, so did the motorist. It didn't take long for a new travel-accommodation industry to emerge. By 1920, over 300 cities had municipal campgrounds (also called "auto camps") that offered an inexpensive way to spend the night. Private campgrounds with small cabins called "tourist camps" appeared. In 1922, over 1,000 tourist camps existed nationwide; by 1928, 3,000; and by 1934, the number mushroomed to over 32,000 tourist camps. Many of these were primitive, with no running water or showers, and the buildings themselves were little more than shacks. In the '30s, as motorists' tastes matured, the demand for more comfortable lodging was met by the "tourist" or "motor court," which featured identical cabins arranged so that guests could park near their unit. The facilities were updated and included all of the basic amenities. By 1935, there were 10,000 tourist courts in the U.S.; by 1939, 13,500; and by the end of the war, upwards of 20,000 served the weary traveler.[90]

A Pasadena, California, architect, Arthur S. Heineman, modified the tourist court idea with a design incorporating attached units and garages into a single structure. Heineman called his first enterprise the "Milestone Mo-Tel" and opened his first unit outside of San Luis Obispo, California, on the famous El Camino Real (now U.S. 101) on September 12, 1925. Heineman referred to the Milestone simply as a "motel," a shorter version of "motor hotel," and seeing the potential of his idea, quickly copyrighted the word "motel" for his exclusive use. The Milestone Motel (more recently renamed the Motel Inn), designed in the popular Spanish Mission style, was a copy of the mission at Santa Barbara, California, complete with a three tier bell tower and restaurant. Heineman's ultimate plan was to build a string of 21 mission-styled motels along the Pacific coast from San Diego to Seattle, with the Milestone Mo-Tel being Motel #4 on the route. Heineman thought that guests would appreciate the convenience of being able to park their vehicles near their room, and the "motel" was created.[91]

The motel concept was slow to catch on, however, as the Depression halted virtually all new construction nationwide. Even Arthur Heineman's grand plans for a chain of motels along the Pacific Coast were dashed by the economic crisis following the Crash of 1929, as no further motels were built after Motel #4. Although tourism fell off sharply in the early '30s, the Depression didn't dampen America's enthusiasm for road adventure. As some of the earlier tourist camps started to age, motorists had to steer clear of older, seamier-looking camps. Female travelers, concerned with safety, often convinced the driver to avoid the more run-down establishments in favor of more modern and cleaner facilities. The travel industry made a gradual recovery by the late '30s, but tourism was interrupted again by wartime.[92]

Top: Campers relaxing along a creek, 1920s. After World War I and a brief post-war shock of high inflation and unemployment, Americans flocked to the great outdoors in ever-increasing numbers. This photo from the 1920s shows a family enjoying a picnic at a wooded campsite on a fine summer day. Rising wages and better employment opportunities in the Roaring Twenties gave a big boost to the domestic travel industry (National Archives [29855]).

Opposite Top: Highway Hostesses with fleet in front of the Phillips Building, Bartlesville, Oklahoma. These highway hostesses are posing next to their fleet of cars with Frank Phillips, ready to "certify" stations throughout the company's territory in the central United States. Looking quite official in their light blue uniforms and cream and-green cars, Phillips' highway hostess campaign was a big success for the company (courtesy, Phillips Petroleum Company).

Bottom Left: Portrait of a Highway Hostess. Another promotional photo of one of Phillips Petroleum's "Highway Hostesses," whose jobs were to check Phillips stations for cleanliness in the 1930s and 1940s. Some of the hostesses were trained nurses who administered first aid to injured motorists, as well as helping disabled vehicles (courtesy, Phillips Petroleum Company).

Bottom Right: Gulf station attendant. Early filling station attendants approached automobile service with an almost military zeal, with each brand training its attendants to provide enthusiastic service and wearing the latest polished uniforms. This Gulf station employee is saluting a mythical customer next to a pump advertising "That Good Gulf Gasoline" (courtesy, Chevron Corporation).

Top: Tent homes, Texas, 1920s. Auto, or "tourist camps," were primitive in the early days, but gradually added amenities such as running water, restrooms, showers, and shelters. Here, a row of tent homes (with numerals at the bottom of each doorway) in a tourist camp somewhere in Texas offers some minimal shelter for travelers. Notice the water tower in the background (National Archives).

Bottom: Tourist camp with rental units. An improved version of the tent home are these small attached cabins in a tourist camp. Though lacking in facilities, tourist camps were popular for those in search of a cheap vacation. By the 1930s, tens of thousands of tourist camps appeared on the nation's roadsides (National Archives).

Roadside cabins on U.S. 50 in West Virginia, 1935. An Esso station and a row of log cabins advertising "CABINS $1.00 & UP" once stood on U.S. 50, approximately 46 miles west of Clarksburg, West Virginia. Tourism took a steep nose-dive in the early years of the Great Depression, but returned to pre–1929 levels by mid-decade (National Archives [35-381]).

Eats

In the early days of auto touring, just finding a decent meal was frequently an adventure. Following World War I, roadside stands, cafes, restaurants, and "greasy spoons" soon lined the nation's thoroughfares, offering food and liquid refreshment. It was always "buyer beware," and the unsuspecting motorist sometimes fell victim to poor-quality fare. The mom-and-pop roadside eateries were the norm in the early decades of auto travel.

The early food service industry adopted the same "service with a smile" attitude as the gasoline filling stations. Food establishments that emphasized customer service often endured for many decades along the nation's motor ways, with uniformed waitresses providing hungry travelers with crisp service at reasonable prices. By the mid–1930s, roadside food service began to emulate the trend set by the gas station industry toward nationally-recognized name brands and ultimately, franchising. However, prior to the "fast food" chains of today, several pioneers in the food industry are worthy of mention.

Kentucky Fried Chicken

The year was 1930. The Great Depression was deepening; banks were closing and bread lines began forming on the streets of American cities. Like many other businesses, Harland Sanders was eking out a living at his gas station/restaurant in Corbin, Kentucky. Harland wasn't a stranger to tough times; his father passed away when he was only 6 years old and his stepfather forced him to leave home at age 12. From a young age, Harland worked a variety of jobs, including two failed businesses prior to the Crash of 1929. Now he was 40 years old, and cash-poor folks in the eastern Kentucky hill country weren't eating out much, and tourism was at a standstill. Things were looking grim. However, using cooking skills and seasoning recipes learned from his mother and combined with his penchant for cleanliness, Harland's restaurant started to gain in popularity among passing travelers. He moved to a larger building on U.S. 25, calling it "Sanders Servistation." Business continued to grow, as travelers gradually learned of Harland Sanders' delicious chicken recipe. By 1935, Governor Ruby

Sanders Servistation, Main Street, Corbin, Kentucky. Several years after opening his first cafe, Harland Sanders expanded his business by adding a filling station which he called "Sanders Servistation," shown on the left side of this photograph, in 1930. The new location had room for a larger restaurant. From there, word of Sanders' Kentucky fried chicken spread beyond U.S. 25 (known as The Dixie Highway), which carried vacationers from the Midwest to Florida (courtesy, KFC Corporation).

Laffon made him a Kentucky colonel in recognition of his contribution to the state's cuisine. Later, Sanders adopted his now-familiar white suit and hat with string tie to complete his Kentucky Colonel image.[93]

Sanders continued to work on improving his chicken seasoning recipe until he was finally satisfied. One problem was that many travelers weren't willing to wait the half-hour it took to fry chicken. Sanders experimented with his recipe further. He discovered that the "pressure cooker," newly available in 1939, greatly reduced cooking time. Sales increased dramatically, and the Colonel's roadside stop became a magnet for tourists traveling on the Dixie Highway. After 1941, wartime gasoline rationing curtailed highway travel, but Sanders survived. With tourism booming after the war, business was so good that he added a motel and enlarged his restaurant to accommodate 142 customers. But, as luck would have it, the federal government bypassed his business with a new highway, once again forcing Harland to close up shop.[94]

Not one to give up, Sanders decided, at the ripe old age of 66, to expand beyond his home state and franchise his fried chicken recipe. In the mid–1950s, Sanders traveled through neighboring states, approaching restaurant owners with his franchise proposal and offering them a sampling of his tasty recipe. Franchisees of what was now officially called "Kentucky Fried Chicken" paid him a few cents for every meal sold under his contract. The idea grew beyond expectations and within four years, he had signed up over 400 franchises in the U.S. and Canada. For the next 20 years, the Colonel continued to visit his franchise locations to ensure good service and food quality, as well as offering helpful tips to KFC employees. By 1964, with over 600 restaurants, the Colonel sold the business for $2 million and a lifetime job. Sanders spent his remaining years advertising and promoting his "finger-lickin' good" recipe, making Kentucky

Top: Interior of Sanders' Cafe. This is the interior of the Sanders Court and Cafe as it appeared in the late 1930s. The slogan above the doorway reads "Good Will: The disposition of a pleased customer to return to the place where he has been well-treated." Sanders always placed emphasis on cleanliness and good service and his restaurant quickly gained a loyal following among travelers on the Dixie Highway (courtesy, KFC Corporation).

Bottom: Sanders Court and Cafe, Corbin, Kentucky. By the late 1930s, Harland Sanders' facilities grew to include overnight accommodations and a Pure service station. After opening his original cafe in 1930 at the age of 40, Sanders became so successful that he was able to franchise his operations throughout the country after World War II, turning a fledgling family business into a major corporate empire (courtesy, KFC Corporation).

Roy Allen (left) and Frank Wright (right) in 1922. Prohibition spurred the sale of soft drinks during the 1920s and countless new soda pop companies proliferated across the country, with root beer being a popular favorite. In June 1919, Roy Allen started selling his own root beer recipe from a roadside stand in Lodi, California. After opening a second location in Sacramento, Allen made an able employee, Frank Wright, his business partner in 1922. They named their restaurants "A & W" by combining their initials. Within two years, the two owned locations in northern and central California, Utah and Texas. In 1924, Allen bought out Wright's stake in the company and continued alone. However, with Wright out of the business early in the company's history, the A & W moniker remained, becoming a popular American trademark (courtesy, A & W Restaurants, Inc).

mula from a pharmacist in Arizona and sold his creamy root beer for a nickel a mug. Although root beer was nothing new, Allen's new beverage quickly gained a following in California's Central Valley. With the success of his small stand in Lodi, Allen opened a second location in Sacramento, which featured "tray boys" offering curb service to customers. The first "drive-in" restaurant was created.[96]

In 1922, Allen took on an employee, Frank Wright, as a partner in the business. Allen and Wright combined their initials, naming the new enterprise "A & W." The two men opened three new locations in Sacramento, selling their "A & W Root Beer." Soon they expanded to northern and central California, Utah and Texas. In 1924, Allen bought Wright's share of the business and trademarked the A & W Root Beer name and logo. Allen then started selling franchises to market his root beer. By 1933, Allen had over 170 franchises in the west and midwestern states. To ensure uniform quality, Allen sold his exclusive root beer concentrate, a trade secret to this day, to each franchise owner. A & W's profits continued to soar, with earnings coming from the sale of the concentrate and a nominal license fee.[97]

During World War II, rationing and manpower shortages affected A & W, with restrictions on sugar, an essential ingredient for root beer. Although no new restaurants were opened during the war, most A & W units remained successful. The period of the late 1940s saw explosive growth for A & W, with the number of franchises tripling to over 450 by 1950. That year, Roy Allen retired and sold the

Fried Chicken a fixture of today's roadside eating scene.[95]

A & W

On a hot day in June 1919, Roy Allen sold his first frosty mug of root beer from a roadside stand in Lodi, California. Allen had purchased the for-

A & W "Root Beer Barrel" building. Although A & W restaurants are best known for their drive-ins (with "car hops"), many may not recall some of the company's eclectic pre–World War II buildings, with some A&Ws resembling giant root beer barrels. This rare photograph dates from the 1930s. By 1933, Roy Allen had over 170 franchises in the west and midwestern states and A & W captured its own niche in the root beer market (courtesy, A & W Restaurants, Inc.).

A & W "Indian Head" building. Some A & W franchises used their own imagination to find ways to attract the attention of passing motorists. Roadside businesses designed structures shaped like donuts, artichokes or other objects or used discarded railroad cars or airplanes to give added flavor to roadside sightseeing. This garish looking "Indian Head" motif appears to date from the 1940s and was located in Kansas City, Kansas. Even for the low price of a nickel a mug, the company made enough profit to continue to expand its operations into the 1960s (courtesy, A & W Restaurants, Inc.).

business to a Nebraskan named Gene Hurtz. The post-war car craze was the perfect environment for A & W Drive-Ins. The food menu was expanded under Huntz's tenure, and the company grew to over 2,000 restaurants by 1960. In the past few decades, the company went through a succession of owners, and some locations were closed. Today, A & W has over 530 restaurants in the U.S. and overseas, and travelers are still enjoying the same frosty-mug taste.[98]

Dairy Queen

While the Colonel was studying chicken, J. F. McCullough, owner of the Homemade Ice Cream Company in Green River, Illinois, was experimenting with ice cream. McCullough believed that ice cream tasted better when it was soft and fresh, not frozen solid, and so he invented his own unique process. With his son and a business partner, they

convinced Sherb Noble to sell the soft ice cream at Noble's ice cream shop in Kankakee, Illinois. On August 4, 1938, they hosted a one-day sale, calling the event the "All the Ice Cream You Eat for Only 10 Cents" sale. The store was mobbed by over 1,600 customers, and Noble feared the crowd would break through his front store window. They held a second sale two weeks later, again with huge success. The McCulloughs instantly recognized that their product had great potential.[99]

However, one technical challenge faced the McCulloughs before they could market their ice cream successfully. The softer ice cream required a freezer that could maintain a temperature at constant 23 degrees Fahrenheit, which freezers of the day could not do. They answered a newspaper ad placed by Harry Oltz, who had patented a freezer that could maintain a constant temperature in 1937, and so they entered into a joint venture with Oltz. In 1939, they signed an agreement allowing

Top: Original Dairy Queen. This old photograph, dated June 22, 1940, is of the first Dairy Queen located in Joliet, Illinois. The opening of this first DQ was a joint effort of J. F. McCullough, his son, and Sherb Noble, an owner of a Kankakee ice cream shop. The three overcame technical problems and other obstacles to found a product that has become almost synonymous with ice cream (courtesy, Dairy Queen International, Inc.).

Bottom: Early Dairy Queen. An early photo of a vintage Dairy Queen location. McCullough devised the name "Dairy Queen," as well as the company's "Cone with the Curl on Top" trademark. The first Dairy Queens sold ice cream cones in just two sizes, priced at 5 and 10 cents. This building was prior to the company's postwar standardized buildings for its franchise locations (courtesy, Dairy Queen International, Inc.).

the McCulloughs to produce the freezers and granting them the exclusive rights to use them in the western United States. In exchange, Oltz had the exclusive right to use his freezers in the eastern states, and was paid a royalty based on the number of gallons of ice cream processed by freezers used by the McCulloughs.[100]

On June 22, 1940, the McCulloughs opened their first store in Joliet, Illinois, with Sherb Noble himself as the owner. However, they needed a name for their new stores. After thinking about the freshness of their ice cream and its source being a dairy product, "Dairy Queen" was chosen. The menu was simple: two sizes of cones with its trademark "Cone with the Curl on Top"; an assortment of flavored sundaes; and take-home pints and quarts. There were ten Dairy Queen stores by the outbreak of World War II and they barely remained open during the war, sometimes closing for weeks at a time when the rationed products ran out. Dairy Queen profited by the postwar consumer spending binge, increasing its franchise locations from 100 in 1947 to 1,156 by 1950.[101]

The decade of the 1950s saw the expansion of suburbia and a booming economy that seemed to produce an endless array of consumer items and modern conveniences. Television and air conditioning, however, tended to keep families at home, so Dairy Queen responded by expanding its menu, adding such favorites as the Banana Split, Dilly Bar, and DQ Sandwich. A territory operator in Georgia experimented with hot food. By 1968, Dairy Queen added the "Brazier Food" line to its menu. Today, you can still occasionally run across an independent ice cream store, with names such as "Dairy Cone" and "Dairy Freeze," that tried to copy DQ's commercial success. By concentrating on a single product—ice cream—Dairy Queen continues to dominate the roadside ice cream business.[102]

Stuckey's

Another American success story of the Depression Era originates from the deep South. In Eastman, Georgia, pecan farmer William S. "Bill" Stuckey, Sr., started selling his surplus pecans from a lean-to shed to passing motorists on U.S. Highway 23. Bill's wife, Ethel, ran the small stand, and tourists bound for Florida eagerly purchased Stuckey's pecans, either as gifts or as souvenirs of the rural South. Ethel began experimenting with an old family recipe using white molasses, powdered sugar and roasted pecans. She eventually made what she called a "pecan log," which they sold at the family stand along with raw pecans. Customers liked Ethel Stuckey's pecan log recipe and sales skyrocketed. In 1937, they built a new building to accommodate the increasing business, and the Stuckey's Candy Shoppe added pecan-based candies such as pecan clusters and fudge to its now-famous Pecan Log Roll. By 1941, business was so good that they opened three more stores; one on U.S. 41 in Unadilla, Georgia; another on U.S. 23 in Folkston; and a third location in Florida. The buildings each proudly displayed a "Stuckey's" sign.[103]

World War II almost caused the demise of Stuckey's, as government rationing forced the closure of all but the Eastman store. However, Stuckey's rebounded after the war and had 29 locations by 1953. The early Stuckey's stores resembled a house with a filling station canopy added. The company entered into a partnership with Texaco in the 1950s, whereby Texaco and Stuckey's products were sold at the same location. To compete with the other roadside businesses, Stuckey's had to rely heavily on advertising, and the company made a big investment in highway billboards. Soon, Stuckey's standard yellow and red billboards appeared on major highways leading to Florida. By the 1960s, with over 6,000 signs, construction and maintenance of the billboards became expensive, so a permanent billboard maintenance crew was employed.[104]

Stuckey's undertook tight quality control to maintain product uniformity, and Ethel Stuckey's kitchen was expanded into a modern candy factory. In 1964, Bill Stuckey, Sr., sold the company's name and franchising rights to Pet Milk, Inc., in exchange for $15 million in Pet stock. The new Stuckey's continued the company's association with Texaco Oil Company, and the company introduced new standardized building designs, with its familiar sloped green roof visible at freeway exits.[105]

The company reached its peak in the early 1970s with over 300 stores, but the 1973 oil embargo and the resulting decline in tourism hurt business. Pet, Inc., started to lose interest in the Stuckey's portion of its operations, and Bill Sr.'s death in 1977 added to Stuckey's decline. Abandoned stores started appearing. However, in 1985, Bill Stuckey, Jr., and a group of partners bought back the Stuckey's name from Pet, Inc., and

Top: William S. "Bill" Stuckey posing next to original shed, Eastman, Georgia. In the late 1930s, William and Ethel Stuckey's pecan farm was producing an oversupply of nuts, so Bill started selling bags of pecans to tourists from a wooden shed on the side of U.S. Route 25. Ethel came up with her own recipe for a "pecan log" and sales were so good that they built a larger building, including a factory. This is a rare photo of Bill Stuckey standing next to his original shed (courtesy, Stuckey's Corporation).

Bottom: First Stuckey's store, 1940s. A photo of the original Stuckey's in Eastman, Georgia, taken in the 1940s. Starting with Ethel's pecan log, the Stuckeys added other pecan-related confections to sell to tourists. The factory with smoke stack is behind the retail outlet (courtesy, Stuckey's Corporation).

Stuckey's and Texaco station, Allandale, Florida. Stuckey's and Texaco entered into a joint venture in the 1950s and both products were sold side-by-side at Stuckey's locations. This early 1950s store was located in Allandale, Florida, a town so small that it is not found on most road maps. This store is typical of the original Stuckey's built before the introduction of the company's standardized architecture of the 1960s (courtesy, Stuckey's Corporation).

resurrected Stuckey's stores and its pecan products. Today, with over 100 locations in 23 states, the Stuckey's tradition is again serving the hungry highway traveler.[106]

Signs of the Times

The earliest roadside advertisement was the filling station itself, as station architecture evolved to entice drivers to pull in for a fill-up. In urban areas, lack of space necessitated posting advertisements on the sides of buildings. As the U.S. federal-aid system was being built, farmers' barns were painted with ads for products such as chewing tobacco, flour, corn syrup, and tire repairs, while others advertised tourist attractions. In exchange for allowing the ad on their barn, the advertiser usually promised to repaint the barn periodically, or paid a nominal fee. Although most of these old barn ads have disappeared, you can still find some

survivors, advertising products such as "Mail Pouch Tobacco."

The traveling public has had a sort of love-hate relationship with highway billboards. On the one hand, reading road signs helped pass the time. Vacationers invented their own highway road games or counted telephone poles for entertainment on the long stretches of open road. However, signs could be gaudy at times and spoil roadside scenery. For the most part, highway billboards were appreciated for their homemade quality and occasional humor. Gas stations, motels, cafes, and other roadside businesses used a variety of techniques to get the motorist to stop.

Several roadside advertisements have made it into American highway folklore. A retired insurance agent from Minneapolis, Minnesota, Clinton Odell, started the fledgling Burma-Vita Company, marketing liniment and their "Burma-Shave" shaving cream in the early 1920s. Odell and his sons, Allan and Leonard, traveled the Midwest selling

Top: Bowes Barn. During the 1920s and 30s, barns were a favorite alternative to billboards for roadside advertisements. No investment in wooden signs was needed and the only cost to the advertiser was a little paint and a modest rental fee to compensate the farmer. Advertisements for "Bowes Seal-Fast Tire Repairs" were painted on barns on many federal-aid highways in the midwest and other areas; only a handful remain today. This barn is located in central Minnesota (photo by author).

Bottom: Blatz Beer Barn Ad. A fading advertisement for Blatz Beer on a barn silo on U.S. 10 in central Wisconsin. Silos as well as barns were sometimes used for product advertisements in locations with good visibility to passing motorists. Beverage products such as Coca-Cola, Miller Beer, and others used grain silos for ads, as they resembled giant drink containers. Many barn ads were painted over or demolished to conform with the Highway Beautification Act of 1965, but a few examples have managed to survive (photo by author).

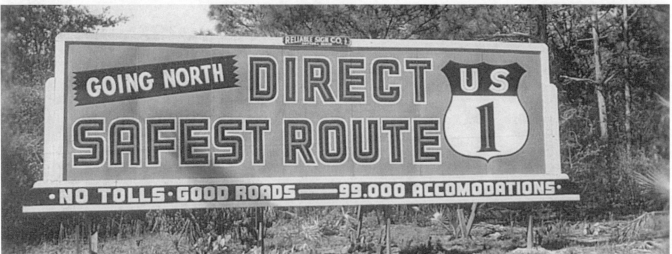

Top: Howard Johnson billboard. A typical early highway billboard with lattice skirt for decoration for Howard Johnson restaurants. Billboard advertisers often signed long-term leases with landowners for the rights to use private property, so decorative signs were produced that would last longer and hopefully require little repainting and maintenance. Signs such as this are rare today, victims of "progress" and highway aesthetics legislation in the 1960s (courtesy, Howard Johnson International, Inc.).

Bottom: "Going North—Direct Safest Route—U.S. 1." A billboard touting U.S. Route 1 as the safest route north from Florida. Highway billboards such as the one pictured, with its stepped borders, were common on American highways in the 1920 through the 1950s. However, billboards gradually multiplied over the years and thickets of competing signs became an annoyance to motorists. In the 1960s, federal legislation required the removal of highway billboards within 660 feet of a highway right-of-way, so thousands of billboards were dismantled across the country (National Archives [52-959]).

Top: Cross-roads of U.S. 221, 321 and 421, Boone, North Carolina. After the American Association of State Highway Officials (AASHO) approved the familiar black-and-white U.S. shield and other road signs in the late 20s, the states marked all federal-aid routes according to the new standards. This intersection is in North Carolina, as noted by the U.S. shields for three federal-aid routes converging in the town of Boone. These signs are rare today, being replaced by a new design with a larger, more visible marker without a reference to the state (National Archives [50-4952]).

Bottom: "You now leave New Mexico—Come Again." For many decades, seasoned travelers on Route 66 passed under this archway on the New Mexico-Arizona border. The Joab family traveled through his location during a scene from the 1940 movie "Grapes of Wrath" starring Henry Fonda, as did many Okies and Arkies journeying to California during the Depression. The movie was filmed at several other locations on U.S. 66 (This photo was taken by T. W. Kines in 1948, National Archives [48-1616]).

their products to small-town drug stores and pharmacies. Sales, however, were disappointing. On one of his sales trips, Allan noticed a series of billboard signs for a gas station, advertising gasoline, oil, and restrooms, with the last sign pointing to the station. They decided to copy the idea, so, with

Wall Drug Store with Ted Hustead, Sr., 1931. Water has long been an important and a scarce commodity for travelers for eons. Locating water for thirsty motorists and auto radiators was especially difficult during the Dust Bowl years of the 1930s when heat waves topped 100 degrees Farenheit for weeks. In 1931, Ted and Dorothy Hustead bought a drug store with a soda fountain in Wall, South Dakota. The Depression virtually halted the tourist trade, and business in Wall was slow. Dorothy Hustead's idea to advertise free ice water to attract patrons became an instant success. To further advertise their store, Ted and son Bill put up the first of the now-famous Wall Drug store billboards on U.S. 16 from Wyoming to Wisconsin, earning the Wall Drug Store a place in highway history (courtesy, Wall Drug Store).

the financial backing of their father, Allan and Leonard bought some old wooden boards and paint and set to work on their new advertising scheme. The Odells cut the lumber into three-foot lengths, and stenciled some crude lettering.[107] Allan and Leonard drove up and down major Minnesota highways, convincing farmers to let them place Burma Shave signs on their land. The Odells put up their signs on open stretches of highway approximately 100 feet apart so that motorists could still read them at highway speeds. Their first signs appeared on U.S. 65 near Lakeville, Minnesota, and U.S. 61 between Red Wing and the

Twin Cities. Soon, sales started to pick up. The Odells decided to be more creative, rhyming the words while adding their own brand of wry humor. Sometimes the ads poked fun at the competition: "It's not toasted; It's not dated; But look out; It's imitated." Some signs gave cautionary messages, what one might call an early public service announcement, to motorists: "Don't pass cars; On curve or hill; If the cops; Don't get you; the mortician will."[108]

The Odells' billboard jingles were such a hit with the public that the ad campaign went nationwide. Soon, they were seen coast to coast. Despite public protest over the steady proliferation of highway billboards in the 1930s, the Burma-Shave signs survived, entertaining a generation of Americans traveling the nation's highways. The company was purchased by Philip Morris in the early 1960s, and the new corporate owners discontinued the Burma-Shave billboard ads. The beloved signs were taken down, thus ending perhaps the most successful roadside marketing concept in highway history.[109]

While the plucky little Burma-Shave signs were sweeping the countryside, Ted and Dorothy Hustead purchased a drug store in dusty Wall, South Dakota, in 1931. It was the height of the Depression, and tourism was slow. The first few years were lean, and only a few hardy tourists stopped in the town of Wall on their way to the Black Hills, Yellowstone, and other points west. Adding to their troubles was a prolonged drought that gripped the Great Plains during the first half of the '30s, with temperatures in excess of 100 degrees, setting all-time records. The store did have a soda fountain, and thirsty customers welcomed the ice cream and liquid refreshments. Dorothy suggested that they should advertise free ice water to entice parched travelers to stop by their store. They already had ice on hand for the store's soda fountain. Each winter, Ted and his 18-year-old son Bill hauled 150-pound ice blocks cut from the frozen Cheyenne River and other local streams, packing the ice in sawdust for the summer months. So, during the summer of 1936, Ted put together a series of signs advertising free ice water. The message of the first signs announced "Get a Soda—Get a Root Beer—Just as Near—To Highway 16 and 14—Free Ice Water—Wall Drug." As soon as the first Wall Drug signs went up, hot and thirsty travelers poured in to their store. The signs were such a success that Ted and Dorothy could not keep up with the hordes of customers that packing into their store, so they hired eight waitresses to help out.[110]

During the following summers up to the outbreak of World War II, Ted and Bill put up more billboards along U.S. 16 from the Big Horn Mountains in Wyoming to La Crosse, Wisconsin. After the war, more signs were erected in other states. Bill gradually took over the job of repairing and maintaining the Wall Drug signs from spring to fall. The signs were fun to read for many motorists driving on long, boring stretches of highway. The road signs also put the town of Wall "on the map," and just about any vacationer who has traveled America by car can attest to seeing at least one Wall Drug sign.[111]

The rest of the story is now highway history. The Husteads' signs have become a national phenomenon, cheerfully advising the motorist of the remaining mileage to see such free wonders as the cowboy orchestra, the outstanding collection of western art, or the new 80-foot dinosaur. Wall Drugs signs survived anti-billboard campaigns and can even be found in some foreign countries.

In the deep South, Garnet and Freda Carter operated "Fairyland" atop Lookout Mountain, Georgia, just across the border from Chattanooga, Tennessee, during the 1920s. Lookout Mountain and the adjacent Chickamauga-Chattanooga military park was the scene of Civil War action as Union forces captured Chattanooga on their way to Atlanta. The Carters envisioned a resort community, complete with a golf course and walk-through gardens. On May 21, 1932, after much work, the business officially reopened as "Rock City Gardens." As the new name suggests, the Carters' 10-acre attraction included extensive wildflower gardens (Freda's contribution) throughout an intricate maze of rock formations. The golf course was scaled down to a miniature golf course, probably the first in the country.[112]

In 1935, Garnet and Fred Maxwell, an owner of a Chattanooga advertising company, decided that ads painted on barns would be a cheap way to spread the word about Rock City Gardens. Garnet and Maxwell's teenage understudy, Clark

Byers, traveled the main highways from Michigan to Florida to Texas, recording locations of favored sites visible to motorists. The pair approached farmers and offered to paint the entire barn at no charge in exchange for the right to include an ad for Rock City. Later, farmers were paid between $3 to $5 for advertising privileges. The color scheme was simple: a black background (using Byers' own formula of linseed oil and lampblack) with white lettering. For the next 30 years, Byer and his crew "barnstormed" across the Midwest and South, painting barn ads freehand using nothing more than four-inch paint brushes. Working full days, they encountered everything from bad weather to angry bulls and labor unions. At its peak in 1956, over 900 barns covered 19 states with the familiar message "See Rock City" or "See 7 States from Rock City—8th Wonder of the World." Highway beautification legislation took its toll on Rock City's barns, and approximately 100 or so remain today. In 1968, Byer put down his paint brush permanently after being nearly electrocuted during a thunderstorm which hospitalized him for one year. In 1996, at age 83, Clark Byer was enjoying a quiet retirement, no doubt reminiscing over the heyday of the Rock City barns. The Rock City of today is even bigger, including a spectacular lighting display during the holiday season. Rock City Gardens is still run by descendants of its founders and is currently owned by Bill Chapin, great-nephew of Garnet and Freda Carter.[113]

Virtually every state has at least one underground cavern to be exploited for commercial gain. Long before the advent of man-made creations such as today's "theme parks," these naturally-occurring wonders were popular tourist attractions for those able to own an automobile and journey into the countryside. Caves are usually found in mountainous regions, such as the Appalachians and South Dakota's Black Hills. The northern half of the Ozark Mountains lies within the State of Missouri, and over 1,000 caves have been identified in the Missouri Ozarks. Names such as Onyx Mountain Caverns, Crystal Caverns, Fairy Cave, Marvel Cave, and Round Spring Caverns, and others too numerous to mention, dot the misty hills.

U.S. Route 66 traverses Missouri diagonally from St. Louis to Springfield in the state's southwestern corner, crossing the northern fringe of the Ozarks. Along this picturesque portion of Route 66, tourist traps hawked locally made "authentic" basketry and other curios. In the 1920s, as the route was improved after being officially designated as U.S. 66, several cave attractions appeared. Onondaga Cave near Leasburg, Missouri, was owned by Lester B. Dill, an avid cave explorer. Dill also purchased Cathedral Caverns and Meramec Caverns. In 1933, while exploring the Meramec Caverns (located 30 miles down the Meramec River from Onondaga Cave), Dill discovered an unknown upper level which eventually led to 26 miles of passages. One of the cave's many marvels was the "Stage Curtain," claimed to be the world's largest cave formation.[114]

The tourism business continued in spite of the Depression, aided by the nation's growing network of highways. Dill embarked on a roadside advertising campaign of his own to pull in more customers. Perhaps borrowing from the success of other successful advertising pioneers of the day, Dill also had ads for his caves painted on barns. At first, Dill's advertisements used only the brief message "Meramec Caverns, U.S. 66, Stanton MO," with white lettering for maximum visibility for passing tourists. Later on, all Meramec Cavern barn ads used the red, yellow and white color scheme that are seen today. Dill also made up "bumper stickers" with the "Meramec Caverns" lettering in bold print. Just to ensure that tourists used them, Dill had his bumper stickers applied to his patrons' bumpers in his parking lot while they were on the cave tour.

Besides running several tourist attractions, Lester Dill is known for his work in helping enact cave inspection legislation in Missouri, which became a model for other states. Missouri earned the nickname "The Cave State" due to Dill's promotional efforts. Among his other accomplishments is his work in organizing the National Cave Association and his opposition to construction of a proposed dam on the Meramec River which would have flooded many local caves, including the Onondaga Cave.[115]

Lester Dill's advertising capitalized on Meramec Caverns' notoriety as a hideout for Jesse James (real name: J. Frank Dalton) and his gang in the early 1870s. The cave is rich in history, includ-

Early Meramec Caverns barn sign on U.S. 40 in southern Illinois. As New Deal programs and private industry slowly created new employment, tourism began to prosper by the late 1930s. The lack of work in hard-hit rural areas prompted some enterprising Americans to start roadside tourist businesses to earn a living. Among the hundreds of "tourist traps" that sprang up on the roadsides was Meramec Caverns near Stanton, Missouri, on U.S. 66. Lester Dill, a local cave explorer, owned and operated several cave attractions in the Missouri Ozarks, including the unique Meramec Caverns, opened in 1933. Dill used the same advertising scheme as Rock City Gardens by painting its ads on barns throughout the Midwest. This photo is of an older Meramec Caverns barn ad prior to the bright red-white-and-yellow coloring used today (photo by author).

MERAMEC
44-66
STANTON, MO.
CAVERNS
JESSE JAMES
HIDEOUT

"Meramec Caverns Bumper Sticker. Since its discovery in 1716, the Meramec Cavern has had a long and colorful history and was used as a haven by Quantrill's guerrillas, then by Jesse James and his gang and other outlaws during the late 1800s. In 1933, the year Lester Dill opened the caves for public tours, Dill discovered 26 miles of previously unexplored passages and soon Meramec Caverns became one of the most well-known cave attractions in the United States. Lester Dill's tour guides used the cave's notoriety to maximum advantage, tantalizing tourists with tales of outlaw bandits and occasionally "finding" rusty guns and other artifact on cave tours. Dill heavily promoted Meramec Caverns with roadside advertising and his ingenious use of complimentary bumper stickers which he had attached to the bumper of every vehicle parked in the Caverns' parking lot (courtesy, Meramec Caverns).

ing its use as haven for Quantrill's Guerillas in 1864. The James Gang's saga includes a famous 1874 incident in which the gang was cornered by lawmen in Meramec Caverns, but escaped through a secret passage. Dill found the gang's escape route in 1940, along with some artifacts left behind. Another cave legend is a curious tale about a 100-year-old man who surfaced publicly in 1948, claiming to be the long-deceased Jesse James. People familiar with the history of the Jesse James Gang checked out the old man's story, and a physical examination revealed bullet scars matching those known to have existed on the body of the infamous outlaw who was gunned down in 1882. No one could disprove his claim, and the man passed away on August 16, 1951, in Granbury, Texas, at the age of 103. Lester Dill himself died in 1980, leaving the operation of Meramec Caverns to his grandson, Lester B. Turilli.[116]

Highway billboards in the early days of roadside advertising consisted mainly of the homemade variety, such as the proverbial "Last Chance for Gas" sign. Billboards evolved into structures designed to last for many years, and ornamentation such as latticework skirts at the base of signs were added, perhaps for a more decorative touch. However, unless the signs were near an electrical source for spotlighting, they were invisible to motorists at night. Billboards located in and near cities and towns were electrically lighted. French scientist George Claude developed neon tubing and patented

its commercial application for outdoor advertisement. The new "glow-discharge electric display lamp" was used throughout Europe, then came to the United States in 1923 when the first neon advertising sign was installed at a Packard dealership in Los Angeles.[117] Soon, neon signs were proliferating along America's highways the 1920s and '30s. Neon lighting came in a variety of colors and its bright glow could be seen at considerable distances, piercing the darkness. The neon sign was a godsend for many a traveler with a near-empty gas tank, or anxiously searching for a place to sleep. Neon signs were in common use until the late 1950s when advertisers started using plastic display signs with fluorescent lighting. Modern plastic signs replaced neon, partially due to the fact that the ad message could be made more versatile than with conventional neon tubing. However, neon lighting has enjoyed a recent resurgence in popularity as the public has rediscovered its practicality for signage, and perhaps a bit of yearning for nostalgic times.

Highway Construction Between the Wars

With aid of federal dollars, the period between the wars saw the nation's road system progress from primarily dirt paths to a 234,000 mile system of hard-surfaced, all-weather highways

by 1940. Civil engineers developed concrete and asphalt road surfaces, as well as cement and steel bridges of all varieties. The early engineers designed bridges and roadways that were "built to last," and today's highway infrastructure is still supported by the U.S. federal aid highway system and many of its original bridges.

However, limited highway funding during the early decades of the 20th century meant that many of the early roads, including federal aid highways, were hastily constructed, leaving sharp 90-degree curves, blind hills and steep grades, making highway travel a white-knuckled affair. Highways were often only 8–10 feet wide, leaving barely enough space for cars, let alone the ever-menacing trailer trucks. During the 1920s, truck registration more than tripled, from 1,107,000 in 1920 to 3,518,000 by

Top: "Gas for Less" neon sign. An independent filling station's bright neon sign promises gas at a discount price. French scientist George Claude's invention of neon tubing for outdoor advertising in 1923 changed the look of the nighttime highway scene. This sign was located at the Tracy Oil Company, Marshall and Hamline Avenues, St. Paul, Minnesota (photo by author).

Bottom: "Gasoline" Arrow neon sign, U.S. 66, Missouri. An ancient neon sign pointing the way to a gas station near Halltown, Missouri. Highway advertising signs used arrows, flashing lights and other visual motifs to direct drivers' attention toward roadside businesses. A handful of antique signs such as this one pictured on old U.S. Route 66 can still be found (photo by author).

Top: Granite block repair, New York City, 1924. Workers repaving a city street with granite blocks. Old materials such as brick paving soon became extinct later in the 1920s as modern methods and machinery became available (National Archives [36597]).

Bottom: Dumping "chert float" on rural road. A base layer of chert (a dull-colored, impure crystalline quartz, also called "hornstone") is dumped on a subgrade on a state road north of Huntsville, Alabama. By J. K. Hillers, 1929 (National Archives [34496]).

Convict labor on State Road 6, south of Blountstown, Florida. This crew is loading sand-clay into trucks on State Road 6 south of Blountstown, Florida, in 1929. New Mexico was the first state to use convict labor for road projects in 1903, a highway between Santa Fe and Las Vegas. Use of prison labor has currently been banned by U.S. courts as unconstitutional under the Fourth Amendment prohibition against involuntary servitude and cruel and unusual punishment (National Archives [35406]).

1930.[118] Many a family vacation was tragically cut short by the combination of narrow roads and bridges, heavy traffic (often caused by a slow vehicle on a long hill), poorly marked roads (especially during night driving), driver error, or reckless drivers disobeying "Do Not Pass" signs. Early motorists gave descriptive nicknames to dangerous stretches of highways, with ominous names that warned drivers to beware. Many highways had their own "Dead Man's Curve." Others had a "Horse Shoe Curve," "Five-Mile Hill," or other hazard. As the 1920s progressed, the motor vehicle death rate soared from 11.7 per 100,000 to 25.7 per 100,000 by 1929. Total annual deaths from accidents nearly tripled during the decade, from 12,500 in 1920 to 31,200 in 1929. However, no one seemed to notice, and crash statistics were obscured by all of the hoopla as the '20s kept roaring on.[119]

State and local governments did what they could on their limited budgets to keep a lid on the highway fatality rate. Railroad grade crossings were more clearly marked. Gradually, electronic signs using flashing lights, bells and occasionally equipped with a mechanical movable arm to prevent vehicles from crossing were used. Dangerous, accident-breeding stretches and hairpin curves were sometimes straightened and steep hills leveled. But with the nation adding between one to two million new vehicles to the road annually during the 1920s, highway construction alone clearly was not doing the job. Local law enforcement could only patrol their immediate cities and towns to catch drivers exceeding the speed limit. Of course, some small-town police and sheriffs were a bit overaggressive in handing out speeding tickets. Motorists, particularly over-the-road haulers, had to keep a sharp eye out for the proverbial town cop lurking behind a tree or billboard. City slickers in their fancy speedsters, eager to reach sunny Florida or some other destination, were easy prey, and many appeared before the local justice of the peace, paying a speeding fine. But on the open highway, law enforcement was nonexistent. Some areas did not have posted speed limits for years. In the early '20s, the area between towns in some states was a lawless no-man's-land, somewhat reminiscent of the Wild West.

However, this didn't last long. Urban police departments in the major metro areas started using cars and motorcycles in the 1910s. The motorcycle was particularly attractive, since it could maneuver easily through traffic jams and were cheap in comparison to cars, so even a modest size town could afford at least one motorcycle. However, to patrol the state highway system and to serve areas not covered by local authorities, each state established its own state highway patrol. Radio communica-

Top: Concrete mixer and crew on federal-aid highway project near Memphis, 1929. One of many road projects financed with federal funds as a result of the Federal-Aid Highway Act of 1921. This highway crew is laying concrete on a road in a rural area near Memphis. The number of motor vehicles on the nation's highways nearly tripled during the 1920s from 9 million to over 26 million by 1930, so projects such as this were sorely needed (courtesy US DOT/FHWA).

Bottom: New concrete bridge, Swan Creek Township, Ohio. The introduction of Bessemer steel in 1855 led to an endless array of uses for the new alloy, from hairpins to bridge construction. Although steel does not corrode as quickly as iron, deterioration remains a factor for highway engineers and steel-reinforced concrete, particularly for shorter bridges, came into use. Concrete bridges using steel mesh for added strength are built by pouring concrete into pre-made wooden forms. This small bridge, dating to 1936, is typical of designs used throughout the United States during the 1920s through the 40s (National Archives [no #]).

tion came later, particularly after World War II, as methods became more sophisticated. Before long, motorists intent on breaking the law had to contend with a this new type law enforcement.

The 1920s and 1930s saw various infestations of insects that ravaged cotton, fruit, and afflicted livestock. State highway patrols, in cooperation with state inspectors, local authorities, and occasionally state national guard units, set up border checkpoints, searching vehicles for pests such as the Mediterranean fruit fly and cattle ticks. The much ballyhooed wealth that was supposedly created during the Roaring Twenties had bypassed much of rural America. Farm prices had been depressed for several years before the 1929 stock market crash. Things only got worse in the '30s, when drought caused crop failures in many areas, and prices fell to historic lows. The situation forced farmers and ranchers to become militant about

Top: Close-up of dynamite for blasting at construction site. A worker places dynamite in a pop hole to remove rock during construction of U. S. 11, north of Winchester, Virginia. Blasting often was necessary to break up solid rock formations for road building. J. K. Hillers August 1937 (National Archives [37-2286]).

Bottom: Interior of tunnel on Blue Ridge Parkway, North Carolina. Among the biggest challenges facing highway engineers are crossing mountains and waterways. Some ranges are too steep for the most able highway designers, so tunneling is sometimes the only alternative. The Roosevelt Administration provided financial aid for road construction to the WPA and federal agencies, and a highway through the Blue Ridge Mountains to the Great Smoky Mountains was one such depression-era project. This photograph is of a power shovel and truck excavating a tunnel on the Blue Ridge Parkway. J. K. Hillers photographed this worksite in June 1940 (National Archives [40-3261]).

Top: "Depression chariots" on crowded street, Greenville, North Carolina, 1933. During the height of the Great Depression, many financially-strapped states were forced to raise taxes at a time when unemployment nation-wide hovered at 25 percent. Deflation in wages and commodity prices added to the nation's desperate economic situation. When North Carolina raised its state gasoline tax by 6 cents per gallon, farmers could not afford to buy gas, so many converted their cars into "depression chariots" by removing the body and rear axle and using four-legged horsepower. The tires were often filled with cotton or corn stalks. The year following the gas tax increase, motor vehicle registrations in the state dropped by over 27,000 vehicles (National Archives [34-203]).

Bottom: Realignment of "Dead Man's Curve" on U. S. 1 near Elkridge, Maryland. The public was so eager for new road construction that the first generation of highways were hastily built, with little regard for factors such as safety. In most cases, hills were not leveled and curves were crowned or sharp, contributing to many traffic accidents during the first several decades of the 20th century. This photo shows an early attempt to straighten U. S. 1's infamous "Dead Man's Curve" by the Maryland Highway Department in 1919 (National Archives [17936]).

Top: Union Pacific signal installation, Sand Creek Junction, Colorado. Another example of electronic grade crossing warning devices is this one with movable gate on U. S. 85 in Colorado. This device was a WPA project. Photograph taken November 24, 1937 (National Archives [37-4524]).

Bottom: A dangerous railroad grade crossing in Maryland, 1922. This railroad junction is using an early bell and stop sign, seen overhanging the crossing in the center. The day of the steam locomotive as pictured here was nearly over, as the diesel engine (developed by German inventor Rudolf Diesel) came into production by 1925. J. K. Hillers (National Archives [26267]).

Top: "Horseshoe curve" on Virginia highway, 1935. Switchbacks and horseshoe curves abounded on early roads when making steep changes in elevation. Highway engineers used the limited means at their disposal in making the first national system of federal-aid highways. Most roads followed the natural contours of the surrounding terrain, such as this winding rural highway near Hill Mountain, north of Roanoke, Virginia (National Archives [35-1396]).

Top: "Arresting" a speeder in Greensboro, North Carolina. The sheer number of new vehicles on the nation's roads increased rapidly during the first decades of this century, along with a corresponding increase in traffic accidents. The Bureau of Public Roads and the states started motor vehicle safety programs as early as the 1920s to educate the public. North Carolina held public demonstrations on rules of the road and safety. The issue of speeding and careless driving was particularly targeted by the states. This is a posed picture taken during a central demonstration sponsored by the North Carolina Highway Commission, showing a "speeder" being ticketed by a policeman. The two men in the car are both employees of the state highway commission. J. K. Hillers, June 6, 1924 (National Archives [29978]).

Bottom: Illinois state policeman on motorcycle, 1928. Larger cities started using motorcycles for law enforcement in the 1910s, and the states and other municipalities followed in the 1920s. The motorcycle had several advantages to automobiles, as they were inexpensive and could maneuver easily through traffic jams. They also were more difficult to spot by lawbreakers. Photo by J. K. Hillers for the Bureau of Public Roads (National Archives [36053]).

protecting their remaining crops and livestock from invading plagues of insects. Border quarantine inspections checkpoints were common in the South and the West. The 1940 movie *Grapes of Wrath* (directed by John Ford and starring Henry Fonda) contains one scene of the Joad family getting rude treatment at a quarantine checkpoint on U.S. 66 as they attempt to cross into Arizona from New Mexico.

President Hoover attempted to hold down the rising unemployment rate by approving several highway appropriations. On December 30, 1930, Hoover signed an emergency bill authorizing $80 million for road projects, to be repaid by the states later. On June 6, 1932, Hoover approved the Revenue Act of 1932, which included the first federal gasoline tax, at one cent per gallon. However, the revenue went into the general fund and little was used for roads. Another measure called the Emergency Relief and Construction Act was signed by Hoover in July 1932, authorizing $120 million in federal aid to the states for highway projects. However, the fiscally-conservative Hoover was not about to give money to the states outright. The funds were still loans that had to be repaid, and states had to raise revenue to match the federal government's share.[120]

When Franklin Delano Roosevelt assumed the presidency in March 1933, the country was flat on its back, with public morale at its lowest and industry shutting down. Banks by the dozens were failing, from Manhattan to Main Street. During President Roosevelt's first 100 days in office, a whirlwind of New Deal legislation was passed in record time by a Congress united in a national crusade to fight the Great Depression. One of the earliest of the Depression-era bills, the Civilian Conservation Corps Reforestation Relief Act, created the CCC, which provided temporary jobs for young men between the ages of 18 and 24 with families on relief. Recruits were paid a wage of $30 a month and given free room and board (usually consisting of a tent outdoors) in camps run by the U.S. Army. The CCC planted over 2 billion trees, built dikes and repaired reservoirs, and renovated national parks and historic sites. One of the early CCC projects was $2 million "Going-to-the-Sun Road" through Logan Pass in Glacier National Park, that opened on July 15, 1933. Later in the 1930s, CCC workers repaired roads and even built bridges, such as the Trinity River Bridge, a 320-foot continuous steel truss bridge, built with inex-

perienced labor in northern California in 1937. By 1935, over a half million men had been employed by the CCC.[121]

The National Industrial Recovery Act, signed into law on June 16, 1933, was another Roosevelt quick-fix effort to end unemployment. In early 1933, for the first time since the Federal-Aid Highway Act of 1916 was passed, no federal funds were

Top: Mediterranean fruit fly quarantine inspection checkpoint. Many states sought to protect crops and livestock by setting up border checkpoints to inspect vehicles for such insects as cattle ticks, the Mediterranean fruit fly, and other pests. Several southeastern states such as Florida experienced an infestation of Mediterranean fruit flies in the late 1920s and early 1930s and the state used its state militia to check all vehicles entering the state. This photograph from 1929 shows Florida National guardsmen stopping cars on U.S. 1 between Jacksonville and St. Augustine (National Archives [35162]).

Bottom: WPA workers laying drain pipe, Tuskegee, Alabama. During the first 100 days of the Roosevelt Administration, a blizzard of legislation aimed at containing the nation's economic crisis passed Congress in record time. President Roosevelt and his brain trusters devised dozens of federally-funded projects to get some of the millions of unemployed to work. The nation had a great need for public works projects, with most areas still using dirt roads, while drought caused wind erosion and flooding to large regions. Highway and other public projects seemed a logical way to promote the public welfare while providing a needed paycheck for desperate citizens out of work (National Archives).

being spent on road projects. The National Industrial Recovery Act restored the federal role when Congress and the president approved $400 million

Top: WPA men spreading asphalt on city street. With a quarter of the work force unemployed and millions working reduced hours, no occupation escaped the effects of the Great Depression. Displaced workers came from all walks of life, and it became clear by 1933 that it would be years before private industry would be in a position to rehire the unemployed in any significant numbers. Many WPA projects did not require skilled labor, so people from disparate occupations were hired for what some critics called "make work" projects. In cities and towns across America, unskilled work for projects such as street repair paid an average wage of $60 a month, a good wage in those days (National Archives).

Bottom: WPA project painting center line, Detroit. WPA workers helped with almost every aspect of highway construction. Besides doing manual labor, WPA hired engineers for road projects at a pay rate of $100 a month. A truck owned by the Detroit police department drives alongside a WPA worker pushing a simple paint sprayer on wheels on a city street in 1935 (National Archives).

for federal-aid projects and $50 million for roads in national parks, forests, and public lands on March 30, 1933. In 1934, Congress revamped the federal aid formula under Hoover's legislation, eliminating the requirement for matching of funds to becoming outright grants to the states. The Hayden-Cartwright Act appropriated $200 million for highway projects, with a minimum of one-fourth to be spent on secondary and feeder roads. The first project completed under the NIRA was a highway between Salt Lake City, Utah, and Saltair Road, on August 5, 1933. The NIRA was appropriated $3.3 billion for public works projects and by August 1934, 16,330 miles of new roads were built.[122]

In addition to building new roads, the NIRA sought to end labor disputes and price cutting, which were worsening the Depression by eroding profits and causing consumer price deflation. Agriculture was already experiencing commodity deflation, and farmers burning crops and dumping milk to drive up prices was a sickening sight to a nation where many were malnourished. The NIRA was well intended and hoped to provide cooperation between business, labor and the government, but the NIRA's Blue Eagle became an unwelcome sight for many, especially businesses. The NIRA never had the opportunity to spend the $3.3 billion allotted for public works programs after FDR put Interior Secretary Harold Ickes in charge of the fund. The program was later transferred to the Public Works Administration (PWA). The NIRA came to an ignoble end when the act was declared unconstitutional by the U.S. Supreme Court on May 27, 1935. During its two years of its existence, the NIRA constructed 27,055 miles of new highways across the country.[123]

The Supreme Court later struck down other controversial New Deal programs. However, such setbacks did not deter FDR from proposing new legislation to replace the jobs programs such as the NIRA. Just one month before the Supreme Court decision effectively abolishing the NIRA, Congress had already passed the Emergency Relief Appropriations Act on April 8, 1935, which authorized a whopping $4.8 billion for public works, a new record for a single congressional expenditure. The act created a new public relief agency, the Works Progress Administration (WPA), headed by brain truster Harry Hopkins. The WPA is probably the most recognized of the New Deal alphabet-soup emergency agencies, and with a large budget, its

Top: CCC workers smoothing blacktop road. The Civilian Conservation Corps was run by the U. S. Army and resembled a military boot camp. Volunteers, mostly men in their 20s, worked in camps located in rural areas on projects such as building dikes and planting trees. Workers were paid $50 a month and the CCC sent all but $5 back to the men's families. Deflation pushed wages for clerks, housekeepers, and others to only $10 a month, so the CCC had no difficulty filling its ranks during its ten years. The CCC, like the WPA and PRA, worked on needed highway projects (National Archives).

Bottom: Preparing earth sub-base for paving. Two CCC men guide a grading machine on a highway project. During the Second World War, the CCC helped improve highways which were of strategic importance for the war effort, including helping build the Alaska Highway to connect the lower 48 states to military bases in Alaska (National Archives).

influence was soon felt in every corner of the nation.[124]

From its inception, the WPA became involved in everything from public facilities to the arts. The agency employed 8 million people until it was dissolved in 1943. During its peak in 1936-37, the WPA gave 3 million workers a steady paycheck, as the country was in a severe recession in 1937. In a seven-year period, WPA constructed over 5,900 schools, 2,500 hospitals, 350 airports, 8,000 parks, and over 570,000 miles of rural roads. The WPA spent $11 billion on public works projects until it was dissolved, but funding depended on the continuing generosity of Congress. Although employment with WPA was only temporary, usually no more than one year, it allowed those in need to find permanent employment in the private sector. Wages usually varied from $100 per month for a skilled engineer to $60 per month for an unskilled laborer, but many workers, particularly in the South, received only $21 per month. WPA employed artists and even paid 2,600 women in Mississippi $20 a month for sewing projects.[125]

Critics of the Works Progress Administration often portrayed it as a "make-work" agency and a waste of tax dollars on unnecessary projects. The image of the typical WPA worker was supposedly a man leaning on a shovel, inspiring a popular song "Leaning on a Shovel." The record shows a different story, one of millions of families escaping impoverished conditions and thousands of physical structures still used by the public today. As Harry Hopkins stated, "Give a man a dole and you save his body but destroy his spirit. Give him a job and pay him an assured wage and you save both the body and the spirit." The WPA's role in road projects was a tremendous shot in the arm for the highway construction sector, as state treasuries had run dry trying to care of its own needy citizens. Without WPA, the American highway system would have had to concentrate on upgrading its two-lane federal-aid highways following World War II, postponing the interstate highway system for perhaps decades.[126]

To address public concerns over traffic safety, the Bureau of Public Roads and many state highway departments conducted tests of road surfaces in the 1920s. An early test in Pittsburg, California, in 1921 and 1922 used various concrete types, over which army surplus trucks with solid tires were driven to simulate heavy truck traffic. In 1932 and 1933, a more extensive test was performed using 63 road surfaces on a two-mile track, again using trucks at the Bates Road Track in Illinois. The results of the tests showed that concrete with thickened edges and longitudinal centerline joints worked best to reduce cracking. Of the various surfaces tested, concrete outperformed asphalt, brick, or other pavement types for durability. Thickened edge concrete slab paving became the standard in highway construction until the 1950s. Testing at both the Pittsburg and Bates sites concluded that wire-mesh reinforcing for concrete also reduced cracking by giving slabs added strength.[127]

If you happen to travel down an old piece of highway, particularly any federal-aid route, you can still encounter vintage stretches of surviving examples of thickened edge concrete roads. Whether you're on the Lincoln Highway (U.S. 30), Dixie Highway (U.S. 25), or U.S. 66, original sections in driveable condition can still be found. Some of these old relics, many over 70 years old now, are located just off of most interstates and second-generation federal-aid highways, especially the main transcontinental routes such as U.S. 10, 20, 30, etc., that were later straightened, bypassed, or improved into four-lane highways. Concrete thickened edge highways are identified by the distinctive sloping curbing and are much narrower than today's standards, with lanes often only 8 to 10 feet wide. You'll find them well-worn, and your right tires may stray off the curbing and onto the shoulder. Also reminiscent is the rhythmic "thump-thump-thump" sound as your tires cross each pavement joint. Even at low speeds, you can appreciate how spine tingling driving must have been in the past, even without the distraction of traffic and poor weather conditions. One explanation given for using sloped curbs was that they would prevent vehicles from driving onto the shoulder by gradually moving the vehicle back onto the roadway. In actual practice, however, the supposed safety feature of concrete curbs was never proven. Some critics argued that sloped concrete curbing caused an additional hazard as compared to ordinary flat concrete slabs, citing the

tendency of the right tire to catch the outside of the curb and perhaps steer the vehicle into the ditch. Moreover, the curbing helped collect rainwater at the bottom of hills, forming miniature lakes that trapped unlucky motorists.

With funding for highway construction always in short supply, federal and state highway departments could not afford to waste precious funds on poorly-planned projects. Although highway construction was booming in the 1920s, improperly designed roads and bridges that needed repair or replacement soon after completion were hampering progress. Many early road failures were caused by weather-related factors or human design error. Hastily-built roads using insufficient subbases washed away after heavy rains or became potholed after temperatures fell below freezing. Concrete "blow-ups" were common, sometimes caused by extreme heat. The over-the-road trucking industry was growing rapidly during the 1920s, but it was soon learned that roads suffered premature damage due to the weight of many long-distance vehicles. A 1927 U.S. Supreme Court decision, *Morris v. Duby*, allowed the states to regulate interstate trucking. The case stemmed from an Oregon Highway Commission regulation lowering the maximum load from 22,000 to 16,500 pounds. The State of Oregon cited studies showing proving that heavy trucks cause far more road damage than autos.[128] It took years of trial and error on the part of highway engineers to find the optimum combination of roadway surfaces, thickness and subbases. However, after all of the experimenting and testing performed during the past 100 years, concrete roads still crack and continue to be require repair work, sometimes using asphalt patching.

New federal-aid highway projects in the 1920s encouraged a burst of bridge construction activity throughout the country, even into the Depression '30s. Some projects were funded under the National Industrial Recovery Act until the NIRA was declared unconstitutional by the U.S. Supreme Court; after 1937, such projects were taken over by the PWA, which used skilled labor. After World War I, many of the nation's great waterways, such as the Mississippi, the Ohio, and others, had few bridges, so ferry boats had to transport motor vehicles, a few at a time. As auto production in the 1920s increased, ferry landings became inundated with impatient travelers waiting for the trip across. In some areas, ferry service was interrupted for weeks at a time due to flooding. Ferries near the confluence of the Ohio and Mississippi Rivers were stopped nearly every spring because of seasonal high waters. When construction of federal-aid highways reached the banks of some great waterway, state highway planners went ahead and built

giant new steel bridges. To help repay highway construction bonds, tolls were usually collected. The Mississippi River Bridge, linking Cairo, Illinois, with Missouri (U.S. 60, 1929), the Mark Twain Bridge at Hannibal, Missouri (U.S. 36, 1935), and the Ohio River Bridge, linking Illinois with Kentucky (U.S. 60, 1938), and others were all built during this period. These are just a few many fine examples of 20th century American engineering, and most of these bridges are still in service today.

Bridge design and construction is an ancient art, practiced and refined by the Romans. Roman architects are usually given credit for the widespread use of the arch bridge design, but

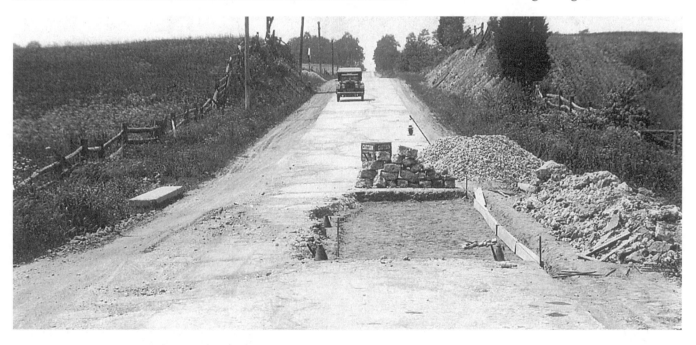

Top: Concrete pavement blowup. Road construction, like most sciences, requires a tedious trial-and-error approach to finding the optimum combination of subbase and pavement design and materials. Many early roads crumbled under the weight of vehicles or fell victim to weather. A frequent problem was cement failure caused by expansion and contraction of pavement during extreme temperature changes. This concrete "blowup" occurred just minutes before a party of BPR personnel, including Herbert S. Fairbanks and photographer J. K. Hillers, arrived. This scene was on Richmond-Fredericksburg Road, 13 miles north of Ashland, Virginia. The date of this photograph is May 26, 1933 (National Archives [33-487]).

Bottom: Concrete repair section on a Maryland road. A 1923 photo of a crumbled section of highway, probably due to a variety of factors such as improperly mixed pavement, unjointed pavement, or weather. Despite years of setbacks, highway engineers gradually learned from earlier mistakes to produce the outstanding highways enjoyed today. This repair project was between Westminster and Taneytown, Maryland (National Archives [27984]).

the arch actually was used centuries earlier in ancient Sumeria, Egypt, and Babylonia. Besides building outstanding bridges, the Romans used the arch design for its 11 aqueducts that brought an amazing 250,000 gallons of water per day to Rome. The arch design was simple yet strong, as both the weight of the bridge and the traffic above kept the stone blocks in place without mortar. After the fall of the Roman Empire, bridge construction stopped for over seven centuries. The Roman Catholic Church ordered construction of several arch bridges between A.D. 1178 and 1188 and the famous London Bridge was built from 1176 to 1209. The stone arch design found its way into the Middle East and China by the 13th century. Bridge building

Top: Patched rural road in Oklahoma. An unidentified highway in a rural area shows numerous asphalt repairs. Civil engineering has evolved from an art in centuries past into more of a science in the 20th century, as heavier use of modern vehicles creates make increasing demands on transportation infrastructure. Asphalt patching provides a temporary yet inexpensive solution to repair minor pavement cracks. Hastily-repaired roads such as this can still be found in most locales today (National Archives [51-939]).

Bottom: Widening of U. S. 1, 5 miles south of Elizabeth, New Jersey. This stretch of U. S. Route 1 bypasses the original route a few miles away due to traffic congestion from nearby cities of Rahway, New Brunswick, and Princeton. This new U. S. 1 was originally located in open country, but new businesses soon lined the highway, as shown above. Highway planners were often vexed by this phenomenon, as the new bypass needed to be bypassed. A third lane is being added to the shoulder area to handle the increase in traffic. Taken in July 1941 (National Archives [41-2403]).

took a much more scientific approach after founding of the world's first engineering school, Ecole des Ponts et Chausses in Paris in 1747, inspiring others in the application of mathematics and other disciplines.[129]

In America, bridges built between 1700 and 1800 were mainly made of wood, many of the covered variety, with a few stone arch bridges. During the 1800 to 1900 period, many of the larger stone arch bridges (often referred to as "viaducts") were built for the early railroads. Several suspension bridges appeared in the 1800s: in Uniontown, Pennsylvania (1801, 70 feet); the Fairmount Park Bridge in Schuylkill, Pennsylvania (1841, 375 feet); the Pittsburgh Aqueduct (1845, 1,134 feet); the Monongahela Bridge in Pittsburgh (1845, 1,504 feet); and the Wheeling Bridge in West Virginia (1849, 1,010 feet). However, the vast majority of the nation's rivers and streams still had to be forded by ferry boats.[130]

One drawback of stone bridges was that their excessive weight limited their size. Bridges using iron, built during the early 1800s, corroded quickly. A breakthrough occurred in 1855 when an Englishman named Henry Bessemer patented a way to mass produce steel, an iron-carbon alloy that resisted corrosion. Bessemer's process gave engineers more flexibility in bridge design, allowing larger bridges to carry heavier traffic. Following the Civil War, the nation still had no major bridge crossing the Mississippi River. St. Louis was the largest city on the mighty river, next to New Orleans, and the growing city needed a major bridge to span the unpredictable Mississippi. The city employed James Eads, a riverboat captain and owner of a profitable diving business that Eads had built up by salvaging sunken vessels on the river. Eads' bridge plans were unprecedented: a steel arch design with 500 feet between each of three stone piers and a total length of 1,524 feet. Eads used wooden falsework underneath the arches, which speeded construction and allowed the project to be completed

Sign with toll rates on bridge over Tennessee River. During the first half of the century, state and local governments had enormous difficulty raising revenue for road construction. Gasoline and other taxes were insufficient to finance a system of hard-surfaced, all-weather roads. Bridge construction was especially costly and many areas had to use ferries to transport cars and goods across waterways. Because of limited funds, many states entered into partnerships with private companies to construct and maintain major bridges. Private toll companies were allowed to charge tolls to help pay for operating and maintenance costs and to repay the bonds. This sign in Tennessee lists the toll charges at a toll bridge over the Tennessee River. Photo taken by J. K. Hillers, October, 1936 (National Archives [37-5176]).

in just six years without interrupting river traffic. When completed in 1874, the Eads Bridge was a monument in civil engineering. In New York City, the celebrated Brooklyn Bridge (also a suspension bridge design), although started in 1869, was not completed until 1884.[131]

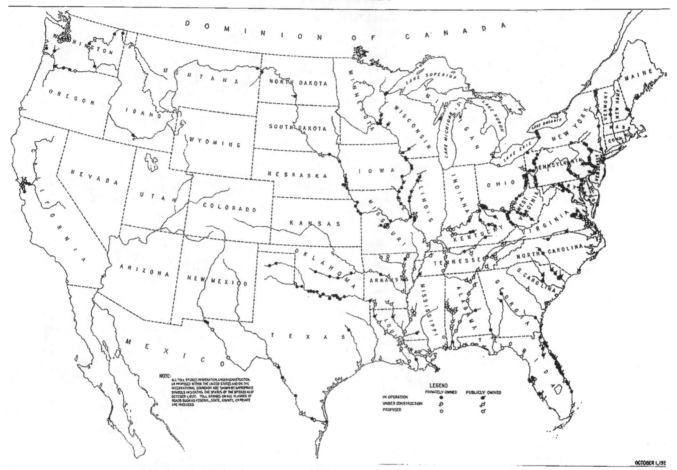

Toll bridges in the United States, 1927. This map shows locations of toll bridges in operation, under construction, or under consideration. Many states enacted special legislation to grant authority to private companies to charge tolls on bridges. Over the years, many states repealed these laws, and former toll bridges have reverted to state control. Toll bridges are becoming less common, with mostly newer and expensive large bridges still collecting tolls (National Archives [33347]).

After 1900, steel became the material of choice for bridge designers, and long span bridges of arch, suspension, and cantilever design were typically used. By World War I, New York City built four major bridges, all crossing the East Hudson River: Williamsburg Bridge, 1,600 feet, 1903; Queensboro Bridge, 2,166 feet, 1909; Manhattan Bridge, 1,470 feet, 1909; and Hell Gate Bridge, 1,632 feet, 1917. The 1920s and '30s saw a burst of bridge construction as the federal-aid highway system expanded. The cantilever design, which used hinged spans between piers to allow for flexing of its steel trusswork, became popular. The Carquinez Bridge, a 3,350-foot-long cantilever-suspension bridge combination, was finished in 1927 to make a shortcut across the south end of the San Francisco Bay. Suspension bridges such as the Bear Mountain Bridge across the Hudson River (1,632 feet, 1924), the Benjamin Franklin Bridge in Philadelphia (1,750 feet, 1926), Detroit's Ambassador Bridge into Ontario (1,850 feet, 1929), and New York City's George Washington Bridge (3,500 feet, 1931), gradually took over as the preferred design as bridge size kept increasing. As the height of skyscrapers seemed to leapfrog into the stratosphere, bridge architects were in a race for building the longest bridge.[132]

Earthquake-prone areas such as the San Fran-

Eads Bridge, St. Louis, 1867–74. Designed by riverboat captain James Buchanan Eads, the St. Louis Bridge (later renamed Eads Bridge) was the largest bridge built in the United States at the time and the first made of Bessemer steel, a relatively new process developed just prior to the Civil War. Eads' project departed from some of the conventional bridge-building techniques of the day, such as sinking piers into bedrock and using a cantilever method instead of scaffolding to construct bridge's arches. The 1,524-foot-long three-span design was the first major bridge to cross the Mississippi River in an area that was particularly hazardous for river traffic. When it officially opened on July 2, 1874, fourteen locomotives filled with passengers crossed the bridge to demonstrate the bridge's strength. The Eads Bridge was acclaimed as a technological wonder and sparked a new era of bridge construction in the United States (author's collection).

each level allowing travel in one direction. The total length of the bridge, including the tunnel, is approximately 43,500 feet, or 8.5 miles, and was opened in 1936. The other bridge left the city north into Marin County through the narrow strait to the Pacific known as the Golden Gate. The Golden Gate Bridge, probably the most photographed of the world's bridges, is a single, graceful suspension design, and was completed one year later. Both bridges withstood the October 17, 1989, Loma Prieta earthquake, with only the Bay Bridge suffering significant damage when a top section of one of the cantilever spans dropped to the roadway below, closing the bridge for only one month.[133]

The nation's economy started a gradual recovery by the late 1930s. As government

cisco area presented a special challenge to bridge designers. The Great Earthquake of 1906 discouraged the construction of tall buildings or bridges throughout the San Francisco Bay area. Being cut off from the mainland was hampering San Francisco's growth, so the city decided to build two great bridges in 1933 during the height of the Great Depression. One bridge would leave San Francisco's bay side of the city northeast to the city of Oakland to over Yerba Buena and Treasure Islands. Known as the San Francisco-Oakland Bay Bridge or simply the "Bay Bridge," the bridge is a combination of two suspension bridges, each measuring 2,310 feet each on the San Francisco side of the islands, a tunnel through Yerba Buena Island, and a 1,400 foot cantilever bridge, followed by five truss bridges. The Bay Bridge has two tiers, with

and industry created new employment, auto purchases began to make a comeback. The total number of vehicles on the road increased sharply from 26.5 million in 1935 to 31 million by the end of the decade, resulting in a corresponding jump in motor vehicle accidents. The 1930s was the most dangerous decade to be on America's highways, with an average death rate for the period of 26.9 per 100,000, compared to under 20 in the 1990s. In 1937 and 1941, the death rate climbed above 30 for the first time. More striking is the measure of total fatalities. In 1937, total deaths amounted to 39,643 with 30 million registered vehicles; in the 1990s, total deaths averaged 45,000 annually, but with over 200 million vehicles on the road. On the positive side, the mortality rate has been gradually dropping since Pearl Harbor, except for the late

Death Rate, Total Deaths, Number of Vehicles

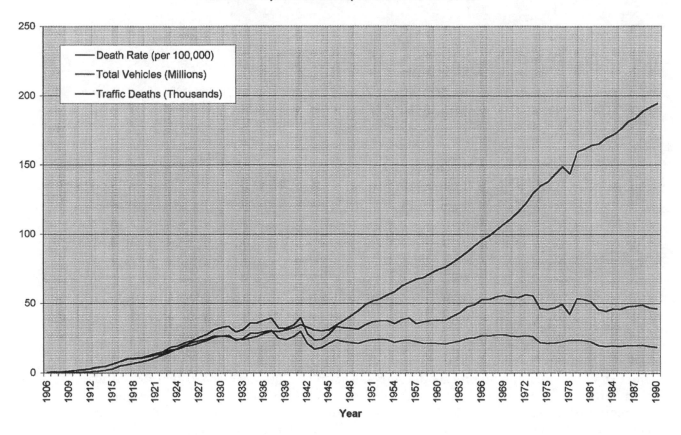

Top: Death Rate, Annual Deaths and Number of Vehicles (by Author Source: National Safety Council).

Bottom: "A traffic accident due to speeding. One man killed and one badly injured." The caption for this photo states the obvious; speeding costs lives. Traffic fatalities rose at an alarming rate in the 1920s and 1930s, caused by poor roads and unskilled drivers. This photo was taken in Harrison, Maryland, in 1920 (National Archives [19093]).

Safety posters, 1940s. The New Deal made widespread use of posters to educate the public on numerous issues and topics, from public safety to social diseases. The states instituted their own ad campaigns as well. These posters were put out by the director of traffic for the District of Columbia to promote a safety campaign in 1944 (National Archives [44-348]).

traffic signals and railroad grade crossing signals developed in the 1930s were a big improvement in controlling traffic and holding down the accident rate. Medians strips were used to reduce the risk of head-ons. More problematic was finding a highway design that would solve urban slowdowns caused by side traffic entering major thoroughfares. The "parkway" concept limited access from side streets abutting the main artery, efficiently moving a large traffic volume in urban areas. New York's Bronx River Parkway was the first to introduce medians as early as 1923. Even with a 35 mile per hour speed limit, the Bronx River Parkway design of limited access worked well in moving heavy urban traffic along its 15-mile route from the Connecticut border to The Bronx.

The early multi-lane designs are credited to Robert Moses, who was in charge of designing new roads in suburban New York in the 1920s and '30s. The Moses model was an urban expressway reserved mainly for passenger vehicles, built for restrained speed, and capable of moving large traffic volumes in cities where space for roads are at a premium. Moses' parkway designs incorporated parks, wetlands, and garden suburbs into the final plans. By 1939, Moses had built over 300 miles of parkways in the New York City area, such as the Henry Hudson Parkway, the West Side Expressway, the Belt Parkway (main feature: cloverleaf interchanges), and the Hutchinson River Parkway. Nearby states copied the parkway concept, such as New Jersey's Pompton Turnpike and Brunswick Turnpike, the Saugus-Newburyport Pike in Massachusetts, and Delaware's DuPont Highway. All across the country, even medium-size cities built short stretches of urban parkways in the years leading up to the second world war.[135]

1960s and the early '70s, when the death rate spiked up again.[134]

Public concern over mounting traffic fatalities began to be heard as the 1930s wound down. State highways departments conducted numerous studies on ways to reduce accidents through better highway design. Vehicles were counted on roads to assess the need for improvements. It was soon learned that most accidents occurred when vehicles either collided head-on, often while making left-hand turns, or due to vehicles entering thoroughfares from side streets. At first, stop-and-go traffic signals at intersections, some operated by hand by policemen, appeared in major cities. The introduction of the first electronic red-yellow-green

Birth of the Superhighway

The individual states and the Bureau of Public Roads' highway research in the 1930s revealed

Auto-train accident, Branchville, Maryland. To this day, most of the thousands of railroad grade crossings throughout the country lack electronic warning devices. It took decades for even the most heavily traveled railroad crossings to have devices installed and auto-train accidents were common. A photographer for the *Baltimore Sun* newspaper snapped a picture of this wreck, with curious onlookers trying to get in the picture. The passengers of the car were no doubt badly injured (courtesy, *Baltimore Sun*).

several feet to the left, often encroaching into the next lane. Another highway study focused on the locations where accidents most frequently occur, and found that many traffic mishaps result when vehicles enter and exit filling stations. "Safety islands" on congested city streets emerged as another attempt to reduce auto-pedestrian accidents.

The Bureau of Public Roads' highway studies were quite sophisticated given the limited technology available at the time. Highway lighting was studied in minute detail and considered all aspects of highway illumination, such as glare from street lights, oncoming cars, reflection from damp pavement and other sources. The consensus was that increasing properly-directed and located light sources was the most important factor for safety during night driving. Since street lighting wasn't practical for rural roads, reflective strips and "buttons" were used on road surfaces and warning signs. The State of Virginia tried precast concrete blocks to separate lanes. Some experiments used varying patterns of painted striping for pedestrian crosswalks. Another method was texturing the roadway or shoulder, or simply painting portions of the road to increase reflection of the driver's headlights. It was noted that concrete was more reflective than asphalt, and a combination of cement and asphalt as used for roadways and curbs to provide contrast. Although tests conducted by the BPR and the state highway departments didn't result in any major solutions to the problem of highway illumination, some aspects of the studies were eventually used and did improve traffic safety.[136]

Other design ideas were floated during the 1930s. Elevated highways were nothing new and had been used in a few locations, such as the Long

that highway officials had a lot to learn about highway design and reducing traffic fatalities. Some studies emphasized "driver psychology" and the effect that the road environment has on motorists. It was learned that objects located near the edge of the roadside caused drivers to subconsciously move

Top: Car accident, Washington, D. C. A bad accident in the District of Columbia, taken by a photographer for *The Washington Post* in 1937. Motor vehicles had few safety features until the 1960s, when the federal government began enacting safety regulations. This photo shows how motorists suffered serious injuries in accidents in older vehicles. *The Washington Post* (reprinted with permission).

Bottom: Automobile graveyard. Auto junkyards, or "graveyards" as they were formerly called, starting filling up with destroyed vehicles as quickly as highways could be built. By the 1960s, hundreds of such junkyards covering thousands of acres became an unpleasant sight to the driving public, until legislation in 1965 put controls on scrapyards. A vintage photo of an auto graveyard at an unknown location (National Archives).

Top: Safety island at Hartford and North Avenues, Baltimore. "Safety islands," some with electronic beacons, have been used as center dividers in urban areas since the 1930s. Medians and cement islands were introduced first in urban areas to prevent head-on collisions. This safety island was located in Baltimore, Maryland, in 1948. T. W. Kines (National Archives [48-421]).

Bottom: Left turn lane islands on California State Route 927 in the San Francisco Bay Area. A 1945 photo demonstrates the efficiency of left turn lane islands in regulating traffic on a crowded California highway. Highway planners in America's growing urban centers such as the San Francisco Bay Area had to stay one step ahead of constantly increasing traffic with new methods of traffic management (National Archives [45-1971]).

Top: Traffic control markings, District of Columbia, 1945. During the 1930s and 1940s, traffic control officials tried out a variety of pavement markings. The Bureau of Public Roads and the states all ran their own tests using different designs for center and barrier (the line on the right edge of the roadway) lines. The District of Columbia experimented with center lines and crosswalks using a broken-line pattern that would be easily visible for drivers. By the 1950s, most states and municipalities settled on universally-accepted standards for roadway markings. T.W. Kines (National Archives [45-2200]).

Bottom: Precast concrete centerline barriers, Alexandria, Virginia. The state of Virginia experimented with precast concrete units for marking center lines during prewar road tests. The photo shows a series of these markers on Quincy Street, looking southwest, in Alexandria, Virginia. Perhaps because of cost, the use of concrete markers was discontinued. C. H. Ritter, April 28, 1950 (National Archives [50-1691]).

Island Parkway (completed for the Vanderbilt Cup Races in 1908) and West Side Elevated Highway along the Hudson River in New York City. However, problems with elevated highways were cited, such as lowering real estate values of adjacent properties. Tire noise from the upper level could be distracting to motorists below. Elevated roads in urban areas also presented an engineering challenge to planners as the two levels of traffic "bottlenecked" as they converged at the terminus of the elevated roadway. Engineers and highway planners quickly learned that design improvements often caused new problems.

The average two-lane highway in America was in a sorry state after 20 years or so of use. The stinginess of the early builders and planners in committing sufficient material and design in construction of the nation's first hard-surface roads was becoming evident with age. Bridges and road width were kept to a minimum, usually barely wide enough to accommodate a vehicle, leaving little margin of error for the driver. Shoulders were practically nonexistent in most places. Hills were seldom leveled, so highways followed the landscape's contours. A chief complaint among drivers was numerous hills and steep grades. Motor vehicles were not as reliable then, and cars and trucks alike often overheated and encountered other mechanical difficulties. Long climbs were especially tough on trucks, busses, and other large vehicles, which slowed to a minimum speed in low gear. Caravans of frustrated drivers formed behind slow-moving vehicles creeping up seemingly endless hills.

An obvious solution to eliminate steep grades was to use heavy excavating equipment to cut through hills to reduce the angle or degree of the roadway. On rural highways,

Super-elevation at Mount Mitchell, North Carolina, 1938. The first generation of highways under the federal-aid system contained many defects, such as crowned or sharp curves, steep hills (causing vehicles to overheat in summer) or narrow lanes and bridges. One solution was to raise the roadbed using earth fill to make grades more gradual and curves safer. This photo shows an improved portion of the Blue Ridge Parkway using a super-elevated roadway. Engineers here made a cut into the hillside on the left side of the road and used the leftover earth and rock as fill for the new roadbed. Taken by G. B. Gordon for the North Carolina Division of Design (National Archives [38-4640]).

expanding urban development would eventually reach the bypass. As new businesses abut the roadway, the new highway would become as congested as the one it bypassed. A completely new innovation was needed to modernize the country's highway system.

Highway engineers and others from around the world took note of the new express roads built in Nazi Germany during the 1930s. American officials and visitors from around the world traveled to Berlin and checked in with the inspector of roads for a tour of Germany's new national highway system. The German "Reichs-autobahnen" (National Motor Road) used the concept of limited access to reduce entering traffic and separated grades by use of overpasses. Road signs were large with highly-visible lettering for easy reading at high speeds. In a country with a much higher population density than the United States, the overall design still moved traffic very efficiently.[137]

The Germans recognized that a large-scale highway program would not only improve transportation but would also boost the economy. Better roads would also stimulate auto industry, which is one of the most important sectors of the domestic economy. German studies found that the auto industry produces more value per person than any other industry, and increased automobile sales could pull the country out of the Depression. The German government managed to sell the public on the idea of the need for a system of superhighways as a necessity for a transportation standpoint, as well as providing instant employment. Government bonds were readily purchased by the public. There was no opposition to the high cost of the project, which cost approximately 500,000 marks per kilometer ($200,000 per mile).[138]

The German autobahn program was a transportation milestone in highway design and served as a model for others worldwide. The German system was completed in only a few years and ahead of schedule, due to innovations in road construction. The Germans employed new heavy machinery for excavation and earth moving. Industrial lo-

"super-elevations" constructed with earth fill were used in the 1930s in some badly-needed locations. One interesting design proposal was the use of "curve spirals" to move traffic to higher elevations. Also called "transitions," a handful of examples of curve spirals were constructed in several national parks and in the state of Oregon. It was thought that drivers would travel the spiral at a constant speed and would not encroach on the inside lanes. Studies noted that oil trails left by vehicles on existing highways show the tendency of drivers to drift into the next lane on curves. The Ford Motor Company's exhibit at the 1939–40 New York World's Fair demonstrated this concept using actual cars driven over an elevated roadway with curve spirals. However, the idea was never used for road construction and quietly faded.

After all of its research and studies, the Bureau of Public Roads and other transportation specialists finally concluded that a major overhaul of the nation's road system was necessary. Building new roads to bypass cities looked promising, but

Example of excellent sight distances on Texas highway. Sharp curves and hills were a common nuisance to drivers on the old highways. A high number of accidents on rural two-lanes were head-ons caused by drivers passing other cars where visibility was limited. Highway engineers sought to correct the shortcomings of the earlier roads by straightening curves and leveling hills. To improve distant vision, planners cleared the shoulder, or right-of-way, of vegetation and other obstructions. This photo shows good sight distances on a Texas highway (National Archives [44-1887]).

Curve Spirals at Ford Motor Exposition, New York City World's Fair. The Ford Motor Company's fair exhibit featured a giant building (in background) with autos driving on a futuristic roadway. The exhibit was a demonstration of the concept of "curve spirals" that some highway engineers touted as a safer alternative to using switchbacks to climb steep elevations. Fairgoers got to drive new Fords on a "Road of Tomorrow" made of an experimental composition of cork and rubber. The idea never made it into actual usage (from the collections of the Henry Ford Museum and Greenfield Village).

Top: Roadmaster's station, National Motor Road, 1937. While the BPR was working on plans for a system of transcontinental expressways, Germany already had a system of limited-access freeways in use. Like FDR, Hitler also used public works projects to reduce unemployment, so he ordered the construction of the National Motor Road. As in the case of road projects of the past, the chief reason for building the "reichsautobahnen" was military rather than civilian. A roadmaster's station on the National Road in 1937 (National Archives [37-2450]).

Bottom: National Motor Road between Hamburg and Lubeck, Germany. A vehicle traveling on a new section of the "autobahn" in Germany's northern lowlands. Highway experts and planners from around the world visited Germany's autobahns to gain insight on modern road building techniques. This series of photos was taken by BRP personnel during a visit to the Third Reich in 1937 (National Archives [37-2430]).

Top: Brick section of National Motor Road with overpasses. A brick section of the autobahn passes under a series of overpasses in the Ruhr district. This photograph reveals that not all of Germany's freeways were concrete paving. The bridges are of well-constructed stonework with single-span I-beams. To build the autobahns, German builders designed and used a variety of new construction machinery and methods to speed highway construction (National Archives [37-2462]).

Bottom: Ausfahrt on Reichsautobahnen, 1937. For convenience, the autobahns positioned gasoline stations at regular intervals for travelers. The station design was of standardized architecture, with no repair facilities. They were government operated, not private. The design with overhanging canopy roof is similar to today's self-service gas stations. Located near Magdeburg, Germany (National Archives [37-2439]).

moved excess earth. The government proudly showed off its new equipment at a fair in Leipzig in the spring of 1937. Large diesel engines of many varieties speeded construction of the project. Many of the vehicles used metal tractor tread or pneumatic tires, with tire tread made of synthetic rubber. While synthetic rubber was more costly, it had longer tread life and stood up well to heavy use. The Germans used antifriction bearings and enclosed gears to minimize oiling, portable crushing and screening plants, and rock drill and pavement breakers, the latter eliminating the need for blasting. A new type of cement was discovered that could harden under water, which greatly accelerated bridge construction. The German "National Motor Road" was acclaimed as the answer for a growing transportation problem projected for the 1940s and beyond.[139]

Bureau of Public Roads officials, including Thomas H. MacDonald, praised the German superhighways as "wonderful examples of the best modern road building." [140] However, MacDonald had some reservations in applying the German model to the United States. MacDonald believed that two-lane highways were sufficient to carry cross-country traffic and that freeways were necessary only in urban areas. Further, MacDonald noted that the autobahns bypassed German cities, and he dismissed the notion that building expensive interstate freeways would be justified from a cost standpoint. However, MacDonald's analysis proved to be incorrect. Germany's superhighways resulted in doubling the output of its auto industry in less than two years, with 945,000 vehicles registered by 1936, exceeding earlier estimates.[141]

comotives pulling dump cars on narrow-gauge track running parallel to the construction site re-

As the federal aid system neared completion

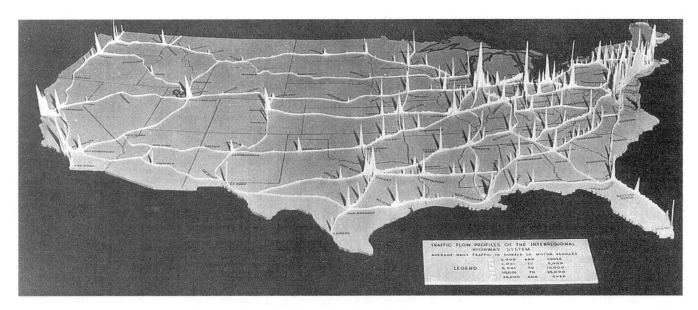

"Traffic flow profile of the Tentative Interregional Highway System, 1937." As the federal-aid system was nearing completion in the 1930s, President Roosevelt believed that the country needed a modern, coast-to coast highway system to meet the nation's growing transportation needs. FDR himself proposed three east-west and three north-south transcontinental expressways and ordered the Bureau of Public Roads to study the feasibility of building such a system. The BPR surveyed traffic volumes nationwide to assess where future routes might be needed. This map is a visual representation of the results of BPR's studies, showing high-volume highway usage in major metropolitan centers and heavily traveled corridors between urban areas. These findings were incorporated into BPR's final report, entitled "Toll Roads and Free Roads," which BPR presented to Congress on April 27, 1939 (National Archives [40-2606-B]).

in the late 1930s, MacDonald and others foresaw the necessity for a new generation of highways. Urban congestion, especially in the larger metropolitan areas, was constantly increasing, as were traffic accidents. During the late '30s, the BPR conducted studies on traffic patterns nationwide. In 1937, Herbert S. Fairbanks, head of BPR's Division of Information, did one survey to calculate traffic flow nationwide to determine the routes for a future cross-country highway system. Based on its estimates, the BPR proposed interstate routes linking major U.S. cities. Highway design plans were a composite of the autobahn and domestic projects already in use. For terminal highways in urban areas, elevated and depressed roadways were proposed to take traffic to the edges of congested areas. Transcontinental routes would link major urban areas and be high-speed, limited-access expressways. Traffic lanes at least 12 feet in width were seen as necessary for safety, as well as banning pedestrians and horse-drawn vehicles from the roadway. Opposing lanes separated by medians and improved sight distances for top speeds of up to 100 miles per hour were proposed. In 1937, Frank

T. Sheets, a former chief highway engineer from Illinois, proposed a "master plan" costing $57 billion. Sheets' plan incorporated some of the above ideas, but suggested that vehicle speed be unrestricted and policing be employed for safety reasons rather than slowing traffic and ticketing motorists. The Sheets plan called for upgrading of main trunk highways (primary and secondary roads), and Sheets estimated that savings in fuel and time would make the project cost-effective. Since the government was already collecting approximately $1 billion in gas taxes, license and other fees, Sheets estimated that his entire plan would take 26 years to complete and would benefit the military and the postal service, as well as the private sector.[142]

President Franklin D. Roosevelt advocated modern interstate highways to create employment during the Depression and for national defense. In the mid–1930s, FDR asked experts to study the possibility of a system of transcontinental highways. Roosevelt himself proposed three east-west and three north-south interstate routes, and FDR convinced Congress to enact the Federal-Aid

Highway Act of 1938. The 1938 Act directed the Bureau of Public Roads to look into Roosevelt's proposed toll highway system. After extensive study and research, the BPR issued its report to President Roosevelt, entitled "Toll Roads and Free Roads." During its study, the BPR noted that state highway surveys revealed that toll charges alone could not cover the construction costs of a project of such scale. Of the six transcontinental routes chosen by FDR, all would operate in the red, except for a 172-mile portion from New Haven to Philadelphia which would just break even. However, the second part of BPR's report to Congress recommended a "Master Plan for Free Highway Development," which proposed a 28,000-mile toll-free interstate highway system that would bypass many federal-aid U.S. highways and attempt to save mileage by straightening routes between cities. Major urban areas would be surrounded by a circular freeway or "beltway" which would carry traffic locally and also divert through traffic around cities. The new expressways would be a minimum of four lanes, divided, and with limited access. The freeway designs in cities specified depressed or elevated roadways proposed in earlier studies and already in existence in most urbanized areas of the late 1930s.[143]

President Roosevelt turned over the findings of the Bureau of Public Roads to Congress on April 27, 1939, and urged swift action, citing the benefits for improved domestic travel as well and for national defense. On July 1, 1939, in a reorganization move, the BPR was renamed the Public Roads Administration (PRA) and the agency was shifted from the Department of Agriculture to the Federal Works Agency. After war erupted in Europe later that year, the U.S. military accelerated wartime planning, charting key transcontinental routes for military usage. On April 14, 1941, two years after submitting "Toll Roads and Free Roads" to Congress, President Roosevelt appointed the National Interregional Highway Committee to take another look at the feasibility of an interstate highway network. The committee was headed by Thomas H. MacDonald, still chief at BPR, Herbert S. Fairbank, and other highway planners. The committee's report, "Interregional Highways," released on January 14, 1943, and written by Fairbanks, was a slight revision of BPR's recommendations in "Toll Roads and Free Roads." The new report called for an expanded network consisting of 40,000 miles of freeways that could handle pro-

jected traffic levels 20 years after the date of completion.[144]

As government-funded road construction failed to keep up with increasing demand in the 1930s, several new projects proceeded simultaneously, one in California and two on the East Coast. The State of Connecticut needed a replacement for the old Boston Post Road (U.S. Route 1), a highly-congested thoroughfare between Boston and New York City that saw an explosive increase in traffic following the First World War. As early as 1923, the Connecticut State Highway Department and several planning associations began studying an alternate route, and by 1925 had enlisted the support of state legislators and Governor John Trumbull for the "Parallel Post Road." [145] In 1931, the state legislature approved funds for a parkway through rural southwestern Connecticut. Plans called for a 37-mile limited-access highway that would move heavy traffic efficiently, yet have a park-like quality. During the planning phase of the project, plans were expanded to include landscaping in areas adjacent to the highway and scenic visas. The roadway was designed for a four-lane divided highway separated by a 21-foot grassy median on a 300-foot right-of-way. Each lane was 13 feet wide, with a sloped curbing that was added after the cement slab was finished. Planners decided to construct a 4- to 5-foot grass shoulder on the right for added "peace of mind" for the driver. For better night vision, a notch in the curbing with "reflector buttons" was added. The road was crowned at the center to divert runoff to the sides of the roadway, where catch basins covered by metal grating safely drained rainwater. The parkway's 72 bridges were styled in the contemporary art moderne or "art deco" design, with each bridge's design being unique. Precast cement ornaments were added for detail, some featuring two-color "sgraffitto" work depicting the state seal, sun-burst medallions, and figures of Indians and colonial settlers. Connecticut Governor Wilbur Cross was not exaggerating when he boasted in 1938 that "There is no more beautiful or more scenic parkway in America." [146]

The original plans for the Merritt Parkway in the 1920s proposed an automobile-only free road, but as the project evolved over the next decade or so, a high-speed expressway emerged. The parkway was named in honor of Schuyler Merritt, a nine-term congressman and Stanford, Connecticut, resident who initiated the effort to build a bypass to

Top: Clearing right-of-way for Merritt Parkway, 1937. A highway crew removes trees and other debris for the last section of Merritt Parkway. Planners routed the new toll-way through Connecticut farmland and woodland, as shown here. A power shovel and three dump trucks comprise a small crew carving a path through a dense forest area. The parkway did not open until 1940, three years after this photo was taken by G. B. Gordon in July 1937 (National Archives [40-147]).

Bottom: Bridge over Merritt Parkway at Greenwich, Connecticut. The state of Connecticut pulled out all the stops when its transportation officials designed the Merritt Parkway in the 1930s. In addition to being a first-class limited-access toll-way, planners envisioned a highway that would be both efficient and aesthetically pleasing, so careful attention was paid to landscaping. Each of the parkway's 72 bridge overpasses has a unique design. After the parkway celebrated its 50th anniversary in 1990, the Connecticut DOT refurbished the roadway and restored the bridges, with their ornamentation, to original condition (photo by author).

the Boston Post Road. The Merritt Parkway made its debut to an enthusiastic motoring public in 1940. During its first year of operation, approximately 15,000 vehicles per day used the Merritt Parkway (compared to 60,000 per day in the 1990s). However, the idea of a free road was dropped and cars were charged a ten-cent toll. Although the concept of the general–service road of early 1930s planners was scrapped, the Merritt was an important first step toward a modern freeway system.[147]

While progress proceeded slowly on the Merritt Parkway, the dream of a modern east-west freeway crossing Pennsylvania was being resurrected. A considerable amount of traffic traversed Pennsylvania from New York City to points west, with the two main routes being the Lincoln Highway (U.S. 30) and the William Penn Highway (U.S. 22). Travel on both highways through rugged, mountainous terrain was hazardous for drivers, often hampered by fog and icy conditions during much of the year. On January 27, 1936, with the help of a grant from the Works Progress Administration, 70 WPA workers surveyed a route crossing the Appalachian Mountains, using teams of five to seven men working in 10-mile sections in all kinds of inclement weather. The survey used Vanderbilt's old roadbed, then explored alternative routes.[148]

On May 21, 1937, Governor Earle signed an act creating a turnpike commission to raise the $60 to $70 million estimated to complete the project. The Pennsylvania Turnpike Commission started the planning phase of the project and decided on a toll road to pay for maintenance and future improvements. Bonds were to be sold to the public, but the Pennsylvania constitution prevented the state from borrowing over $1 million in bonds without voter approval, so other revenue sources were needed. After the state offered some support services to jump-start the project, state WPA director Walter A. Jones suggested using WPA labor. However, it was decided that unskilled WPA workers should not be used on a project of this magnitude. Private financial sources were reluctant to sell turnpike bonds based on the risk without being backed by the state. Global events convinced President Roosevelt that the turnpike was a necessity, and FDR directed the RFC to purchase $35 million in turnpike bonds in October 1938, which also allowed approval of a $29 million grant from the Public Works Administration to help

fund the project. Four days later, the first construction contract was advertised for a ten-mile section in Cumberland County near Shippensburg.[149]

Some of the turnpike's design concepts were borrowed from earlier American efforts and Germany's autobahns. The new turnpike covered a distance of 160 miles from Carlisle (west of Harrisburg) to Irwin, 10 miles east of Pittsburgh. Some of the project's seven tunnels used tunnels abandoned by Cornelius Vanderbilt for his South Penn Rail Road during the 1800s. Vanderbilt's project was started in the 1840s, but was delayed for several decades and interrupted by the Civil War. Major work on the project did not get underway until 1881, when 300 men began surveying the 5,000 miles of location lines for the 208-line route. Thousands of laborers were hired to fill ravines and build tunnels and stone piers for bridges. Vanderbilt's crew used a crude version of the power shovel to move over 5 million cubic yards of grading, and by 1885, 41 miles of tunnels had been excavated. After making a deal with rival Pennsylvania Rail Road, Vanderbilt suddenly abandoned the project, after considerable cost and the loss of 27 workers killed during its construction.[150]

However, Vanderbilt's effort was not completely in vain, as his ill-fated South Pennsylvania project saved considerable work for the new turnpike. Design innovations such as special tunnel lighting designed to ease the transition for drivers from artificial to outdoor light was a unique feature for 1940. Plans called for a four-lane divided freeway with limited access at interchanges placed in key areas, with 1,200 foot-long entrance and exit ramps and a 200-foot right-of-way. Other safety features included limiting grades to just 3 percent (compared to 9-12 percent on the Lincoln and William Penn highways), maximum curves of six degrees, and a minimum 600-foot sight distance for the driver. While the Lincoln Highway has a cumulative total of 13,880 feet of grades, the turnpike's plans reduced the total climb to 3,940 feet. Planners projected that the reduction in grades on the new expressway would bring significant fuel savings and save other vehicle costs to motorists. Highway studies estimated that a truck's operating costs roughly doubled from a 3 percent to a 9 percent grade. The trip from Philadelphia to Pittsburgh on the new highway would save trucks five to six hours, well worth the modest toll of six cents per mile (toll for cars was one cent per mile).

Top: Construction of tunnel on Pennsylvania Turnpike. Heavy-duty dump trucks haul away large rocks at a construction site on one of the Pennsylvania's seven tunnels. The Pennsylvania Alleghenys were a formidable barrier to generations of travelers crossing their rugged terrain. In the 1840s, railroad tycoon Cornelius Vanderbilt sent a large work crew to survey right-of-way and dig several tunnels for his South Penn Railroad. After several decades of work, Vanderbilt ultimately abandoned the project. However, much of the ill-fated railroad's right-of-way and old tunnels were used for the Pennsylvania Turnpike. The photo here is of a new tunnel under construction (courtesy, Pennsylvania Turnpike Commission).

Bottom: Continuous concrete pour on stretch of Pennsylvania Turnpike. Engineers and planners of the Pennsylvania Turnpike employed new cost-saving methods. A continuously-moving cement paving machine speeded the project to completion in just three years. This photo is of a continuous cement pour operation on the turnpike (courtesy, Pennsylvania Turnpike Commission).

Top: Military convoy on completed section of turnpike near Bedford, Pennsylvania. As events in Europe and Asia increased American fears of an impending war, Roosevelt convinced Congress to beef up the armed forces and aid allies such as Great Britain. State national guards also were put on alert status. On August 6, 1940, the Pennsylvania National Guard staged a practice drill, with units using a finished portion of the turnpike to "free" the city of Bedford from a foreign invader (courtesy, Pennsylvania Turnpike Commission).

Bottom: Opening day at Irwin toll gate, October 1, 1940. Eager motorists line up for the grand opening of the turnpike at 12:01 A.M. A similar scene was played out at the other end of the 160-mile long toll road at Carlisle, just a dozen miles west of the state capitol at Harrisburg. Motorists could enjoy the scenic Pennsylvania Appalachians at speeds of over 60 miles per hour without stopping, just in time for the final weeks of the 1939–40 New York World's Fair (courtesy, Pennsylvania Turnpike Commission).

Vanderbilt's engineers wisely used south and west slopes for maximum sun exposure during the winter months to help melt snow and ice.[151]

After two years of planning and ground preparation, the first concrete paving began on August 31, 1939. Cement was mixed on-site, and the final phase of the project took approximately one year. In 1940, with war raging in the Atlantic and Pacific, the Pennsylvania National Guard used a portion of the nearly-completed turnpike near Bedford for military maneuvers. When the turnpike finally opened on October 1, 1940, eager motorists lined up at the Carlisle entrance at midnight for the grand opening. The Pennsylvania Turnpike started a new chapter in automotive history. Travelers could now ride nonstop (except at toll booths) and dine or relax at convenient "service plazas" with a gasoline station and restaurant (Howard Johnson had the exclusive franchise rights to the restaurants). The Turnpike had no speed limits when it first opened, but on April 15, 1941, Governor James signed legislation limiting speeds for passenger cars to 70 miles per hour (truck speeds varied from 50 to 65 mph, depending on weight). When the United States officially entered World War II in December 1941, all civilian traffic was limited to 35 miles per hour to save fuel for the war. However, most cars of the day could barely go 60 mph, let alone 80, and tires and cooling systems could not handle sustained high-speed driving. The Turnpike truly earned its title, "superhighway."[152]

By the end of 1940, after only being open for three months, over 500,000 cars and 48,000 trucks used the Pennsylvania Turnpike. In subsequent years, revenue exceeded projections and turnpike bonds were repaid ahead of schedule. Before the Turnpike's completion, Commission Chairman Walter Jones unveiled his own proposal for an 1,800-mile extension of the Turnpike, with routes running from Philadelphia to St. Louis, Pittsburgh to Chicago, Indianapolis to Chicago, and Richmond to Boston. The financial suc-

Top: Cars passing through toll gate. The toll booths for the turnpike were a distinctive hexagon style, as shown in this photo taken shortly after the turnpike's opening. The toll booths were remodeled several decades later (courtesy, Pennsylvania Turnpike Commission).

Bottom: Interior of Howard Johnson restaurant. Howard Johnson used a tasteful colonial design for its turnpike restaurants, with a grey stone exterior. In later years, Howard Johnson lost its exclusive rights to turnpike locations, and currently, several "fast food" chains use the original buildings. At the Bedford service area, historic plaques commemorate the original Howard Johnsons and the role they played in America's first super-highway (courtesy, Pennsylvania Turnpike Commission).

cess of the Turnpike stood in stark contrast to Bureau of Public Roads' studies which claimed that toll superhighways were not feasible. When asked by President Roosevelt to look into the possibility of a system of national toll roads, BPR director MacDonald dismissed the idea, pointing out that BPR's own studies found that tolls would not cover construction costs and motorists would drive out of their way to avoid paying tolls. BPR's "Toll Roads and Free Roads" report estimated that the route following the Pennsylvania Turnpike would rank only 19th in traffic volume. In the end, the Turnpike had disproved the theories of MacDonald and BPR engineers.[153]

On the West Coast, thousands of Americans funneled into California during the Depression to escape the Dust Bowl, or find fame and fortune in the land of Tinsel Town. The state added 1,230,000 new residents during the 1930s, a 21 percent increase.[154] Closed factories, and dreary, aging eastern cities with breadlines stood in sharp contrast to the opportunities that awaited those willing to pull up stakes and move west. The allure of the sun-drenched Golden State beckoned with a siren song almost too irresistible for many desperate Americans down on their luck, or on their last dime. In the years between the two world wars, the film industry provided fantasy lands of escape for Americans, and Hollywood had considerable influence over popular culture. The West Coast was starting to compete with the Eastern Seaboard as the birthplace of national economic and social trends. With a year-round climate, Californians have more time to enjoy their cars. The state was an early pioneer in establishing national trail routes, and some of the nation's earliest auto clubs (such as the Automobile Club of Southern California, established in 1903) originated in California. The American Car Cul-

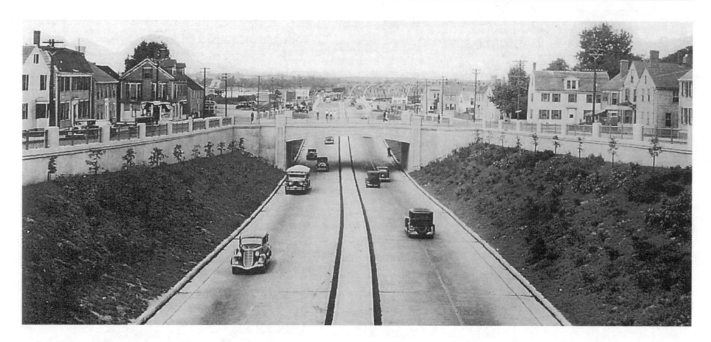

Early divided highway, Newton, Massachusetts, 1935. Cities across the country built short stretches of divided urban parkways in the middle to late 1930s, as auto sales gradually returned to pre–Crash levels. Even smaller cities managed to fund early freeway projects such as this one with a depressed roadway, in Newton, Massachusetts (courtesy, US DOT/FHWA).

ture got its start in Southern California during the late 1930s while the rest of the country was preoccupied with the economy and international politics. The drive-up restaurant, drive-in movie theatre and other car-related cultural novelties made their first appearance on the West Coast.

The great influx of migration into the state in the 1930s resulted in a population boom in California, particularly in the Los Angeles area. The Los Angeles metropolitan area experienced spectacular growth during the period, and the city had outgrown its highway infrastructure. As the Pennsylvania Turnpike, Merritt Parkway, and other smaller projects were under way during the late '30s, it was now California's turn. The route between the business districts of the city of Pasadena and downtown Los Angeles was one area that needed a new expressway, particularly during major events such as the Pasadena New Years Festival and the Rose Bowl parade. In 1937, planning for a modern parkway linking the two cities was started as a joint enterprise of the California Highway Department, the U.S. Bureau of Public Roads, and the cities of Los Angeles, Pasadena and South Pasadena. The state highway department took over the most of the design and all of the construction of the project at an estimated cost for the six-mile

freeway of $3.5 million. The WPA and PWA were also involved, and $500,000 from the Public Roads Administration helped fund the project. The parkway route skirted Arroyo Seco Park between Los Angeles and Pasadena, so the new highway was named the Arroyo Seco Parkway.[155]

In 1930, before the Arroyo Seco project got started, the city of Los Angeles excavated tunnels through the Elysian Park hills at the southern end of the route near downtown Los Angeles, then built the Figueroa Street viaduct in 1936. The parkway's design plans included a six-lane expressway with two 35-foot roadways divided by six-foot medians. The median strips were lined with six-inch sloped curbs, while 12-inch gutters on the shoulder diverted runoff. One special feature was that the lane nearest to the median was constructed of asphaltic concrete, while the remaining two lanes were made of portland cement. Traffic lanes were 11 feet in width, wider than most highways at the time. Pedestrians were banned from the parkway and stopping was prohibited. The route along the Arroyo Seco and Elysian Parks was lined with a chain-link fence (hidden by shrubs for esthetics) to keep children and others from entering the highway. A total of 24 overpasses kept traffic away from the parkway, which had no entrance or exit ramps. The

General Motors' "Futurama" exhibit, New York City World's Fair, 1939–40. The New York World's Fair showcased the latest technological wonders, from television to microwave cooking. In keeping with the fair's theme, General Motors lead the way with its "Futurama" exhibit using ideas from designer Norman Bel Geddes. A scale model of a City of 1960 with vehicles traveling on multi-lane freeways portrayed the future as an orderly, efficient world. This philosophy led to "slum clearance" and "urban renewal" efforts of the 1940s through the 1960s (copyright, General Motors Corporation. Used by permission).

way was dedicated on December 30, 1940, just in time for Pasadena's Tournament of Roses festivities with a lavish ceremony including Governor Culbert Olson and the Queen of the 1941 Tournament of Roses, and others. Governor Olson proclaimed that "This, fellow citizens, is the first freeway in the west. It is only the first. And that is the great promise of the future of many more freeways to come." However, further freeway building was abruptly halted with the outbreak of World War II.[156]

With highway congestion in urban areas and major highways of the U.S. system on the rise, the more populous states built short segments of multilane urban expressways. At the same time, the Bureau of Public Roads made a policy shift during the Depression, focusing on urban traffic concerns instead of rural highways. The BPR studied new ways to alter traditional perpendicular traffic patterns to ease urban congestion. Some of its designs proposed a depressed, multilane divided highway with cross streets on bridges. This concept was demonstrated at the 1933 Century of Progress Exposition in Chicago, which included a dramatic display of the history of road development from 1792 to the present. Exhibits featured changing maps and dioramas beginning with the Lancaster Turnpike to a modern four-lane freeway of 1933, with bus stations at grade-separated intersections and bordering sidewalks for pedestrians. Later in the decade, General Motors' "Futurama" exhibit at the 1939 New York World's Fair, inspired by designer Norman Bel Geddes, depicted a moving scale model of a futuristic city of 1960, complete with multi-lane freeways and "cloverleaf" entrance and exit ramps, much like today's interstate highways. Speeds on the open highway would be approximately 100 mph and 50 mph in urban areas. In cities, traffic accidents would be reduced by separating local and high speed traffic on multilevel roadways, and distance between vehicles would be regulated by radio signals from a central control. The GM exhibit included scale models of some sample freeways to

planners extended the parkway further into downtown Los Angeles, and the final distance measured a total of nine miles. When the Arroyo Seco Parkway (renamed the Pasadena Freeway in 1954) was opened on December 1, 1940, excited southern Californians got a glimpse of things to come. The park-

Cloverleaf design for future freeways, "Futurama" exhibit, New York City World's Fair. The GM fair exhibit gave visitors a range of design concepts for the highways of the future. This view shows inner lanes exiting the freeway in a rather complicated pattern. Such imaginative ideas were put on hold with the outbreak of World War II (copyright, General Motors Corporation. Used by permission).

show what future highways might look like. To the millions of fairgoers who saw the exhibit in 1939 and the following year, the future of American motoring looked bright. However, Futurama was way ahead of its time, and dreams of glamorous future-cities and superhighways would have to wait until the war's end.

The BPR continued its research, calculating the cost of delays under the current, inefficient system versus the price tag for a replacement of the old federal-aid system. As events in Europe and Asia continued to worsen, President Roosevelt began to prepare the public for the possibility of war. After the outbreak of war in Europe in September 1939, the U.S. government started Lend Lease and other programs to aid Britain, the Soviet Union, and other allies. In 1940, the military mapped out strategic military routes across the country in case of war. However, these were mainly existing two-lane U.S. highways. Neither the highway infrastructure nor the military were ready for a major war.

On February 1, 1941, the Public Road Administration issued its "Highways of National Defense" report, urging rapid improvement of the 1,500 miles of roads on military reservations and 2,830 miles of access roads for strategic purposes. Two months later, FDR appointed a National Interregional Highway Committee headed by Thomas MacDonald to refine BPR's 1939 "Interregional Highways" and "Tolls Roads and Free Roads" reports.[157] An early defense project was the war department's approval of a $35

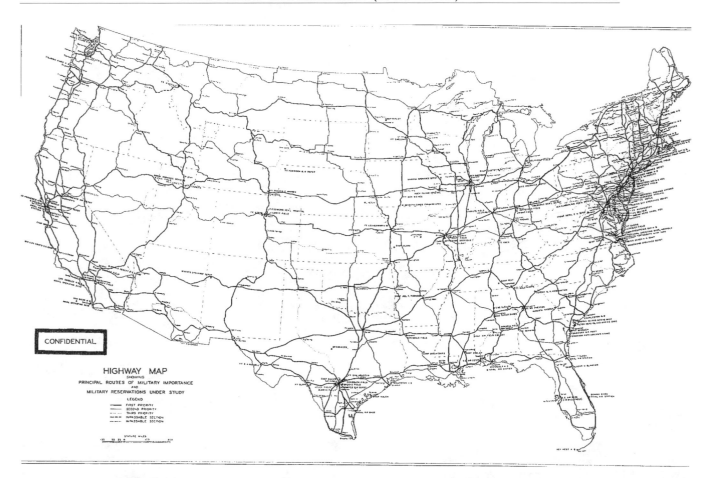

Principal routes of military importance. With war moving ever closer to American shores, President Roosevelt, with heads of the armed forces, developed a classified plan for routing troops and supplies across the continental United States in the event of war. National defense was a major impetus for building the interstate highway system after World War II. This official map is marked "Confidential" and states in small print in the right corner "Revised to October 23, 1940" (National Archives [40-2854]).

million parkway system servicing the new war department building being built by the Federal Works Agency. The highways for the future Pentagon building were to be divided highways with cloverleaf interchanges as proposed by General Motors' Futurama and other earlier designs. On November 19, 1941, just weeks before Pearl Harbor, FDR signed the Defense Highway Act, authorizing $150 million to build roads certified as important to the nation's defense by the secretary of war, and $50 million to upgrade deficient roads.[158]

The travel industry became dormant from 1942 to 1945 as the public sector of the economy took a back seat to the war effort. Most traffic on the nation's highways consisted of military convoys or other vehicles with war related purposes. The auto industry stopped producing cars after December 1941, with the 1942 models interrupted

in midyear, and retooled for war production. The war caused shortages in everything from tires to silk stockings as materials were diverted for tires and parachutes. Gasoline rationing made pleasure travel a luxury. In early 1942, President Roosevelt urged state governors to enforce a 40 mile-per-hour speed limit to help the war effort based on PRA data claiming lower speeds save both fuel and tires. Although the U.S. highway system was finished just in time for the war, the military found it outmoded and travel slow. The first-generation national highway network was still a two-lane system with many of the same built-in hazards of the original roads designed 20 years earlier. Large military vehicles found cross-country travel difficult, with frequent stops for numerous towns, narrow roads and bridges, some only 18 feet wide, with steep hills and sharp curves. The PRA helped

Top: Sketch of urban expressway, *1944.* Taken from "Interregional Highways," this wartime drawing shows an elevated section of an urban freeway. Ideas such as this were later incorporated into interstate highway designs. The original caption read: "Show window at the elevated level dressed appropriately with the kind of large display that would be needed for comprehension by express traffic" (courtesy, US DOT/FHWA).

Bottom: Artist's drawing of divided four-lane highway, *1945.* A drawing from the early 1940s showing exit ramps but cross-traffic entering the highway from local roads. Highway planners were in almost universal agreement that highways of the future would not be true "free ways" unless access from side roads was limited. The final design for the interstate highways corrected the problem of unlimited access that was a major flaw of the federal-aid system by limiting access to the main thoroughfare (courtesy, US DOT/FHWA).

Top: Cahuenga Pass Freeway, Los Angeles, 1944. The city of Los Angeles became a focal point for national defense during World War II because of its strategic location, naval and air bases, and war production factories. New highway construction across the country ended during the war, with materials and labor diverted for the war effort. Several new freeways were built in the L. A. area from 1941 to 1945 to accommodate military and related ground transport throughout the Los Angeles basin. The eight-lane Cahuenga Pass Freeway was completed during the war, crossing the Santa Monica Mountains to link Los Angeles with the San Fernando Valley. This shot looks south towards downtown Los Angeles (National Archives [44-1296]).

Bottom: Arroyo Seco Parkway looking north toward city of Pasadena. A 1945 photo showing the Arroyo Seco Parkway on its final approach to Pasadena. Although the parkway had been open for only five years, planners were dissatisfied with some aspects of its original design. The photograph's caption notes vegetation beginning to encroach on the roadway and the lack of space for disabled vehicles to park in case of emergency. Planners proposed building safety turnouts for emergency stops (National Archives [46-576]).

many military road projects during the war, including the Alaska Highway linking airfields in the United States and Canada. The Alaska Highway project alone used 14,000 civilian workers and 1,850 PRA employees, as well as the U.S. Army Corp Engineers and units of African-American soldiers during the peak of construction in 1943.[159]

As the nation was preparing for the invasion of France in 1944, General Dwight Eisenhower, as supreme commander of the allied forces in Europe, publicly expressed his frustrations over the delays in moving military transport across the country on existing roads. This prompted Congress to renew its debate over a new highway system to meet the nation's transportation needs after the war. That same year, the Bureau of Public Roads released its latest report, "Interregional Highways," which again proposed a "National System of Interstate Highways" to replace the U.S. federal-aid highways. As usual, urban and rural interests were at odds over the shape of the legislation, and many states preferred more control over future highways and less federal involvement. The result was the passage of the Federal-Aid Highway Act of 1944, which proposed a slightly larger system than BPR's highway routing plan. The 1944 act did not provide any details or funding for such a system, so actual construction for an interstate system would be postponed until after the war. However, with the end of the war imminent, the nation began to look ahead to peacetime and a resumption of highway improvements.

The Golden Age (1946–1969)

With the final wrap up of World War II, the nation was set for a speedy return to civilian life. The Roaring Twenties seemed like a distant memory after a decade and a half of Depression and war, and the country was eager to get back to work and resume normal family life. The United States was the only major allied nation to escape the war's devastation and emerge with its economy intact. The war weakened Great Britain, France, the Soviet Union, and other allies. Both Churchill and de Gaulle were voted out of office in 1946, and Stalin replaced the Axis Powers as the new threat to democracy. To fill the power vacuum in the West, the United States assumed a new role as the preeminent leader of the Free World. America now believed in its own invincibility, and a feeling of boundless optimism prevailed. Even the Korean conflict failed to dampen the national mood.

In the years just following the war, pent-up demand for durable goods far outstripped supply. Auto production was also slow to recover and did not reach prewar levels until 1950. The transition from military to civilian production and the cost of re-tooling for new models was a major undertaking for the automotive and other heavy industries. Detroit's 1946–48 model years were merely made-over 1942s with some cosmetic changes. There were also shortages of certain raw materials, and some models were delivered to car dealers minus bumpers and other nonessential parts. However, consumers just wanted something with four wheels that could be driven away, so appearances were a minor concern.

Road construction resumed, but government-funded roads could not keep up with the 18 million new cars on the road between 1945 and 1950. Total expenditures at all government levels nearly doubled, from $2.4 billion in 1939 and to $4.2 billion in 1949.[160] While the public eagerly pressed for the building of superhighways, the reality was that funds were badly needed to repair the existing roads, which were in a bad state of disrepair after four years of neglect. Bridges were weak and roads narrow. The size and speed of vehicles slowly started to increase, and it became clear that the country would have to make a greater commitment towards a nationwide road-building effort.

The Public Roads Administration didn't wait for the end of the war to start freeway planning. The PRA asked state and local officials for their recommendations for a future interstate network and worked with AASHO on design standards. The AASHO did not approve standardized designs for the entire system, opting for a more flexible approach based on topography, population, and expected traffic volume. For example, four-lane divided freeways would be the rule, but two-lane highways with some at-grade railroad and highways crossings would exist in low traffic areas. Access would still be limited and highways would be designed to handle traffic 20 years after completion, as proposed in BPR's Interregional Highways report. These standards were approved by the PRA

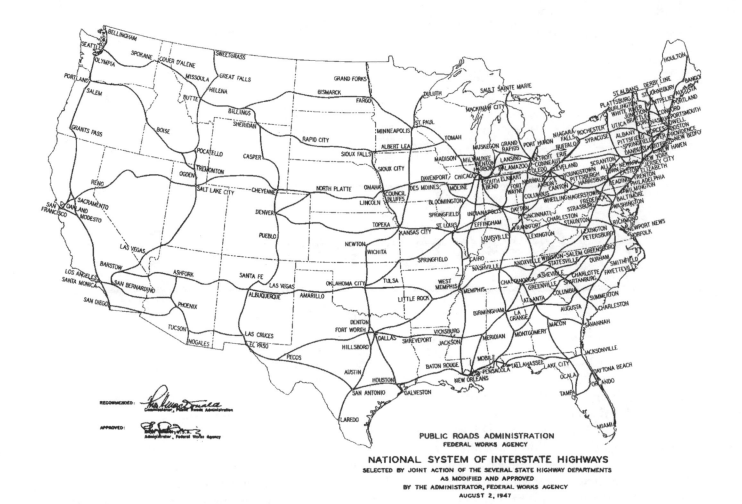

PUBLIC ROADS ADMINISTRATION
FEDERAL WORKS AGENCY

NATIONAL SYSTEM OF INTERSTATE HIGHWAYS

SELECTED BY JOINT ACTION OF THE SEVERAL STATE HIGHWAY DEPARTMENTS
AS MODIFIED AND APPROVED
BY THE ADMINISTRATOR, FEDERAL WORKS AGENCY
AUGUST 2, 1947

Top: Concrete paving in Arlington, Virginia. Road construction after the Second World War employed prewar methods. This photograph shows a paving crew finishing a portion of new concrete highway on Globe Road and Arlington Boulevard, in Arlington, Virginia. Photo by T. W. Kines for BPR, September 1953 (National Archives [53-2056]).

Bottom: Installing lastite expansion joint. Early roads did not allow for expansion and contraction due to temperature changes. Engineers learned that expansion joints between cement slabs helped prevent premature road damage. Highway workers in Kansas are placing a lastite expansion joint on a new concrete road in 1948 (National Archives [48-1320-A-D]).

Opposite Page Top: National System of Interstate Highways, Public Roads Administration, 1947. After World War II, the Public Roads Administration continued its efforts to implement an interstate highway system proposed by the Federal-Aid Highway Act of 1944. As a result of several years of input from state and local transportation officials, the PRA unveiled its final proposal for a 37,000-mile system. The map shows the routes planned by PRA, which were later used for the planning of today's interstate system (courtesy, U.S. DOT/FHMA).

Opposite Page Bottom: Chain reaction accident on Arroyo Seco Parkway, 1950. Traffic headaches came to southern California before most areas of the country in the postwar years. On the West Coast, road construction could not keep up with the influx of new residents that moved into the state. The state's population increased by 3,679,000 during the 1940s, up 53 percent. Modern freeways (and traffic jams) became a trademark of the Los Angeles area, with new highways constantly being planned or under construction. In 1954, the Arroyo Seco Parkway was renamed the Pasadena Freeway (National Archives).

Top: Construction of Memphis Highway Bridge over Mississippi River, October 1945. Looking west toward the state of Arkansas, this view shows a construction site building a new bridge over the Mississippi near Memphis, Tennessee. One crew is building the concrete footings on land, while another is ready to pour cement into a mold driven into the river bottom. A railroad bridge with telephone poles is at the right, while the old highway bridge is barely visible at the far right (National Archives [46-400]).

Bottom: Workers on I-beams on Memphis Highway Bridge. Road and bridge construction was hazardous work, with much labor still requiring skill and muscle. These highway construction workers are carefully positioning I-beams for riveting on the new Memphis Highway Bridge over the Mississippi (National Archives).

Top: Closeup of worker on Memphis Highway Bridge. A hard-hat inspects rivets on the Memphis Highway Bridge. The project, started in 1945, took over five years to complete, and replaced a narrow old bridge. C. H. Ritter photographed this construction worker in action in April 1949 (National Archives).

Bottom: Dedication ceremony of opening of bridge, District of Columbia. People were so enthusiastic about new highways that even a new highway bridge was cause for excitement. With the Jefferson Memorial serving as a nice visual backdrop, a podium is set up on a stage, with flags flying for the big celebration. Taken by C. H. Ritter, May 9, 1950 (National Archives [50-2039]).

on August 1, 1945, shortly before the end of the war in the Pacific. The PRA also decided on its chosen routes for a future interstate system and asked the states for suggestions. On March 28, 1946, Nebraska became the first state to accept PRA's map plan. On August 2, 1947, PRA unveiled its final

highway routes for the 37,000-mile interstate highway system. However, states were unwilling to use scarce federal-aid funds for interstate highways. Despite PRA's bold initiatives, a federally-backed interstate highway network was again sidetracked. By 1949, the Public Works Administration became the Bureau of Public Roads once again, placed under the General Services Administration for one month before being transferred to the Department of Commerce.[161]

Interest in privately-funded freeways resurfaced as Americans took to the road in increasing numbers. The State of New York started planning a statewide freeway system as early as 1942 when the state legislature passed a bill authorizing planning of a route spanning the state from New York City to Buffalo. For years, New York sorely needed a modern freeway system to link New York City with other areas of the state, such as the state capital at Albany and the cities of Rochester and Buffalo. Pennsylvania, Connecticut, and California already had their own toll roads, and the Empire State, being the nation's most populous and placed strategically in the nation's urban northeast, was a logical location for a new high-speed expressway. Due to the mountainous topography of the state's south-central region, the preferred route from New York City to Buffalo followed an L-shaped path through Albany. At the time, the over 600-mile journey traveled over twisting, curvy two-lane highways that followed the historic Hudson and Mohawk River Valleys, with the east-west section between Albany and Syracuse passing the Genesee Trail, dating to the 1790s, and the Erie Canal, completed in 1825.[162]

New York Governor Thomas E. Dewey was a staunch supporter of the plan for a new cross-state freeway. During his tenure during the 1940s and early '50s, Dewey was instrumental in getting a series of bills enacted by the state legislature to make the project a reality. A shorter, more direct route from New York City and Buffalo was considered, but construction costs to traverse the Catskill

Mountains and the hundreds of miles of rough terrain would have been prohibitive. In addition, many argued that the state capital should be included on the freeway route plans. The final route selected for the new expressway basically followed the same 600-mile path of the existing two-lane federal-aid highways.

In July 1946, Governor Dewey appeared at the ground-breaking for the first freeway construction of a four-mile segment between Canandaigua and Victor. However, work proceeded at a snail's pace, taking the state two years to complete this modest initiative. A second project, a 3.6-mile piece from Walden Avenue and Cleveland Drive in Buffalo, wasn't started until January 1949. After realizing that the state could not afford the high cost of highway construction, the legislature created the New York State Thruway Authority on March 21, 1950. As an independent legal entity, the Thruway Authority could finance the costs of construction and maintenance of the freeway through the sale of bonds underwritten by the state and by the collection of tolls by freeway users. The following year, the state legislature approved a measure amending the state constitution to allow the state to financially back the Thruway bonds, making them far less risky and more attractive to investors.[163]

After New York state voters approved the constitutional amendment granting the state authority to back Thruway bonds, some minor freeway work started in the fall of 1951, with the 3.6-mile section in Buffalo finally being completed in October. The year 1952 saw little change, with only 24 miles between Liverpool and Canastota opening in January. More financial maneuvering the following year yielded only a new 3.2 mile piece at the western end of the Thruway's Ontario section and a 9.4 mile section from Saugerties and Kingston. Up to this time, all completed portions of the Thruway were toll-free. In January 1954, Governor Dewey signed legislation allowing the Thruway Authority to issue bonds not backed by the state. The new strategy stimulated a sharp increase in the sale of Thruway bonds. The new revenues financed the completion of a 115-mile stretch from Rochester and Lowell (west of Utica) that was officially opened for traffic on June 24, 1954, after a dedication ceremony with Governor Dewey present. The Thruway charged its first tolls with the opening of this new section of the system. In August 1954, a 63-mile stretch from Rochester to

Buffalo was finished. The governor made another photo-op at the inaugural motorcade for the opening of a 118-mile section from Westmoreland to Newburgh on October 26. By the year's end, 381 miles of Thruway were completed. The final mileage for the main line of the Thruway from New York City to Buffalo now totaled 426 miles.[164]

More mileage was added to the Thruway system during the 1950s. The Thruway was connected to New Jersey's Garden State Parkway in October 1957, and an extension to the Massachusetts state line via State Route 9 was completed the following year. The Thruway's new safety improvements included a wide grass center median or "mall" averaging 1,025 feet in width, with 1,000-foot sight distances, and 1,200 foot acceleration and deceleration lanes. All highway and advertising signs had to be a minimum of 660 feet from the nearest edge of the right-of-way. By the end of the '50s, after the completion of the 6-mile Niagara section in Buffalo, the New York Thruway system reached a total of 553 miles.[165]

The Thruway used the travel-plaza concept similar to the Pennsylvania Turnpike to control the number of businesses on the system. The services were again limited to just two items: food and fuel. The downside of the federal-aid system was the unlimited number of businesses and side roads that could enter the highway at any point. The private toll roads sought to bring some reliability and order to the traveling experience. Also like its predecessor, the Thruway solicited bids for the exclusive rights for gas service stations and restaurants located at its 11 plazas. The first filling stations allowed to sell petroleum-related products on the Thruway were an obscure brand, "Calso." In 1959, American Oil and Mobil Oil companies landed contracts for the exclusive rights for filling station locations on the Thruway. They were joined by a succession of brands in later years, such as Arco, Chevron, Exxon, and Sunoco. Currently, 12 Mobil and 15 Sunoco outlets serve the Thruway.[166]

On September 1, 1964, the New York Legislature voted to name the New York Thruway "The Governor Thomas E. Dewey Thruway" in honor of the former governor's visionary support for the toll way. Over the years, the Thruway Authority acquired the Second South (and North) Grand Island bridges (1962, 1964, respectively), the Cross Westchester Expressway, and Interstate 84 (both in 1991). In addition, the Thruway Authority operates

Top: Clearing roadbed for New York Thruway near Syracuse. A photo of construction of the New York Thruway, authorized by an act of the New York legislature in 1942 under a proposal by Governor Thomas E. Dewey. Construction began in 1946, but state funds were inadequate and the project proceeded slowly. A 1950 law created the New York Thruway Authority, a private company engaged to build and maintain the freeway. The 1950 law allowed the Thruway Authority to sell $500 million in bonds to fund the project. This early 1950s photo of the Thruway's construction at Syracuse looks west toward the LeMoyne Avenue bridge, with the U. S. 11 bridge in the background. Later, I-81 would intersect with the Thruway beyond the curve at the top of the picture (courtesy, New York Thruway Authority).

Bottom: First open section of New York Thruway near Catskill, New York. The pace of construction of the Thruway increased immediately when funds became available from the sale of thruway bonds. The photo shows a 9-mile section of the Thruway that was opened to traffic on a temporary, toll-free basis on July 14, 1950. This area is south of Albany (courtesy, New York Thruway Authority).

Top: Construction of New York Thruway near Saugerties, New York. Wagon drills are used to drill holes for blasting rock on this section of the Thruway project. By the time the Thruway and additional routes were completed in the late 1950s, the project's total cost was almost $1 billion. This portion of the Thruway was opened on October 26, 1954 (courtesy, New York Thruway Authority).

Bottom: Governor Dewey dedicating opening of New York Thruway. On June 24, 1954, the first toll section of the Thruway was opened, a 115-mile piece between Rochester and Lowell. Governor Dewey, a longtime advocate of a statewide toll road, cuts the ribbon at the official ceremony at the Canastota Interchange. The Thruway has been renamed "The Governor Thomas E. Dewey Thruway" in honor of the governor's role in building the Thruway. Pictured from left are: Sen. Wheeler Milmoe, Mrs. Tallamy, Thruway Vice Chairman David J. Martin, Mrs. Ketchum, District Engineer Lacy Ketchum, Thruway Chairman Bertram Tallamy, Gov. Dewey, Mrs. Dewey, Thruway Secretary-Treasurer R. Burnell Bixby, Assemblyman Harold Tyler. The two children holding the ribbons are Patricia Waldo, 7, and Jimmy Spencer, 4 (courtesy, New York Thruway Authority).

a 524-mile canal system for barge traffic. As the Thruway celebrated its 40th birthday in 1990, the system underwent a major facelift. The original travel plaza buildings were replaced with larger, more modern facilities, with 16 new service plazas added. The Burger King restaurant chain (operated by Howard Johnson Motor Hotels) owned the right to tollway locations by the late 1990s. With the addition of the new plazas, officials expanded Thruway food facilities to include some familiar names such as McDonald's, Roy Rogers, Bob's Big Boy, Sbarro's, Nathan's, Popeye's, Dunkin' Donuts, Mrs. Fields' Cookies, and The Country's Best Yogurt (TCBY). At 641 miles, the New York Thruway is the nation's longest privately-run toll road system.[167]

New Jersey's highway system was experiencing the same traffic woes as New York and other populous states by the late 1940s. The corridor between Philadelphia and New York City was a major headache for drivers and was served by two outdated federal-aid highways: U.S. 1 and U.S. 130. Congestion

and accidents continued to mount annually. In 1947, the New Jersey legislature created the New Jersey Turnpike Authority, with retired General W. W. Wanamaker of the Army Corps of Engineers as its executive director. The Turnpike Authority plotted a 117.5-mile bypass of U.S. 1 and U.S. 130 and divided the construction project into seven crews under the supervision of eight architectural firms. This approach may have been in-

Top: New York State Thruway Patrol. Two officers from Troop T of the New York Thruway patrol standing next to their vehicle with emergency kit. Thruway police patrolled the system, aiding motorists and keeping law and order on the highway (courtesy, New York Thruway Authority).

Bottom: Thruway travel plaza, 1950s. The New York Thruway's planners copied the Pennsylvania Turnpike's concept of limiting restaurant and service station franchises to only a few select businesses. The Thruway also used standardized architecture for service plazas. The above service area, a Calso gasoline station with restaurant, was one of 22 that were built in 1955–56. The service plazas, like this one at Pattersonville, were remodeled in the 1990s and now include several familiar national and regional fast food brands (courtesy, New York Thruway Authority).

Toll gate, New York Thruway, 1950s. One of the original toll plazas for the New York Thruway as they appeared in the 1950s. This toll gate was located at Utica, New York. The Thruway Authority completely revamped its toll plazas in later years (author's collection).

motorists. The official turnpike pamphlet instructed motorists to place a white handkerchief between the glass and frame of the driver's side window to alert Turnpike State Police or authorized service tow trucks for help. Other innovations included two-way radio connecting every toll station, tunnel supervisors, police, and AAA-authorized service personnel in case of roadside emergency.

The early 1950s saw more private investment in toll roads. Illinois, Indiana, and Ohio created turnpike authorities to build east-west toll roads through their states. The three states coordinated on a route linking the Pennsylvania Turnpike on Ohio's eastern border, through northern Ohio and Indiana, to Chicago. Illinois built three tollways in the Chicago area: the Northwest, East-West and Tri-State tollways. The toll roads gave the same exclusive rights to locations at exit points as the other private toll roads. The Illinois Toll-way featured the first "oasis" design, which incorporated a restaurant/gift shop on a bridge above the highway, plus a modern, multipump service station. The first restaurants were the Fred Harvey chain, followed by Howard Johnson and currently McDonald's, Burger King, and others. The Ohio Toll-way was the first to be completed in 1955, with the Indiana and Illinois Toll-ways opening the following year. Motorists could drive nonstop from New York to Chicago, exclusive of toll stops. Since the 1950s, only a handful of privately-operated toll-ways have been built, mostly in western states, such as Oklahoma (Will Rogers and Turner Turnpikes and four new toll roads) and the Kansas Turnpike in Kansas.

Following the Second World War, Detroit's design experts started copying aircraft for its auto designs, particularly those of the new jet airplanes. Hood ornaments resembled missiles and cars were given celestial names such as Star Chief, Constellation, Galaxie, and Comet, and powered by "Rocket V-8s." While the car makers were busy making space-age exteriors, something was developing under the hood as well. In 1953, Dodge introduced its first V-8, the 241-cubic-inch hemi that delivered an amazing 241 horsepower. Two years

spired by the Allies' multifront war strategy during World War II. Like the highly-successful Pennsylvania Turnpike, the New Jersey Turnpike also limited access on and off the system, as well as controlling the number of business franchise at its service plazas. The Turnpike ultimately constructed 13 service plazas on the system.[168]

On November 5, 1951, despite the ongoing Korean War, the first 53 miles of the Turnpike between Deepwater and Bordertown opened to the public. Later that month, the route was extended an additional 40 miles from Bordertown and Woodbridge. By December 12, another 12 miles from Woodbridge to Newark was finished, and on January 15, 1952, the final 9-mile stretch from Newark to Ridgefield Park completed the project. Several small additions were built later. In 1956, the Holland Tunnel, the 8-mile Newark Bay-Hudson County Extension, and a 6-mile section linking the New Jersey Turnpike to the Pennsylvania Turnpike opened, putting the total turnpike mileage at 148 miles.[169]

During the 1950s, the Pennsylvania Turnpike made improvements and added new mileage to its toll-way system. A 100-mile segment from Carlisle to Valley Forge was opened on November 20, 1950, followed by the western extension from Irwin to the Ohio state line on December 26, 1951. On November 17, 1954, a 33-mile extension from Valley Forge to the Delaware River opened to traffic. Several years later, the northeastern extension to Scranton was finished on November 7, 1957.[170] The Turnpike added roadside assistance for stranded

(continued on page 151)

Top: Pennsylvania Turnpike in the 1950s. Following the Second World War, new mileage was added to the Pennsylvania Turnpike. The eastern end of the turnpike was extended by 100 miles from Carlisle to Valley Forge, and the western end from Irwin to the Ohio line. Work at both ends was completed by the end of 1951. Other new sections, including the 110-mile northeastern extension from Philadelphia to Scranton, were added during the 1950s. Today, the turnpike has a total of 506 miles (courtesy, Pennsylvania Turnpike Commission).

Previous Page Top Left: Construction of Passaic River Bridge for New Jersey Turnpike. While work proceeded on the New York Thruway, the New Jersey legislature created its own turnpike authority in 1947. New Jersey learned from New York's experience that state funds alone could not finance freeway construction, so the New Jersey Turnpike Authority was allowed to sell bonds. This bridge project is located near Essex City, New Jersey (courtesy, New Jersey Turnpike Authority).

Previous Page Top Right: Lifting final section of Chaplain Washington Memorial Bridge, New Jersey Turnpike. Another bridge over the Passaic River in eastern New Jersey nears completion. The Chaplain Washington Memorial Bridge (named for a World War II veteran) was completed in 1952, not long after the first sections of the toll-way were opened for traffic (courtesy, New Jersey Turnpike Authority).

Previous Page Middle: Newly-opened straightaway on New Jersey Turnpike near Cranbury, New Jersey. This section of turnpike between Trenton and New Brunswick cuts through prime New Jersey farmland. Exit 8-A is pictured in the distance (courtesy, New Jersey Turnpike Authority).

Previous Page Bottom: Signs on New Jersey Turnpike, 1952. To satisfy the public's eagerness to drive on the toll-way, turnpike authorities opened newly completed portions between freeway exits for public use. The final nine miles of the turnpike from Newark to Ridgefield Park opened on January 15, 1952 (National Archives [52-459]).

Top: Pennsylvania state policeman posing along Turnpike, early 1950s. State police were employed since the opening of the Pennsylvania Turnpike to assist motorists. The toll-way originally had no posted speed limits until Governor James signed into law a bill limiting speeds for autos to 70 mph on April 15, 1941. To conserve fuel during the war, speeds were reduced to only 35 mph for civilian traffic. This state trooper is standing next to his Ford patrol car on the shoulder of the turnpike (courtesy, Pennsylvania Turnpike Commission).

Bottom: Ohio toll-way gate. The state of Ohio started its own toll road in the early 1950s. Texaco was given the rights for the first toll-way station locations. The Ohio Turnpike joins the Pennsylvania Turnpike on the state's eastern border and ends at the Indiana border. Total length of the turnpike is 241 miles (author's collection).

Top Left: New York Thruway logo (courtesy, New York Thruway Authority).

Top Middle: New Jersey Turnpike logo (courtesy, New Jersey Turnpike Commission).

Top Right: Pennsylvania Turnpike logo (courtesy, Pennsylvania Turnpike Authority).

Bottom: Glass House Restaurant, Indiana Toll-way. Indiana and Ohio finished their east-west toll roads in 1956, with Indiana's toll-way crossing the northern edge of the state from Ohio to Chicago, Illinois. Gasoline stations and dining facilities such as the Glass House Restaurant were located just off the toll-way's service exits. These buildings now house contemporary food outlets (photo by author).

later, Chevrolet offered its own 265 c.i.d. V-8 power-plant. Marketing emphasized the space age, and cars grew tail fins that resembled jet wings.

America's love affair with the automobile reached its apex during these years as the car became the center of modern civilization. Peoples' lives, as well as urban and suburban design, were modified to accommodate the auto. Drive-in movie theaters and car washes (and later on the West Coast, drive-in churches) appeared in the late 1940s to serve America's newest icon. Drag racing and hot rodding reached its peak of popularity, and the automobile claimed

Top: Fred Harvey "Top-of-the-Toll-way" Restaurant and gift shop on Illinois Toll-way. The Fred Harvey restaurant chain was the first to have oasis locations on the Illinois Toll-way, with five modern facilities straddling the roadway. The unique design allows guests to view the traffic passing beneath the restaurant. Over the years, the oasis restaurants changed hands, from Howard Johnson in the 1960s and 1970s to McDonald's, Wendy's and Burger King today (author's collection).

Bottom: Aerial view of oasis on Illinois Toll-way. Illinois' first toll roads were built while similar projects were under construction in neighboring Indiana and Ohio. The above photo is of an "oasis" on the Northwest Toll-way, which bypasses downtown Chicago and connects the Indiana Toll-way with I-94 in southern Wisconsin. The Tri State Toll-way runs north from Chicago to the Wisconsin border at Racine, while the East-West Toll-way travels from Chicago to the western metropolitan area. The Illinois Toll-way had ten Standard Oil service stations on the system to serve motorists when it first opened in 1956 (author's collection).

General Motors experimental cars with GM Design Dome in background, Warren, Michigan. The introduction of the jet engine and rocket research revolutionized the airplane manufacturing industry after World War II, and aerospace design made an big impact on Detroit. The Big Three automakers designed cars looking more like spacecraft, with galactic names such as Constellation, Galaxy, and Comet, with "rocket V-8" engines and "swept wing" styling. Some prototypes proposed in the 1950s appeared to be jet airplanes on wheels. From left to right are three of General Motors' entries: the 1954 Firebird I, the 1956 XP500, and 1956 Firebird II (courtesy, GM Media Archives).

a new niche in the country's social psyche. Speed limits were increasing, as was the mood of optimism shared by the public. American life was becoming more fast paced, causing a new revolution for the nation's travel industry.

Motels

The prosperity following World War II gave the travel industry a needed shot-in-the-arm as millions of Americans took to the highway on family outings. A boom in motel construction ensued, and thousands of individual owner-operator establishments seemed to spring up overnight. Although motel architecture varied, a standard design emerged: a row of rooms connected to a single structure, with the proprietor living on-site behind the small motel office, making them available on a 24-hour basis. Approximately 50,000 tourist and motor courts were still in service in the early 1950s, but they were aging and were gradually being replaced by the newer motels by the end of the decade. The American Automobile Association

(AAA) would only recommend 3,522 tourist courts as having acceptable quality in 1950. Following the same trend set by the oil companies, more national brand names of motels appeared to compete with the mom-and-pop operators. By 1950, the motels exceeded the number of hotels for the first time. America had entered the Age of the Motel.[171]

Although the boom in postwar motel construction was adding needed units to the nation's stock of lodging facilities, supply failed to keep pace with demand. Like many products and services in the years following World War II, the shortage of hotels made the overnight stay unpredictable. First-rate accommodations were even harder to find. The older downtown hotels were often expensive and in dilapidated condition, and the food at the hotel restaurant was notoriously disgusting. Most hotels had not seen any improvements since their original construction and many lacked modern amenities such as air conditioning. Many hotels were still located near the railroad line, and the noise from passing trains disturbed the sleep of hotel guests. The only alternative for the traveler was the tourist and motor courts or outdoor camping, which meant few facilities, especially for families with young children. Thousands of tourist camps were showing their age and in poor condition.

Postwar highways gradually improved to make traveling marginally reliable, and vacationers could now take longer trips. The oil companies had already offered travelers complementary membership to travel clubs which helped plan trip routes and provided road maps and information on tourist spots and points of interest. In 1929, the "Ray Walker Guide to Motels and Cottages" began publication, listing recommended lodging for travelers, as travel organizations such as AAA had already been providing for its members. In 1946, M. K. Guertin, a California hotelier, and 66 other motel-inn owners formed the Best Western Motels as a referral system. Motel owners who joined agreed to share expenses, direct business to each other, and improve the quality of hotel/motel service. Guertin spent $2,332.62 of his own money to set up the organization, which initially involved inspecting 507 motels in only 29 days throughout the western states. Guertin pioneered the use of

Top: Trailer Court on U.S. 61, Baton Rouge Louisiana. A typical trailer court offering permanent and temporary rentals on U.S. Highway 61 near Baton Rouge, Louisiana. Trailer courts and trailer "camps" had few amenities but provided an alternative for those in search of a cheaper way to travel. After the Second World War, consumers began to demand more uniformity and comfort in overnight accommodations and aging, outdated trailer camps and courts were soon avoided in favor of newly-constructed postwar motels. By the mid–1950s, most of the trailer camps and motor courts had vanished from the American roadside (National Archives [51-1826]).

Bottom: Quonset village, Colfax, California. The U.S. military ordered thousands of "Quonset huts" (portable corrugated steel shelters, named for the town in Rhode Island where they were developed) during World War II for temporary housing and other uses. After the war, many were sold off as war surplus. A set of Quonset huts here are converted into cabins at a resort on U.S. 40 near Colfax, California. A Chevron station attends to two customers in the foreground. T. W. Kines, August 14, 1948 (National Archives [48-1540]).

mattresses, linens, and air conditioning in the hospitality industry. The organization distributed free of charge its own "Best Western Travel Guide" to aid motorists; a modern version is still in publication. In 1962, Best Western was firmly established west of the Mississippi, and its new gold crown logo was introduced for its members' motel signs. In 1964, with many new locations in the eastern United States, Best Eastern was established. In 1966, Best Western made Phoenix, Arizona, its central headquarters. Today, over 3,500 hotel and motel establishments worldwide claim membership to the Best Western system.[172]

As the decade of the 1950s started, Best Western's logo was slowly appearing on the nation's highways, recommending a quality night's stay for the increasingly-picky tourist. Unfortunately, most American travelers still had to make due with old prewar tourist courts and hotels. The time seemed ripe for someone to meet the obvious need for reliable overnight lodging. Even back in the 1920s,

author Sinclair Lewis lamented the deplorable conditions which beset the hapless traveler at the typical hotel. Lewis envisioned a day in which hotels were clean, affordable, and located on all national thoroughfares. He wrote that the hotel guest of the future would not "waste money on gilt and

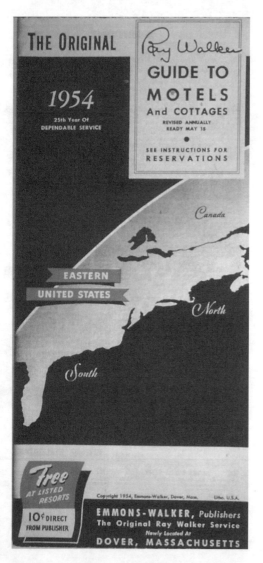

Left: Tee Pee Village, San Antonio, Texas. One of the pleasures of traveling the American highway during the 1940s through the 1960s was the amusing variety of weird businesses and tourist attractions on the road. Some motels modeled themselves after an Indian tee pee village for an exotic night's rest. The "Tee Pee Village Lodge" pictured here may have copied the famous "Wigwam Village," a chain of a dozen or so motels that flourished mainly in the western two-thirds of the country, from Kentucky to California. Most of them are now gone, except for three still operating in Cave City, KY, Holbrook, AZ, and Rialto, CA. Photo by T. W. Kines, January 12, 1950 (National Archives [50-176]).

Right: Ray Walker Guide to Motels and Cottages. The Ray Walker guide to lodging facilities started in 1929, and included useful information on the services of places advertised. The pamphlet claims that unlike other such referral guides, listings are chosen based on their merits, but does not explain how it assures quality for all of the motels and resorts in its brochure. The guide was limited to accommodations in the eastern United States (author's collection).

Left: Superior Courts brochure. Several minor chains of motels existed just prior to and after World War II, including the Alamo Plaza Courts, United Motor Courts, and Superior Courts. Some, like United Motor Courts and Superior Courts, merely lent their name to a lodging "system," and did not share common architecture. They were also regional, like Superior Courts, which only served the Atlantic coastal states. A few isolated Superior Courts can still be found today (author's collection).

Right: Best Western logos: 1947; 1962; 1966; 1993 (courtesy, Best Western International).

onyx, but he is going to have agreeable clerks, good coffee, endurable mattresses and good lighting." [173]

Holiday Inn

After returning from a family vacation to Washington, D.C., in 1951, Klemmons Wilson, a successful Memphis, Tennessee, home builder, experienced first-hand the plight of the American tourist in search of decent travel accommodations. Wilson, like many traveling salesmen and vacationers of the day, had fallen victim to the dark, dingy downtown hotel, with its often indifferent hotel clerks, bell hops, and bell captains always expecting a gratuity. Wilson's vacation travails got him wondering why no one was marketing better travel facilities with at least some minimum quality standards. Already a major success as a mass-producer of homes during the postwar housing boom, Wilson redirected his entrepreneurial talents towards his own vision of a totally new concept in lodging.[174]

Klemmons Wilson is a typical American success story. Born in Osceola, Arkansas, in 1913, Klemmons lost his father when he was just nine months old. Shortly after his father's death, Klemmons and his mother moved to Memphis, where she worked as a dentist's assistant, an auditor's assistant, and a bookkeeper to support the small family. Klemmons worked as a drug store delivery boy until he broke his leg in an auto accident. After graduating from high school, the young Klemmons started his first business selling popcorn to movie theaters using a popcorn machine he purchased. Klemmons managed to convince the owner of the Memphisian Theater to rent him space for his popcorn machine for $2.50 a week, plus electricity. Klemmons later boasted that he was earning a princely income of $30 per week, a lot of money in those days. Before long, the enterprising youngster became owner of 40 movie theaters, not an easy task in the lean years of the Great Depression. Klemmons next went into the home building business, using mass-production methods similar to the Levittown developments on the East Coast. In the late 1940s, Klemmons Wilson became known in the mid-south as "Mr. GI Housing." [175]

Besides being a savvy businessman in the housing field, Wilson recognized that consumer tastes were becoming more sophisticated. Americans were demanding higher quality, standardized, and reliable goods and services. The most successful businesses appeared to concentrate on cultivating brand loyalty and a customer's identity with a product and its corporate logo. Suburban America saw explosive growth as ex-soldiers and their families rushed to purchase new housing with low-cost GI loans. Being in the housing business himself, Wilson also noticed that the postwar consumer preferred the latest in ultra-modern designs, so he decided to furnish his motels with modern furniture, sliding glass patio doors, wall-to-wall carpeting, air conditioning, and of course, television. Naming his new motel "Holiday Inn," Wilson's innovations would soon become a model for the entire industry. Wilson made his mother, Ruby "Doll" Wilson, vice-president and placed her in charge of interior decorating in the early years.[176]

Wilson opened his first motel on Summer Avenue on the eastern fringe of Memphis in 1952, only one year after his ill-fated family vacation. Like many others to follow, the original Holiday Inn offered free parking, air conditioning, telephones, free ice, a swimming pool, and a restaurant on the premises. Wilson's new motel was designed to be "family-friendly" long before anyone thought of the term. In addition to offering babysitter services and dog kennels, children could stay for free, starting an industry-wide trend. Wilson's first Holiday Inn contained 120 units in a single structure.[177]

After the debut of his first prototype, Wilson opened three more motels in the next year-and-a-half. Although the first motels were a commercial success, Wilson ran out of funds to expand further. Wilson sensed an opportunity to start a nationwide chain of motels and he needed a partner who shared his business philosophy. In 1954, Wilson approached Wallace E. Johnson, also a highly successful home builder. In a single evening, the two enthusiastically agreed on a joint venture and formed Holiday Inn of America. The following year, they tapped attorney William B. Walton to help organize the new company.[178]

The first 75 Holiday Inns were single-story structures styled in the ranch-house design popular at the time. The buildings were placed on cement slabs, with glass and wood walls and wooden roofing. Doll Wilson saw to it that the interior color schemes were bright and cheerful, in contrast to the dark, outdated décor of the older hotels. In 1957, a subsidiary, Inn Keepers Supply Company, was created to manufacture all of the

furnishings, including the carpeting, furniture, mirrors, lamps, even the paint. At the company's "Holiday City" corporate headquarters on Lamar Avenue in Memphis, construction plans for the motels were standardized and local firms hired to design, build, and make all of the furnishings.[179]

The new motel chain needed one final touch, something that motorists would instantly recognize on the highways, day or night. The result was the now-famous "Great Sign," a 50-foot green-and-yellow neon beacon complete with flashing

Top: Ribbon-cutting for opening of first Holiday Inn, Memphis, 1952. Following World War II, many hotels in central cities had become dilapidated, outdated, and expensive. In 1951, Klemmons Wilson took his family from Memphis to Washington, D. C., for a vacation, and found poor conditions in the hotels, with few lodging facilities to accommodate families with children. A successful home builder, Wilson decided that the time was ripe for someone to start a motel business with an emphasis on good quality and a casual, family-style atmosphere. He opened his first motel in Memphis, and added several more in the next two years. In 1954, Wilson and another major home builder, Wallace E. Johnson, formed Holiday Inns of America (courtesy, Holiday Inns International, Inc.).

Middle: First Holiday Inn, Summer Avenue, Memphis. Klemmons Wilson followed the postwar industry practice of locating motels on the edge of cities, away from the older hotels and enabling motorists to bypass metropolitan areas more easily. His first motel was located at the outskirts of Memphis, a modest one-story building that became Holiday Inn's standard design for dozens of units to follow. Wilson took an assembly-line approach to the hostelry business much like Henry Ford, with subsidiary companies supplying everything from carpeting, furniture, even paint. Klemmons employed his mother, Ruby "Doll" Wilson, as vice-president and placed her in charge of interior decorating for the new motels (courtesy, Holiday Inns International, Inc.).

Bottom: Klemmons Wilson with Holiday Inn "Great Sign." Klemmons Wilson recognized that advertising is a key ingredient to any business's success, so he paid careful attention to marketing his new idea to the motoring public. The first order of business, after selecting a name, was an effective advertising sign for his new motel chain. Wilson decided on the now-famous "Great Sign" for Holiday Inns, a 50-foot green-and-yellow neon sign complete with an arrow and flashing lights (a throwback from Wilson's early days working in and around movie houses) (courtesy, Holiday Inns International, Inc.).

lights reminiscent of the marquees of the old movie houses of Wilson's younger days. The company registered its slogan, "The Nation's Innkeeper" (now "The World's Innkeeper"), with the U.S. Patent Office, and also holds a registered service mark for its standards in food service and availability of its facilities (another industry first). Vacationing families, over-the-road truck drivers and traveling salesmen all loved the new inns' uniform quality and conveniences. As Holiday Inns were starting to gain in popularity, hotel occupancy rates were dropping, down from 85 percent to 67 percent during the period 1948 to 1958. By the end of 1956, 20 Holiday Inns were in operation.[180]

The success of his motels prompted Wilson to add Trav-L-Park, offering the same clean, modern facilities to campers as its Inns. Trav-L-Parks came complete with swimming pools, miniature golf, shuffleboard courts, restrooms, laundry facilities, and a store with a gift shop. Recreational vehicles were becoming popular, and Trav-L-Parks put a maximum limit of 15 vehicles per acre to avoid crowding guests.[181]

The new interstate highway system paved the way for rapid expansion of Holiday Inn. Businesses such as restaurants, filling stations, and motels all rushed to purchase property near freeway interchanges and competition was fierce. Holiday Inn had a slight advantage since its franchisees, being local people, were familiar with their hometowns and often bought the prime locations before other competing businesses. Gulf Oil even entered into a joint venture with Holiday Inn so that Gulf could purchase adjacent property for its service stations. By 1960, Holiday Inn had over 100 motels, with two new units opening each week. That same year, Holiday Inn surpassed Howard Johnson in the number of motel locations.[182]

Holiday Inn motel, 1960. A 1950s-style Holiday Inn with restaurant, typical of the first motels. Klemmons Wilson insisted that each Holiday Inn include above-average dining facilities, along with other industry firsts, such as free parking and ice, and swimming pools. Children could stay for free. Wilson applied his experience at mass-producing homes to building motels. Motels were of simple construction, with walls made of cement block masonry. By 1960, Holiday Inn had over 100 locations across the United States, with two new outlets opening weekly. This one is located on U.S. 45 in Columbus, Mississippi (author's collection).

**Holiday Inn SOUTH
AUSTIN, TEXAS**

Modern Holiday Inn, 1960s. As the Holiday Inn chain expanded in the 1960s, motel architecture departed from the early standardized motel floor plans. This modern Holiday Inn design, with circular tower, was used in many areas of the country. Holiday Inn later added "Holidomes" to some its newer motels, complete with indoor pool, as the company embraced a greater variety of building designs. Pictured is the Holiday Inn South, in Austin, Texas (author's collection).

Throughout the 1960s, Wilson continued to work tirelessly to further expand Holiday Inn. Not one for day-to-day corporate details, Wilson traveled nationwide and eventually overseas, putting in 12- to 14-hour days. By 1963, Holiday Inn opened its 500th location, then doubled that number just four years later. Holiday Inn dominated the hostelry industry into the 1970s. Over time, the company grew into a conglomerate of over 50 companies, including the Trailways Bus Company, a cardboard manufacturer, and a meat-packing business. However, the company's for-

tunes started going in reverse. The Arab oil embargo of 1973–74 caused a sharp decline in travel, drastically cutting Holiday Inn's profits. The company's stock lost 80 percent of its value from 1972 to the end of 1973. Holiday Inn's largest shareholder, Roy Winegardner, went directly to Memphis to find out what was going wrong. He discovered that the top leadership was unable to coordinate the vast Holiday Inn empire, and the company was in disarray. Like many successful entrepreneurs, Wilson was gifted at setting up a successful company, but was unable to juggle a major corporation owning unrelated subsidiaries. Many older Holiday Inns had become outdated and were in desperate need of renovation. Holiday Inn's reputation for high-quality lodging began to suffer, and it was losing business to new competitors. Winegardner was no stranger to the hotel business, since he owned and later sold 24 of his hotels in the late 1960s to purchase $41 million worth of Holiday Inn stock. With so much personally at stake, Winegardner gathered several other major shareholders and franchisees to meet with Wilson and Johnson. The group convinced Wilson and Johnson to turn over control of the company to Winegardner. Wilson later stepped down from his corporate post.[183]

Winegardner's first move was to sell off unprofitable Holiday Inn businesses to cut costs and upgrade the older motels. In 1979, Holiday Inn went into the gaming business, which later proved to be extremely profitable and helped get the company out of the red. In the 1980s, Holiday Inn expanded its lodging locations under new hotel brands, such as Hampton Inn, Crowne Plaza, Intercontinental Hotels and Resorts, Embassy Suites, Holiday Inn Express, and its latest entry, Staybridge Suites. Today, Holiday Inn is a subsidiary of Bass Hotels and Resorts and is based in

Great Britain, which operates 2,600 hotels and resorts worldwide, and hosting 150 million guests annually.[184]

Howard Johnson

Although the West Coast can claim credit for the invention of the motel, the modern motel-chain concept got its early beginnings on the East Coast. In 1925, the same year that the Milestone Mo-Tel opened in California, Howard Dearing Johnson purchased a small patent medicine store in Quincy, Massachusetts, with $500 in borrowed money. Johnson's store included a soda fountain, where he sold just three flavors of ice cream: vanilla, chocolate, and strawberry. He perfected his ice cream after experimenting with an old-fashioned hand-cranked ice cream freezer in his basement. Johnson added frankfurters, hamburgers, and other items to the menu and the little drug store became the Howard Johnson Restaurant. Business was so good that he opened a second store in 1929 and by 1935, there were 25 Howard Johnson roadside ice cream and sandwich stands in Massachusetts, bearing the friendly "Simple Simon and Pie Man" logo.[185]

Howard Johnson made another business first when it became the first restaurant on a freeway. In 1940, Howard Johnson was awarded a contract for nine restaurant locations on the newly-completed Pennsylvania Turnpike in 1940. After the war, Howard Johnson became the exclusive restaurants serving the Ohio and New Jersey turnpikes. Howard Johnson restaurants offered standardized yet family-style service and expanded rapidly after World War II to over 400 units by 1954. That year, Howard Johnson decided to enter the lodging industry, and opened its first motor lodge in Savannah, Georgia. The Howard Johnson Motor Lodges incorporated the familiar orange-roofed restaurants into its motel design and retained its franchising formula that had been very lucrative for its restaurant business. Like Holiday Inn, Howard Johnson went through a brief period of decline in the last few decades but has made a strong comeback. Currently, over 500 Howard Johnson lodging facilities can be found in the U.S., Canada, and Mexico.[186]

Other new motel chains came on the scene in the mid–1950s, copying Howard Johnson and Holiday Inn's successful formula. In 1954, a group of investors in Flagstaff, Arizona, opened a motel

Howard Johnson logos, 1950s–60s; 1996 (courtesy, Howard Johnson International, Inc.).

Howard Johnson motel and restaurant, 1960s. Howard Johnson went into the lodging business, opening its first motel in Savannah, Georgia, in 1954. Pictured is an ultra-modern Howard Johnson Motor Lodge (again, the word "motel" is avoided) with its orange-colored roof which has been the trademark of Howard Johnson. Howard Johnson had divided its resources in two industries—hostelry and cuisine—and managed to retain its edge in both fields in the 1960s. Despite growing competition with the new "fast food" franchises, Howard Johnson for years outsold McDonald's, Kentucky Fried Chicken and Burger King combined (author's collection).

Ramada Inn Roadside Hotel, Memphis. In the same year (1954) that Klemmons Wilson and Wallace E. Johnson teamed up to form Holiday Inn, a group of investors started the Ramada Inn hotels in Flagstaff, Arizona. Choosing the Spanish word "Ramada" (meaning "a shaded resting place"), the new chain sought to be a bit more sophisticated than its competitors by calling itself an "inn" as opposed to a mere "motel," and using formal American colonial architecture. The original signs had a friendly colonial-era innkeeper to welcome travelers (author's collection).

in the hopes of establishing their own franchise system. The group adopted the name "Ramada Inn" (Ramada being Spanish for "a shaded resting place") for their motel chain. By 1963, Ramada Inn grew to 40 company-owned and franchise locations, and over 500 by 1973.[187] Another well-known name in lodging, Travelodge, also started on the West Coast prior to World War II. In 1935, a San Diego businessman named Scott King opened up a motor court to accommodate the business traveler. He came up with the name "Travelodge" in 1939, but did not incorporate the name until 1946. Like many new entries into motel business following the Second World War, Travelodge enjoyed spectacular growth during the postwar years, claiming 52 locations in California by 1954. By this time, the company needed a new logo or mascot for its corporate image. The symbol of California on its state flag, the Golden Bear, was chosen. Travelodge adopted its "Sleepy Bear" mascot to remind travelers that a good night's sleep awaited them. By this book's printing, over 500

Travelodge and Thriftlodge locations are found throughout the United States, Canada, and Latin America.[188] Other motel chains, such as Motel 6, would come later. The interstate highway system encouraged motel construction, with new lodging facilities appearing wherever a new freeway opened to traffic. To add a touch of class and perhaps to distinguish themselves from the average run-of-the-mill motel, the new franchises preferred to call their establishments "inns" or "lodges" for a more intimate image.

By the 1950s, it had again become apparent that America needed more modern multi-lane highways. Other than the few private toll roads that either existed or were under construction, most of the country was starting to feel the transportation crunch starting to intensify as the total number of vehicles continued to increase. The first-generation two lanes were now obsolete, with the nation's highways clogged with vacationers and commercial traffic competing for road space. Driving, especially cross-country, was becoming more

Travelodge Motel, South Sioux City, Nebraska. The Travelodge motel chain actually started before World War II. In 1935, businessman Scott King purchased a motor court in San Diego, California, which he renamed "Travelodge" in 1939. The name was incorporated in 1946, just after the war. Over the next several decades, Travelodge moved beyond its west coast home base to become one of the country's biggest nationwide chains. The company's "Sleepy Bear" mascot was modeled after the bear on the California state flag (author's collection).

time consuming, with travel time actually increasing, much to the dismay of motorists who were accustomed to constant improvements. New highway safety studies only confirmed what the prewar studies had identified as the two chief causes of highway congestion: increasing number of vehicles driving longer distances and unlimited access to main arteries from side traffic. Since the highway department experts could not do too much about the first problem, they focused on the issue of unlimited access.

The traffic situation on the mainly two-lane U.S. system and in urban centers was becoming acute. Many of old highways were built for the Model A, if not the Model T, and with traffic volume predicted to continue to increase into the 1960s, a transportation crisis appeared inevitable. The original roads still had dangerous curves, speeds of 25 or 30 mph, narrow bridges, numerous intersections, and other hazards. America's first

hard-surfaced highways were also crumbling due to age and increasing truck traffic. The Bureau of Public Roads' 1955 surveys revealed some disturbing statistics. The BPR listed a portion of Los Angeles' Hollywood Freeway as the nation's busiest expressway, where BPR counted 290,760 vehicles on July 18 (172,000 on an average day). Also worthy of mention is a stretch of Lake Shore Drive (U.S. 41) in Chicago and Highway Bridge (U.S. 1) crossing the Potomac into Washington, D. C. *Life* magazine gave the American highway system an R.I.P. in a 1955 article entitled "Death of the Open Road: What's Happened to Our Highways?" The article focused on the 30-mile section of U.S. 1 between Baltimore and Washington, D.C., from colonial times to the 1950s, illustrating the need for a new interstate freeway system. This short stretch of U.S. 1 had an accident rate three times the national average. Although the highway had four lanes, each lane was only ten feet in width and not separated by a median. It had its own "Dead Man's Curve" that remained a major killer despite several efforts over the years to relocate and rebuild it. Aptly referred to as "Death Highway" by many veteran drivers, the deadly road claimed 30 to 40 lives a year until it was finally bypassed by a new expressway.[189] However, numerous other American highways were suffering from the same traffic strangulation as highlighted by *Life*'s article, and many were demanding a federally backed plan. President Truman did sign the Federal-Aid Highway Act of 1952, which approved the first funding for an interstate system under the 1944 Highway Act, but the $25 million appropriated was too little to put a dent in the nation's highway woes.[190]

The call for a new national highway system based on prewar plans renewed public debate for action at the federal level. Businesses and developers hoping to profit from a new freeway system lobbied state and local officials. One of the arguments was that a high-speed interstate freeway system similar to the German autobahns was necessary in case of war or other national emergency, which seemed plausible during the early Cold War days. President Dwight Eisenhower recognized the need for good roads long ago when he witnessed the poor condition of the nation's highways during the U.S. Army's 1919 transcontinental convoy. Although the convoy used the Lincoln Highway, one of the better of the transcontinental roads that existed at the time, travel proceeded at a snail's pace, with constant delays due to flimsy wooden bridges collapsing under the weight of heavy trucks and roads that turned into swampy bogs, entrapping soldiers and vehicles. Numerous small towns slowed progress, and the convoy was further held up by speechmaking politicians and others along the route. After two months, the exhausted troops finally arrived in San Francisco on September 5, 1919, greeted by parade of jubilant well-wishers. Eisenhower and others believed that the trip was far too long for motorized travel in the 20th century. During World War II, Eisenhower was annoyed by the delays in moving the military cross-country. State highway appropriations alone could not meet the demand for more modern roads, as evidenced by the slow pace of construction of the few new toll roads.[191] While campaigning for president in 1952, Eisenhower told the Hearst newspapers that "The obsolescence of the nation's high-

Civil Defense sign, 1952. During the Cold War, proponents of interstate highways often argued that national defense made such a system vital for national security. General Dwight Eisenhower raised such concerns during World War II after seeing first-hand how inadequately the federal-aid system handled military traffic. By the early 1950s, the country was being prepared by the government for possible enemy attack, and a civil defense system was developed to give the public the assurance of some protection. The social and political climate at the time was one of paranoia, with the Soviets having built an atom bomb, a war in Korea, flying saucer sightings and the McCarthy Red Scare going on all at once (National Archives [52-1664]).

way system presents an appalling problem of waste, danger, and death." By the time he took office in January 1953, only 6,416 miles of interstate highways were completed. But before he could tackle the nation's highway problems, Ike first had to honor a campaign promise to find a solution to the deadlocked Korean peace talks and end the war.[192]

During 1953, Congress held hearings on a new highway bill. The following year, Congress enacted the Federal-Aid Highway Act of 1954. The bill was a compromise between city-versus-country and special interests who almost routinely surface during any congressional debate on the issue of highways. As usual, a major sticking point was the allocation of federal aid funds. The eastern states wanted population to be a factor in distributing funds, while many large western states pressed for land area and distance. The bill's formula for apportionment of federal funding attempted to satisfy everyone, with one-half based on population and one-half based on a federal-aid formula (one-third on highway distance, one-third on population, and one-third on land area). Although President Eisenhower had some reservations about the bill, he nevertheless signed it into law on May 6, 1954.[193]

After settling the Korean Conflict, President Eisenhower resumed his quest to build the world's most modern superhighway system. Eisenhower envisioned a "Grand Plan," a coast-to-coast ribbon of concrete designed to last for decades. Although the Congress debated highway issues annually, Eisenhower was impatient with the pace of congressional deliberations. A governing body of 400-plus members caused the process to become bogged down from infighting between rival factions. Past efforts by Congress to tackle the highway problem usually resulted in watered-down compromises. Although Congress had just passed the 1954 Highway Act, Eisenhower privately believed that the Act did not go far enough to ease the transportation trouble that experts were predicting in the future. Eisenhower started by appointing a high-level commission to formulate plans for a interstate highway system. In July 1954, Ike appointed the "President's Advisory Committee on a National Highway Program," picking his longtime advisor, General Lucius D. Clay (who was also an engineer) as chairman of the committee. Other committee members included Bill Roberts of Allis-Chalmers (manufacturer of farm implements), David Beck of the International Brotherhood of Teamsters, Sloan Colt of the Bankers' Trust Company, and Steven Bechtel of the Bechtel Corporation. Francis C. (Frank) Turner of the Bureau of Public Roads served as the committee's advisory secretary. Turner brought considerable expertise to the process due to his extensive knowledge of highway issues while serving at BPR since 1929.[194]

As the Clay Committee deliberated, suggestions from all quarters came in, from the oil companies and the trucking industry to farmers and urban planners. The consensus throughout the country and among most transportation experts was that a total replacement of the current U.S. highway system was needed to solve the gridlock that was projected to take place in the 1960s. The states lobbied against increasing the federal gasoline tax. However, using BPR's data, the committee projected the total cost for an interstate project would be a minimum of $100 billion, and gas taxes could provide an instant revenue source. Another argument in favor of gasoline and diesel taxes and

other "user fees" was that they appear logical from a fairness standpoint since they primarily affect those who benefit directly.[195]

The Clay Committee borrowed from the work of its predecessors who were involved with the Federal-Aid Highway Act of 1944 and proposed an interstate system of limited access, multi-lane freeways of standardized construction. The committee recommended 12-foot-wide lanes, with 180 to 250-foot rights-of-way, wide enough to accommodate adding future lanes if necessary. "Service roads" running parallel to the freeway would allow businesses to locate near the roadway but not abut the roadside, thereby preserving the concept of limited access. Other proposals included increasing the number of lanes in the system by 50 percent, with 2,300 miles of six-lane freeways, 28,000 four lanes, and approximately 7,000 of two-lane highways. The two-lane routes would not be divided, but shoulders would be at least 10 feet in width, allowing disabled vehicles to pull off the roadway. Highway experts estimated that drivers automatically slow for stopped vehicles on the roadside, reducing traffic capacity by 60 percent. The Committee chose the same interstate routes proposed in 1947 by the PRA, although some funding would be used to upgrade some existing routes, and recommended the formation of a new Federal Highway Corporation to sell $25 million in highway bonds, to be repaid by federal gasoline and diesel taxes over a 30-year period. The cost to complete the system was estimated at $101 billion. While this figure seemed enormous, transportation officials argued that the nation would still have to spend in excess of $50 billion by the mid–1960s for road construction even without a new interstate system. In addition, the federal-aid system would continue to add unnecessary costs to the economy in the form of higher auto insurance rates resulting from accidents preventable by newer roads, added wear to tires and vehicles, increased fuel consumption due to traffic delays, and lost time and productivity for industry. The Clay Committee presented its final report to the president on January 11, 1955. Eisenhower was completely enthusiastic about the committee's recommendations and forwarded the report to Congress on February 22, 1955.[196]

While the Clay Committee was busy with its project, some members of Congress were also studying the interstate highway issue. Senator Albert Gore, Sr. (father of the current vice-presi-

Eisenhower with Clay Committee, January 11, 1955. Heeding the call for an interstate highway system, Congress passed highway bills in its 1952 and 1954 sessions, both without adequate finding. In July 1954, Ike appointed a committee to develop a plan and report its findings to the president and Congress. Pictured here, the "Clay Committee," headed by General Lucius Clay, hands its report to Eisenhower on January 11, 1955. Their recommendations became the foundation for the present interstate highway system. From left: Gen. Lucius Clay, Frank Turner, Steve Bechtel, Sloan Colt, William Roberts, and Dave Beck (U.S. DOT/FHWA).

dent), served on the Public Works Committee prior to becoming chairman of the Senate Subcommittee on Roads in 1955. Gore introduced a bill allocating $10 billion a year through 1961 for interstate highway construction. The Gore proposal would have expanded the mileage of the system and increased the federal share to 75 percent. However, the Gore bill did not specify how to raise the additional revenue. Furthermore, the Constitution mandates that all spending bills must originate in the House of Representatives. The Gore bill presumed that future congressional and state appropriations would finance the system. Several governors and New York's famed highway architect and planner Robert Moses attacked the bill. Moses in particular faulted the Gore plan for failing to account for the high costs of acquiring land for the system and the "pay-as-you-go" approach as unfair to future drivers who

would not have to pay for the new freeway system.[197]

Congress simultaneously debated the Gore bill and the Clay Committee's proposal. Fiscal conservatives such as Virginia Senator Harry F. Byrd, Jr., were adamantly against any federal borrowing to finance a highway system. Gore's bill would have to clear the Committee on Finance to address the lack of funding, and as chairman, Byrd's opposition could doom the bill. On May 25, 1955, the Senate defeated the Clay Committee's bill by a 60–31 margin, while the Senate overwhelmingly approved the Gore bill on a voice vote. In the House, Rep. George H. Fallon of Maryland, chairman of the House Committee on Public Works, introduced his own bill. Fallon worked with the House Ways and Means Committee to come up with a financing mechanism that would satisfy recalcitrant members. After seeing the Clay proposal go down in defeat in the Senate and the House version facing opposition, Frank Turner supplied Fallon with valuable BPR data to help formulate a sound bill. The Fallon bill proposed increasing the federal gasoline tax and other highway user taxes to pay for the new system and increase the federal government's share to 90 percent. Since supporters for interstate highways kept emphasizing national defense in favor of the new system, the Fallon bill was entitled "National System of Interstate and Defense Highways." [198]

On July 27, 1955, the Clay Committee's bill was defeated in the House of Representatives on a 221–193 vote. As the House debated the Fallon bill, opponents of increased user fees (oil companies, the trucking industry and tire manufacturers) brought considerable pressure on House members. In the end, the Fallon bill fared worse, with the House voting it down by a 292 to 123 vote. The interstate highway system would have to wait another year.[199]

The following year, interstate highway proponents regrouped after getting encouragement from President Eisenhower, who renewed his pledge to get Congress to approve interstate highway legislation in his 1956 State of the Union speech. The Bureau of Public Roads adjusted its routing plans and added 5,636 miles of urban freeways. In September 1955, BPR issued its "General Location of National System of Defense Highways" report, which kept the routes proposed by PRA in 1947, while adding the new urban freeway mileage. Rep. Fallon introduced a revised version of his previous bill on January 26, 1956, entitled the "Federal-Aid Highway Act of 1956." The new bill proposed a 40,000 mile system with the federal government paying 90 percent of construction costs, or $24.8 billion, to be completed in 13 years. Funding to the states would be based on a ratio of each state's costs and the BPR's estimates of the costs to complete the entire system. The ratio would be adjusted periodically by BPR as the construction progressed. A unique provision of the new Fallon bill was the proposal to create a Highway Trust Fund to collect highway user fees for highway construction.[200]

The House Ways and Means Committee, with authority over legislative financing, debated methods of funding a new interstate system. Committee Chairman Hale Boggs of Louisiana added his own proposal to increase the federal gas tax by 2 to 3 cents per gallon and adding several new user fees. The Fallon bill (Title I) and Boggs' bill (Title II) were combined into a single bill and approved by the House Public Works Committee. The full House passed the Federal-Aid Highway Act of 1956 on April 27 by a wide 388–19 margin. The bill went on to the Senate, where the Public Works Committee considered Title I, and Byrd's Finance Committee deliberated on the Title II portion of the bill. The Public Works Committee deleted most of the Fallon bill, substituting Gore's bill, except for the 13-year target date for completion and the 90–10 proportion of federal state financing. The new version also changed the federal funding to the states, with two-thirds based on population, one-sixth on road distance and one-sixth on land area. Meanwhile, Byrd's Committee added the provision that would allow the secretary of the treasury to reduce funding on a proportionate basis if construction costs exceed Highway Trust Fund revenues. The complete bill, including the Byrd Amendment, passed the Senate on a voice vote on May 29, 1956.[201]

A joint Senate-House conference committee convened to iron out the differences between the two bills. After a month of negotiations, the final version slightly expanded the system to 41,000 miles at a cost estimate of $25 billion, to be completed by 1969. The funding for the interstate system for the first three years used the Gore formula, while the final ten years used the Fallon formula. The compromise kept the federal share of costs at 90 percent. The bill easily passed the Senate by 89–1, and the House approved the bill on a voice vote the same day. The president quickly signed the bill on June 29 while recovering from an intestinal disorder in Walter Reed Army Hospital.[202]

The stated purpose for the Federal-Aid Highway Act of 1956 was to carry out the provisions of the Federal-Aid Road Act of 1916 and "all Acts mandatory and supplementary thereto." The Act declared that it is essential to the national interest to provide for the early completion of the "National System of Interstate Highways" as authorized under the Federal-Aid Highway Act of 1944, and to complete the new system in 13 years. It further states that "Because of its primary importance to the national defense, the name of such system is hereby changed to the 'National System of Interstate and Defense Highways,' or simply referred to as the 'Interstate System.'"[203]

The Federal-Aid Highway Act of 1956 contained Eisenhower's request for uniform design standards to be decided by the Bureau of Public Roads and AASHO, both missing from earlier proposals. The Act did allow some two-lane segments and at-grade crossings in lightly traveled areas with limited access, and toll roads and bridges were added to the system. One lingering issue that was debated was whether states should be reimbursed by the federal government for any freeways constructed with less than 90 percent federal funding (such as state or privately financed toll roads). This proposal was deferred for several decades until passage of the Inter-modal Surface Transportation Efficiency Act of 1991.[204]

The 1956 Act established a Highway Trust Fund, which receives revenues for federal-aid highway projects from federal taxes collected on the sale of gasoline and diesel fuel and other federal highway user and excise taxes. Title II of the Act (entitled the "Highway Revenue Act of 1956") raised the federal gasoline tax for autos and diesel fuel for trucks from 2 to 3 cents per gallon, increased taxes for tires and inner tubes (taxed by the pound), and added some new user fees, such as a tax on trucks in excess of 26,000 pounds gross vehicle weight, vehicle registration fees, and other "excise" taxes. The sellers of taxable items such as tires, or certain users such as the interstate truckers, would pay their taxes to the Internal Revenue Service, which then deposited the funds into the Highway Trust Fund. The states would be reimbursed for any amounts spent in excess of the 90 percent federal share after the states actually incur such costs. The trust fund was scheduled to expire in 1972 after the projected completion date for the interstate system. However, interstate highway construction ultimately failed to meet its expected 1969 target date, so Congress extended the expiration date of the trust fund several times (it is currently due to expire on September 30, 1999).[205]

Another key feature of the Federal-Aid Highway Act of 1956 is that Congress gave the federal government the authority to condemn and purchase land for rights-of-way for interstate highways and provided funding to make land purchases. This is important because many states did not have the legal authority nor the funds to acquire land for the interstate system, so the Act allowed the federal government to convey title of the land to the states. States were expected to start interstate projects with their own funds. However, based on years of past experience, it was expected

that many states would have difficulty in raising sufficient revenues to start interstate projects to meet the 1969 completion date under the Act. To compensate for this dilemma, the Act allotted each state a proportion of highway funds as a line of credit that states could withdraw to start interstate construction. The states later billed the federal government after they had incurred construction costs for federal reimbursement.

The 1956 Act created a new Federal Highway Administration (FHWA), with the Bureau of Public Roads becoming one of several departments within the FHWA. John A. Volpe was appointed the first interim FWHA administrator on October 22, 1956, until Bertram D. Tallamy (chairman of the New York Thruway Authority) could take over in 1957. On July 12, 1956, AASHO adopted its initial geometric design standards for the interstates.[206] The Federal Highway Administration, in cooperation with AASHO, set highway design standards as mandated by the 1956 Act for uniformity and safety. The original design required traffic lanes (with a few exceptions) to be at least 12 feet in width and designed for speeds of 70 miles per hour, grades not to exceed 6 percent, and bridge clearances at a minimum of 14 feet. Other geometric and construction standards for the new interstate highways were approved by the U.S. Commerce Department in cooperation with state highway departments. The final design for the interstates was a culmination of decades of input and research from auto clubs, civil engineers, and state and federal highway officials.[207]

While the old U.S. highway system's primary objective was to serve all population centers over 50,000, the new system sought to reduce total mileage and serve fewer cities. The designers projected that fewer interstate highways could efficiently handle the same traffic as under the old system. The interstates adopted a new highway numbering scheme to distinguish itself from the federal aid system. In August 1957, AASHO settled on a new numbering system and a design for route markers for the interstates. The east-west, north-south and even-odd numbering of the U.S. system was simply reversed, so that numbers increase on east-west routes from the southern states to those in the country's northern tier (for example, I-10 travels east-west through the southern states, while the northernmost interstate highway, I-94, serves the northern states). The same is true of routes traveling north-south, with U.S. 1 being bypassed

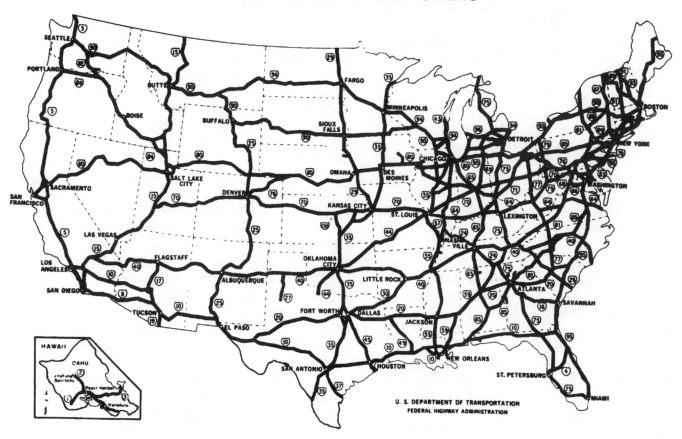

**THE DWIGHT D. EISENHOWER SYSTEM OF
INTERSTATE AND DEFENSE HIGHWAYS**

U. S. DEPARTMENT OF TRANSPORTATION
FEDERAL HIGHWAY ADMINISTRATION

National System of Interstate Highways. The Bureau of Public Roads and AASHO coordinated on the final free-way routing following passage of the Federal-Aid Highway Act of 1956. This map is nearly identical to the routes proposed by BPR in its 1937 report and the Public Roads Administration in 1947. In actuality, the new interstate routes closely follow federal-aid highways that they replaced. The network as approved by Congress was for a 41,000-mile system to be completed in 1969. Additional mileage was added in later years (U.S. DOT/FHWA).

by I-95 on the East Coast and U.S. 101 bypassed by I-5 on the West Coast. Interstate routes intersecting beltway systems encircling major metropolitan areas are assigned their own three-digit numbering by adding a third numeral (an even or odd number depending on the direction of the through route). An example is I-95, which intersects the Washington, D.C., metro area; the D. C. area beltway route is designated as I-495.

The AASHO received approximately 100 suggestions from the states for designs for the interstate highway's new route markers. On August 14, 1957, AASHO decided on a design for interstate highway signs using proposals from Missouri and Texas. The new federal shield, proudly bearing its patriotic red-white-and-blue coloration, firmly es-

tablishes the interstate highway as a truly national system. The design was later patented by AASHO in 1967.[208]

Construction of the interstates began immediately, with vast acreage acquired for new right-of-way. Missouri became the first state to award an interstate highway construction contract under the 1956 Federal-Aid Highway Act. On August 2, 1956, the state awarded three contracts: a 13.3-mile bypass of U.S. 66 in Laclede County; 2.6 miles of I-70 in St. Charles County to bypass U.S. 40; and 0.6 miles of I-70 in downtown St. Louis. The three projects cost a total of $5 million, but would have cost upwards of $74 million today, according to Missouri DOT experts.[209]

Missouri has a competitor to claiming the first

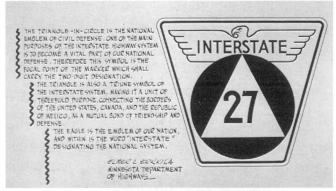

Proposed interstate highway marker designs. The AASHO solicited and received over 100 suggested designs for the new interstate highway route markers from the states. The final design chosen by AASHO was based on proposals from the states of Missouri and Texas. Among the designs submitted were some from the following states: (from left to right): Nevada, Minnesota, Indiana, North Carolina, New York, and Arizona (courtesy, AASHTO and U.S. DOT/FHWA).

Above: Highway officials posing with sign for first interstate highway, Missouri, 1956. The birth of the interstate highway system begins on June 29, 1956, the day President Eisenhower signed the Federal-Aid Highway Act of 1956 into law. Many states immediately put in requests for federal funding for proposed projects that have been delayed for years. On August 2, 1956, Missouri was the first state to officially sign contracts for freeway construction for three projects. One was for a section in Laclede County to bypass U.S. 66, another north of St. Louis in St. Charles County to bypass U.S. 40, and a third in downtown St. Louis. The men in the photo are standing at the site of the I-70 project in St. Charles County. On August 10, 1996, to commemorate the 40th anniversary of these historic projects, the state of Missouri held a public celebration on this site (courtesy, Missouri Department of Transportation).

Above Right: Interstate highway system marker. The AASHO (renamed AASHTO in 1973, to include transportation officials, whether or not they were highway-related) approved the numbering for the interstates, which basically reversed the numbering formula used by the U. S. federal-aid system, and also using three-digit routes for beltway freeways. The AASHO also approved the official marking symbol for the new system, a red-white-and-blue shield with each state shown at the top. The Portland Cement Association placed this advertisement in a 1957 *Life* magazine to promote the highway construction industry's role in building the new interstates, as well as advertising its new "sound-conditioned" concrete (courtesy, Portland Cement Association).

interstate highway, however. Kansas started a freeway project prior to the enactment of the 1956 Highway Act, an 8-mile bypass of U.S. 40 between Topeka and Valencia, and the state had already awarded a contract to complete the project. On September 26, 1956, the Kansas project was finished, making it the first interstate highway project completed under the Federal-Aid Highway Act of 1956. This modest yet important milestone in America's quest for modern roads was marked by a ribbon-cutting ceremony on November 14, 1956, with Governor Fred Hall taking part. Governor Hall dedicated the new I-70 as the country's first section of interstate highway.[210]

High speed travel with maximum safety were the hallmarks of the new system. Civil engineers put their many years of knowledge and experience to the test. The interstates' dimensions called for a wide 180- to 250-foot right-of-way, with grades minimized and sharp curves eliminated. Shoulders and medians were wide and ditches made more gradual to reduce injuries in the event of vehicles leaving the roadway. Cloverleaf interchanges, popularized in some prewar freeway designs, were incorporated into the plans to enable traffic to keep moving at a constant speed near a nationally-set speed limit. Upon completion, the interstate highway system would become the most ambitious road project in world history, surpassing the efforts of the Romans.

The Bureau of Public Roads (and its successor, the Federal Highway Administration) continued to use the Bates Road test facility in Illinois well into the 1950s. Tests were performed to measure thermal and moisture gradients, subgrade friction, and load transfer between slabs. The BPR's testing of concrete pavements in 1923 and 1938, along with the new test data, confirmed that continuously reinforced concrete pavement (CRCP) was a superior surface for longer life. After these tests, continuously reinforced concrete was used almost exclusively in highway projects to follow. While CRCP used wire mesh reinforcement to add strength to pavement, this allowed engineers to reduce pavement thickness, thus saving material and costs. Projects using continuously reinforced concrete were also less expensive than the old thickened-edge types since pavement could be laid much quicker with new machinery, again reducing construction costs. The introduction of the slip form concrete paver required only 25 workers, while at least 100 men were required on a typical paving crew using older methods.[211]

The Federal Highway Administration was aware that the public demanded a superior

Highway officials in Kansas posing with sign, 1956. Kansas has its own claim to being the first state to build an interstate highway. Kansas started construction of portion of future I-70 west of Topeka to bypass old U.S. 40 several months before the passage of the Federal-Aid Highway Act of 1956. Although the state didn't actually award the construction contract for this project until August 31, the final paving was finished on September 26, 1956, making Kansas the first state to complete a project using federal aid under the 1956 Highway Act. Kansas Highway Commissioner Ivan Wassberg wrote the date "9-26-56" in the fresh cement to commemorate this transportation milestone. Pictured from left to right is Ivan Wassberg, George C. Koss (Koss Construction Company), W. S. McDaniels (Assistant State Highway Engineer), and John Beuerlein (Manager, Kansas Division of Koss Construction Company) (courtesy, Kansas DOT).

Top: Laying continuous reinforcement on I-80 project, western Iowa, 1966. After completing the roadbed subbases, the paving crew sets up forms and joints, then lays steel mesh reinforcement. Freeway construction proceeded rapidly in plains states like Iowa. The cost per mile of interstate highways varied greatly. Freeways in urban areas are expensive due to the high price of land acquisition, while in marshy or rugged terrain, blasting highways and tunnels through mountain areas, or additional bridgework greatly increase construction costs (courtesy, U.S. DOT/FHWA).

Bottom: Urban freeway construction. A late 1950s construction site preparing the roadbed through an major U. S. city. The interstates were welcome in virtually every corner of the country, particularly farmers and truckers who rely on long-distance highway transportation. In cities, freeways helped ease traffic congestion but often displaced people while destroying long-established neighborhoods (courtesy, U.S. DOT/FHWA).

Left: Freeway bridge construction. A section of a modern freeway bridge is hoisted into place by a stationary crane obscured by the bridge at right. New, state-of-the-art construction equipment was developed for the interstate system, such as larger earth-moving equipment and cranes (courtesy, U.S. DOT/FHWA).

Right: Construction of twin bridges at Yakima, Washington. Not since the German autobahns has any nation undertaken a major national highway project such as the American interstate highway system. The interstate project was a public works marvel unmatched by previous efforts. Engineers had to build an entirely new system across a vast land area with rugged topography. Outside of Yakima, Washington, planners had to build two bridges across a deep gorge formed by the Yakima River. An elaborate wooden "false-work" was constructed to support the bridge work (courtesy, AASHTO).

freeway system that would be built with the best modern scientific methods available. Americans also wanted the most from their tax dollar and didn't want to see highways become obsolete by the time they were finished. The federal government and the states were poised to spend billions of dollars, and officials felt that they could not afford the embarrassment if interstate highways suffered from premature pavement or bridge failures or design defects. Widespread construction problems could jeopardize public support in the new system, throwing the entire program into disarray and delaying its completion. As the interstate project was just getting started, a July 1960 *Reader's Digest* article entitled "Our Great Big Highway Bungle" claimed that "waste, mismanagement, and outright graft are making a multi-million dollar rat-hole" of the interstate system. State and federal governments had already learned that delays in construction projects always increased costs. Therefore, the FHWA made highway design, construction methods, and use of newer materials among its top priorities.

Top: Completing final surface on new "fresh" on construction of I-465, Indianapolis, 1967. This crew is using new technology in finishing a section of fresh concrete on the eastern leg of the I-465 beltway project outside of Indianapolis, Indiana. The Bureau of Public Roads, AASHTO, and the state DOTs shared their experience and expertise, resulting in more efficient freeway construction (courtesy, U.S. DOT/FHWA).

Bottom: A paving crew on a rural section of I-75, Georgia, 1967. The prosperous 1960s witnessed a dramatic increase in vacation travel, touching off a frenzy of new interstate highway construction across the country. States appeared to be in competition to see who could complete their projects first. Several smaller states with short mileage were able to finish their projects early, while some rural states also made great headway. Construction budgets increased with each passing year due to labor costs and inflation, and the interstate system missed its 1969 target date for completion. By 1967, only two states (Missouri and Ohio) had completed at least one interstate highway from border to border (courtesy, U.S. DOT/FHWA).

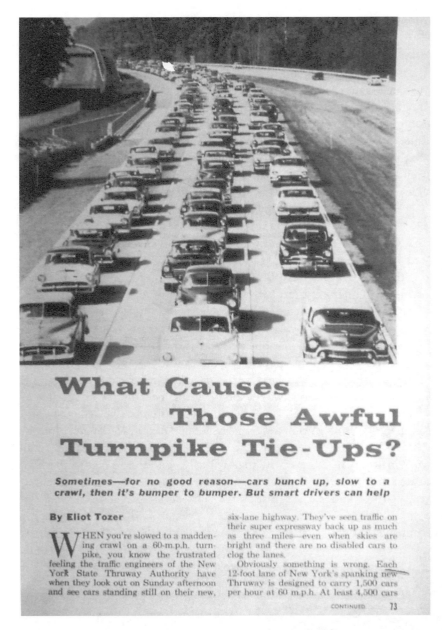

What Causes Those Awful Turnpike Tie-Ups?

Sometimes—for no good reason—cars bunch up, slow to a crawl, then it's bumper to bumper. But smart drivers can help

By Eliot Tozer

WHEN you're slowed to a maddening crawl on a 60-m.p.h. turnpike, you know the frustrated feeling the traffic engineers of the New York State Thruway Authority have when they look out on Sunday afternoon and see cars standing still on their new, six-lane highway. They've seen traffic on their super expressway back up as much as three miles—even when skies are bright and there are no disabled cars to clog the lanes.

Obviously something is wrong. Each 12-foot lane of New York's spanking new Thruway is designed to carry 1,500 cars per hour at 60 m.p.h. At least 4,500 cars

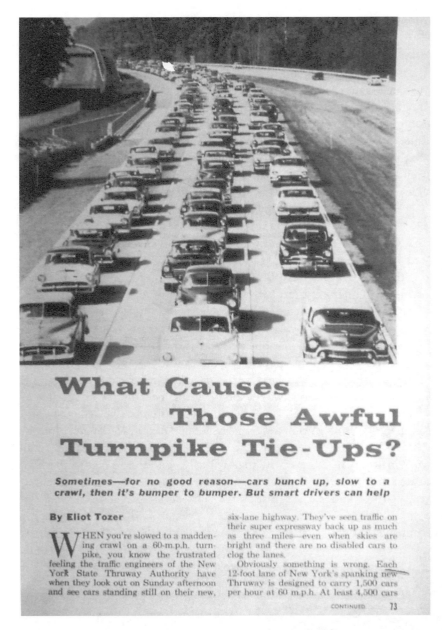CONTINUED 73

"What causes those awful turnpike tie-ups?" Despite interstate construction projects in progress in virtually every state, articles such as this one in *Popular Science* magazine still complained about traffic congestion. In May 1955, *Life* magazine's "Death of the Open Road" cover story predicted a transportation crisis in the 1960s unless the nation built an interstate highway system. This September 1959 article highlights the public's impatience with traffic "tie-ups" (courtesy, *Popular Science* magazine).

The AASHO lent its expertise to the Federal Highway Administration for the interstate highway system. The AASHO built a new test facility near Ottawa, Illinois, in a rural area west of Chicago. From 1958 to 1960, AASHO ran experiments on a test track using six loops to test the effects of trucks on various pavements. The AASHO road tests found that properly graded granular subbases using doweled joints worked best for longer pavement life.

As construction of the interstate highways bypassed some of the old U.S. system, areas adjacent to the new highways were immediately affected. Generations of families and businesses in urban neighborhoods were uprooted to make way for the new freeways. In rural areas, cities and towns on federal aid routes saw a sharp decline in traffic and tourism. Merchants in bypassed areas saw their business drop to a trickle the day following the opening of a new section of interstate. Some businesses relocated to the nearest freeway interchange to survive; those who didn't often were forced to close. Many of the smaller hamlets withered away, becoming little more than ghost towns. In major cities, large areas were cleared and urban neighborhoods uprooted in the path of the interstate.

The politics and economics of interstate highway routing often resulted in low-value properties being condemned, which meant the leveling of housing where the cities' neediest citizens resided. During the New Deal and after the war, major cities began the process of revitalizing aging urban core areas by demolishing substandard housing and replacing them with complexes of high-rise apartment buildings, a process referred to as "slum clearance." Later, urban planners discovered that freeway construction could provide a shortcut way to remove blighted areas. In the 60s, "urban renewal" became the euphemism for this new type of urban planning, skirting the social issues it raised.

The 1950s and 1960s were exciting times to be on the American Road. Motorists were treated to an eclectic mix of down-home versus space-age accommodations, of scary two-lane roads and modern superhighways. The American highway landscape gradually evolved into a cornucopia of new businesses lining the interstates. National brands of motels, restaurants, and gas stations, like pearls connected by a string of nonstop freeways, wholly dependent on the interstate.

The evolution of the American gasoline service station reached its zenith during this era. The number of filling stations peaked by 1970 at 216,959 units.[212] Competition among the major oil companies was fierce, with many regional brands eventually going under. Some companies merged to survive. Some national and independent outlets offered dishes, tableware, and trinkets of all sorts, often using redeemable stamps for free gifts to attract customers. The stations themselves continued to get larger to accommodate more autos for repairs. The independent stations pioneered some trends in the late 1940s and '50s that the big companies didn't copy until the 1970s. In 1947, George Urich, an independent station owner in Los Angeles, opened the nation's first cut-rate self-service filling station. Urich's station had 20 pumps and the first customers didn't seem to mind having to pump their own gas to save a few cents per gallon.

The concept also allowed Urich's patrons to enter and exit the station in just two minutes, roughly half the time it normally takes for a station attendant to serve the motorist. A *Newsweek* article described Urich's station as "Five or six pretty girls in sweaters and slacks, [who] roller skate from island to island making change and collecting. A supervisor in a glass booth directs them by loudspeaker and keeps an eye out for customers violating the no-smoking regulations." The concept was so successful that Urich opened several more locations. The idea soon spread and within a year, approximately 25 self-service stations were operating in the Los Angeles area. *Life* magazine called it the "Gas-A-Teria" and hailed it as "California's newest contribution to the drive-in way of life." Other publications, such as *Business Week*, dismissed the self-service station as a "a strictly local phenomena." However, more self-service stations appeared across the country, prompting irate competitors to resort to desperate tactics. During the early years in business, Urich and other self-service station operators became the target of vandalism and even death threats. The self-serve station nevertheless gained public acceptance, and the concept gained a toe-hold in the gasoline retail market, particularly on the West and East Coasts.[213]

Just as the self-service gas stations were entering the automotive scene, the first multi-pump stations appeared during the postwar period. By 1950, several national brands located on toll roads were large operations, but the megastation of today was again pioneered by risk taking independents. One regional independent that appeared in southern Wyoming called "Little America" was a complex of 55 gas and diesel pumps, with a 300-capacity coffee shop and dining room, a 150-room motel, and a cocktail lounge. There were many others, of course. Truck terminals likewise expanded in size, becoming "truck stops" and later, "travel plazas." A good number of truck stops, such as "The Diamonds" west of St. Louis on U.S. 66, claimed to be the country's largest. Despite all of the changes in highway traveling, one fact remained: Truck stops still had the best food on the highway.

By the 1960s, many brands such as

"Slim Olson—43 Pumps." A portent of things to come, an early multi-pump operation on U.S. 91 in Salt Lake City, Utah. Following World War II, gasoline filling stations began to increase in size, particularly on high-traffic highways. Photo by T. W. Kines, June 1953 (National Archives).

Top: Early self-service station. A rare photo of a self-service filling station in 1950. This independent brand was on Williamson Road in Roanoke, Virginia. The self-service filling station concept was started by George Urich, an independent station owner who opened up the nation's first cut-rate self-service gas station in Los Angeles in 1947. The idea was so successful that he opened several locations, and Urich and others who copied his idea were the object of vandalism and death threats from competitors (National Archives [50-4844]).

Bottom: Truckers terminal on U.S. 1 near South Hill, Virginia. "Simmons Terminal" truck stop offered Pure gasoline and probably good food at its restaurant on U.S. 1, two miles south of South Hill, Virginia. Truck stops were a haven for grizzled truckers and road stories. The size of truck stops, like gas stations, increased over the years into "truck plazas" (National Archives).

Top: Ranch-style Shell station. The Shell Oil Company was one of the first to revamp its station architecture. In the late 1950s, Shell chose the ranch-style design which was much in vogue for homes for its new look. The goal was to make the structure appear less like a service station and more like a home, an idea similar to the cottage-style designs of the 1920s and 1930s (courtesy, Shell Oil Company).

Bottom: Little America Travel Center, Wyoming. By the 1960s, gas stations, particularly on the interstates, became larger in size. A chain of independent stations called "Little America" located along I-80 in southern Wyoming boasted 55 gas and diesel pumps. Calling itself a "travel center," Little America had everything a traveler could want, including a restaurant seating 300, coffee shop and dining room, fountain, cocktail lounge, and a 150-unit motel. Little Americas are still operating currently. This postcard shows how the self-proclaimed "Queen of the Highways" appeared in the early 1960s (author's collection).

Cities Service, Skelly, and others vanished from the road scene due to mergers, victims of steady competition. Sometimes familiar brands were replaced by new ones. Cities Service became Citgo and Skelly merged into Getty. Today, the Getty Oil Company is history. The remaining oil companies scrambled for a slice of the motorist's dollar by continuing to emphasize customer service. Corporate image was becoming foremost in the minds of petroleum CEOs. Some took the more obvious route toward company refurbishment by simply demolishing older filling stations and replacing them with modern station designs to create a newer image. Shell Oil was an early participant, introducing its "ranch style" stations in the late 1950s. Shell continued its station renovation campaign into the 1960s, placing ads in *Life* magazine claiming the Shell didn't want a "grease smeared shack" bearing its company logo. Phillips Petroleum opted for a ultramodern design, a triangular carport supported by an oil derrick-styled pole and a revolving Phillips 66 shield at the top. Mobil streamlined its buildings and logo, with the word "Mobil" given more prominence over its famous Flying Red Horse. Texaco opted for a less austere design, with its green mansard roof to make its stations appear more homelike.

As the speed of highway travel increased, the roadside food industry was also about to get faster. With Kentucky Fried Chicken, A & W, Dairy Queen, and others already firmly entrenched, a second wave of "fast food" restaurants made their debut. The pioneer, of course, was the venerable chain of McDonald's restaurants. In December 1948, Dick and Mac McDonald opened a drive-thru restaurant in San Bernardino, California. Several drive-up restaurants already existed at the time, but they were mainly confined to southern California. The early drive-ups featured female car hops that served customers while they sat in their vehicles. The McDonalds modified the idea and took a slightly different approach that would serve customers quicker and eliminate the need for unnecessary employees. The McDonald brothers named their

restaurants after themselves, and several of the first "McDonald's" restaurants opened up in the Los Angeles area in the early 1950s.[214]

In 1954, a Multimixer salesman from Oak Park, Illinois, named Raymond Kroc visited the McDonald brothers and, after studying their operation, became their franchising agent. On April 15, 1955, Ray Kroc opened the first McDonald's restaurant outside of Southern California, in Des Plaines, Illinois. Kroc believed that an assembly-line format with a limited menu could deliver quality food with even faster service. In July of the same year, another location was

Above: American Icon: The last original McDonald's, Downey, California. In 1948, Dick and Mac McDonald opened a drive-up hamburger stand in San Bernardino, California. After adding several new locations, Illinois salesman Ray Kroc became the McDonalds' franchising agent. Kroc opened the first McDonald's restaurant outside of Southern California in Des Plaines, Illinois, in 1955. With Kroc's sales experience, the chain grew to 100 locations by 1960. In 1972, McDonald's converted its original "golden arches" restaurants with the current architecture to include more inside seating and drive-thru service. The new design helped increase sales dramatically, making McDonald's a Fortune 500 company. Only this Downey, California, golden arches–style outlet survives today and is marked with a plaque designating it a national historic building (courtesy, McDonald's Corporation).

Right: Speedee sign, Downey, California. As the fast-food industry matured, McDonald's found that it needed to convert its original restaurants to drive-thrus to stay ahead of the competition. McDonalds had planned for years to demolish its Downey location, as it was losing about $50,000 per year. Concerned preservationists, area residents and the local chamber of commerce petitioned the fast-food giant to save the remaining golden arches restaurant. The original sign with the "Speedy" mascot is at the Downey McDonald's (courtesy, McDonald's Corporation).

opened in Fresno, California. To promote its faster service to the public, the company adopted a jolly hamburger character named "Speedee" as its mascot for its advertising signs. The company opened 11 additional units in 1956 in the Chicago area and in Southern California. Success continued, and McDonald's had 40 restaurants and $4,446,000 in sales in 1957. By 1960, McDonald's boasted 200 locations nationwide, as its "Look for the Golden Arches" jingle was beginning to air on local radio stations throughout the country. In 1961, Kroc bought out the McDonald brothers for $2.7 million and continued the company's phenomenal growth over the ensuing years.[215]

The 1960s saw a proliferation of new fast-food franchises, all borrowing from Ray Kroc's formula. As McDonald's franchises were spreading throughout the country, its sales were still minuscule compared to Howard Johnson, which had been around since before World War II. In the 1960s, Howard Johnson's sales exceeded the combined total of McDonalds, Kentucky Fried Chicken, and Burger King.[216] The fast-food restaurant, conveniently located at freeway exits, was a perfect match for travel on the interstates.

Construction of the interstates continued in the 1960s, with each state competing to be the first to finish their freeways, or for bragging rights to claim the most modern highways. The East Coast and Southern California led the way, with expressways eight lanes or more wide, with Chicago also joining in. Progress varied greatly from state to state, depending on factors such as politics, funding, and the state's land area. Many of the bigger states with more mileage, particularly in the West, took nearly 25 years to complete their projects. Gasoline was cheap and vacationing by auto was encouraged, and the slogan "See America Best—By Car" was coined by the travel industry to promote tourism. Their efforts were successful, and a record number of Americans took to the road, with total vehicle miles increasing from 719 billion in 1960 to over 1.07 trillion by the decade's end.[217]

In the wild 1960s, the public, particularly younger drivers, wanted cars capable of higher top-end speed and more horsepower. The Detroit car makers responded with the "muscle car." The U.S. auto industry rolled out an array of sporty Chargers, GTOs, and Stingrays, not to mention others that began to stalk the highways. Cubic inches increased, and some models came standard-equipped

with tachometers, roll-bars, and other racing accessories. As the decade progressed, the popularity of auto racing, particularly on the national level, was at its peak. Speed limits began to increase, up to 75 miles per hour on the interstates in some western states. A few mavericks like Montana had no speed limits on state highways. Some experts predicted that 100 mile-per-hour speed limits were just on the horizon. A late–1960s *Parade* magazine article forecast 100 mile-per-hour speeds within ten years.

In the early 1960s, Americans believed that there were almost no limits to what the nation could achieve. President John F. Kennedy promised an American lunar landing by the end of the decade and NASA delivered, one year ahead of schedule. Despite Kennedy's assassination and the Vietnam War, a heady confidence prevailed. Urban riots and campus demonstrations started focusing attention to social issues by the decade's end. As is typical with modern times, nothing continues indefinitely.

The role of the automobile in modern society came into public scrutiny for the first time. The focus shifted from civil rights and war protests to consumer issues such as air, water, noise, or other pollution. Perhaps the nation's extended peacetime prosperity gave America the luxury to embark on an extended excursion into national soul-reaching. Nevertheless, the automobile was beginning to be portrayed as more of a villain during the second half of the century. First, it was safety. Seat belts were installed on the 1964 models. As the auto makers earnestly pursued crash testing, Ralph Nader's landmark exposé, *Unsafe at Any Speed*, raised safety concerns about defective automotive design and its cost to the nation and the driving public in terms of property damage and loss of life. By the late 1960s, as much of the nation's traffic was already being serviced by the new interstates, some critics argued that even the newest highways had built-in design flaws. A 1969 *Life* magazine article blamed many unnecessary accidents on new, as well as old outdated roads. As 1970 approached, crash statistics began to mount in spite of better highways and safer cars. Some of the deadlier highways earned their own grim nicknames. Indiana's U.S. 12 just outside of Chicago-Gary, neglected after being bypassed by I-80 and I-90, came to be called the "Missing Link." The heavily-traveled Dixie Highway (U.S. 25, from Detroit to Miami) became known as the "Dixie Die-way." Motorists cruising

Top: Grand opening of Kentucky Fried Chicken, 1950s. This long line for a grand opening of a new KFC in the 1950s was typical of the enthusiasm generated wherever a new Kentucky Fried Chicken outlet opened. Harland Sanders personally toured the country after the Second World War, signing up potential franchisees by giving them a sample of his famous chicken recipe. The Colonel's "finger lickin' good" cuisine continued to sell well with the public, and the company experienced spectacular growth in the decades following World War II. Above is one of franchise-owner Don De Laria's locations in Minneapolis, Minnesota (courtesy, KFC Corporation).

Right: The Colonel helping a KFC employee. Harland Sanders believed that good food and good service were the two most important ingredients to any successful restaurant. The Colonel routinely visited his restaurants to check up on quality during the 1950s and 1960s. By 1964, with over 600 locations, Sanders sold the business for $2 million and a lifetime job to promote Kentucky Fried Chicken. The Colonel here is giving some helpful tips to a young KFC employee in the 1950s (courtesy, KFC Corporation).

Top Left: KFC logo, (courtesy, KFC Corporation).

Top Right: Dairy Queen logo (courtesy, Dairy Queen International, Inc.).

Middle: A & W logos; 1960s–1990s, and late 1990s (courtesy, A & W Restaurants, Inc.).

Bottom: 1950s-era Dairy Queen. The Dairy Queen company, like many businesses, started using standardized restaurant architecture following World War II. The signs retained the blue-and-white lettering from the original restaurants and added the "Cone with the Curl," the company's longtime trademark. The all-glass building was typical of postwar modern design. This vintage DQ is located at Lexington and Larpenteur Avenues in Roseville, Minnesota (photo by author).

Top Left: Continued postwar prosperity in the 1960s meant steady growth for the travel industry. As Americans enjoyed higher incomes and more leisure time, vacationers took to the road in record numbers. The "See America Best—By Car" campaign (here rendered as "Discover America Best by Car") supported by the travel industry was successful in stimulating tourism (author's collection).

Top Right: Mobil attendant with customer. Public relations ads by the national gasoline brands still focused on customer service in the 1960s. To stay competitive, many filling stations still gave away freebies such as thermometers, ice scrapers, and road maps, while regional and independents gave customers dishes, glassware, and other merchandise with redeemable coupons on each gas purchase (courtesy, Mobil Corporation).

Bottom Left: "Citgo Zzooommm." Many older gasoline brands were forced out of business during the 1950s and 1960s, while new ones were formed through mergers and acquisitions. The "Cities Service" brand was phased out and became Citgo in 1965, while Skelly Oil Company merged with Getty Oil. Citgo kicked off its inaugural advertising campaign with ads such as this, which capitalized on the 1960s obsession with speed (courtesy, Citgo Corporation).

Bottom Right: Ultra-modern Gulf station, 1965. In the 1960s, virtually all design and marketing of consumer and other products was strictly "ultra modern." Gas station architecture likewise went "space age," and a few national brands experimented with bold, flamboyant designs. The Gulf Oil Corporation introduced several eye-catching station styles, such as this one connected with a Holiday Inn in Memphis. However, "Jetsons" architecture died out after the 1960s, when the counterculture movement became a new influence on design and popular culture (courtesy, Chevron Corporation).

at highway speeds on one stretch of the Dixie Highway on the north approach to Dayton, Ohio, could not adjust to the sudden series of stoplight intersections. This four-lane section of old road claimed 340 accidents in 1968 and was given the ominous nickname "Blood Strip." [218] There were other high accident highways too numerous to mention here, which made long-distance driving a white-knuckled experience for many motorists. Annual fatalities exceeded 50,000 for the first time in 1966. The death rate for the years 1966–69 was 27.2 per 100,000, the highest since the late 1930s. The highway carnage resulted from several factors, among them reckless driving behavior inspired by rebellious 1960s attitudes. Average highway speed had been slowing rising for decades, topping 60 mph by 1969. Perhaps the racing stripes and 140-

Top: 1965 Pontiac GTO ad. The muscle car of the 1960s actually began a decade earlier, with each automaker building larger-displacement engines each year. Big-name auto racing was gaining national attention, and Detroit responded with cars worthy of the racetrack. The tiger was a typical sales prop to symbolize power, and was used for Pontiac's GTO, Uniroyal "Tiger Paw" Tires, and gasoline ("Put a Tiger in Your Tank"). Safety reports, rising traffic fatalities, Ralph Nader's book on the Corvair, and an increasing anti-automobile attitude dimmed the muscle car era before emission controls and skyrocketing gas prices ended it. Copyright, General Motors Corporation (used with permission).

Bottom: Phillips 66 station, circa 1965. The Phillips Petroleum Company introduced its own modern standardized station design in the mid–1960s, a gull-wing canopy supported by an "oil derrick" pole topped by a revolving sign. The unique design made Phillips stations easy to spot on highways and freeway exits. This vintage Phillips station is in Sidney, Nebraska, on U.S. 30 (photo by author).

AC spark plug ad, "Cyclone by Cadillac." This ad uses a late 1950s General Motors concept car, the "Cyclone," to fire up enthusiasm for AC's spark plugs and related automotive products. Detroit's Big Three (plus American Motors Corporation) promised the public a new generation of forward-looking designs, and their ad campaigns of the 1960s sought to acclimate buyers with tantalizing new models for the future (copyright, General Motors Corp. Used with permission).

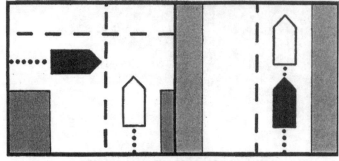

You will. Will he?

Maybe you obey stop signs and signals. Some drivers don't. So never assume the right-of-way blindly. Always protect yourself by driving defensively. ☐ If someone follows you too close, don't speed up. Slow down a little and encourage him to pass. Remember, being in the right isn't enough. You could be dead right.

Watch out for the other guy!

mile-per-hour speedometers played some role. In any case, America's speed curve seemed overdue for some sort of correction.[219]

The federal government got more heavily involved in highway safety during the 1960s in response to public and media pressure. In reality, however, federal highway agencies had been performing road testing and public safety promotions for decades. As early as 1924, Secretary of Commerce Herbert Hoover convened the first National Conference on Street and Highway Safety in Washington, D. C., where over 900 members of police departments, automobile, educational and civic groups met to discuss highway safety and other issues. In the year just prior to the conference, over 22,000 motorists died on America's highways, with 678,000 injured. In November 1963, the Bureau of Public Roads participated in a meeting including law enforcement agencies from Illinois to California to discuss increased patrolling of U.S. 66. The highway's accident rate was well above the national average, despite the fact that much of "Bloody 66" was already bypassed by new interstates.[220]

In March 1964, President Lyndon Johnson asked Secretary of Commerce Luther Hodges to step up safety programs throughout the country by instituting safety spot checks of motorists when necessary. Much of the nation's highway infrastructure was aging, being designed and built decades ago. Bridges especially were neglected and thousands were in poor condition from corrosion and weakened by heavy traffic. Bridge inspections were ordered following the December 15, 1967, collapse of the Silver Bridge (U.S. 31) between Point Pleasant, West Virginia, and Gallipolis, Ohio, in which 46 people perished. The Federal-Aid Highway Act of

Public service safety ad. During the late 1960s and early 1970s, traffic fatalities and injuries reached levels not seen since the late 1930s and early 1940s, as the death rate hit 30 per 100,000 and total deaths exceeded 50,000 annually. Public service announcements on television, radio, and the print media, using catchy slogans such as "Look Out for the Other Guy," were put out by the National Safety Council to educate the public on highway safety (courtesy, National Safety Council).

Top: Aldrich Cheese Mart, Aldrich, Minnesota. A typical family-run business just off U. S. 10 in Aldrich, Minnesota, population 90 when this picture was taken in 1960. Many "tourist traps" selling "authentic" Indian curios, souvenirs, and other novelties have come and gone over the years, but the Aldrich Cheese Mart is still going strong today (author's collection).

Bottom: Ginkgo Gem Shop, Vantage, Washington. "Rock shops" were a favorite stopping place for "rock hounds" in search of gemstones, dinosaur fossils, and Indian arrowheads for their collections. For a small fee, some rock shops provided customers with a shovel and allowed them to dig for their own rocks at a large rock pile located on the premises. Rock collecting is largely a thing of the past, so gem shops are rare today. The Ginkgo Gem Shop was an extremely popular stop in Vantage, Washington, located in central Washington state (author's collection).

1968 established National Bridge Inspection Standards, and a 1970 federal-aid act created the Special Bridge Replacement Program to help replace old bridges.[221]

Aesthetics was also becoming a big issue with a public becoming less enchanted with the automobile. The country's car culture was blamed for being the chief cause of air pollution, blighting the landscape with gaudy highway billboards, scarring neighborhoods and gobbling up farmland. Environmentalists and anti-auto advocates pursued their case, while the media often portrayed the auto

as having a negative impact on modern society. In 1965, at the urging of Lady Bird Johnson, Congress passed a measure cryptically titled "Control of Outdoor Advertising." The purpose of the new law, later called the "Highway Beautification Act of 1965," as stated in Title I, was to "control" outdoor advertising on interstate highways and the primary system, and "to protect the public investment in such highways, to promote the safety and recreational value of public travel, and to preserve natural beauty." The law required all outdoor advertising signs, displays, and devices within 660

Ultra-modern hotels, 1960s. Lodging facilities, such as filling stations, restaurants, and other vestiges of late–20th century life, gained in size during the 1960s. Pictured are four examples of '60s-style architecture in motel designs.

Top, Left to Right: **The Thunderbird Resort Motels had locations in several major cities, this one being on Ocean Blvd. and 185th Street in Miami, Florida. The sprawling Colony 7 Motor Inn (with Schraffi's Restaurant), was on the Baltimore-Washington Parkway midway between the two cities, and adjacent to the Laurel Race Track.**

Bottom, Left to Right: **The Franklin Motor Inn, near the Schuylkill Expressway in downtown Philadelphia, had a 300-room capacity. The Airport Marina Hotel was adjacent to the Los Angeles International Airport, offering 535 soundproofed rooms with tropical pool area in the inner courtyard (author's collection).**

feet of the nearest highway right-of-way to be removed. Exempt were signs which promoted natural wonders, and scenic and historical attractions. The spacing and size of future advertising signs beyond 660 feet of the right-of-way was to be decided by mutual agreement between the states and the FHWA. Congress appropriated $40 million as "just compensation" to sign owners forced to remove or cover advertising signs, and a January 1, 1970, deadline was set for states' compliance. Under the act, all billboards, barns, and other outdoor advertising had to either be taken down or painted over. The result was the destruction and removal of over 600,000 highway billboards across the country.[222]

Title II of the Act, entitled "Control of Junkyards," was aimed at regulating scrap metal yards near highways. Auto junk yards, like highway billboards, were the villains of the "Beautify America" activists whose agenda was to protect the public from the sight of heaps of ugly, rusted metal. Like Title I, Title II affected interstate and primary highways, and required scrap yards, junkyards and automobile graveyards to "be screened by natural objects, plantings, fences, or other appropriate means so as to not be visible from the main traveled way of the system, or shall be removed from sight." The law mandated that any such business within 1,000 feet of the highways designated in the Act is within its jurisdiction, and also as in Title

I, states which failed to comply stood to lose 10 percent of their federal highway funds. The Congress allocated $40 million to pay for costs to fence off or hide offending junkyards. Today, the absence of outdoor billboards and scrap yards on federal-aid and interstate highways confirms the efficiency of the federal government's effort to enhance the quality of highway scenery for the traveling public, although some might argue against its merits.[223]

In the mid–1960s, Congress decided to unify all transportation agencies into one cabinet-level department. On October 15, 1966, President Johnson signed the act creating the new Department of Transportation. On April 1, 1967, the USDOT's first secretary, Alan Boyd, led an inaugural ceremony on the Capitol Mall. The Department of Transportation, which included the Federal Highway Administration, became the fourth-largest federal department. Several Commerce Department agencies, including the Bureau of Public Roads, the National Traffic Safety Agency, and the National Highway Safety Agency, were merged into the FHWA. The Department of Transportation was reorganized in 1970, eliminating its bureau system, including the Bureau of Public Roads. Currently, the U.S. DOT contains agencies related to transportation, such as the Federal Railroad Administration, the Federal Aviation Administration, the Urban Mass Transit Administration, and the Coast Guard.[224]

*Chief Administrative Officers from
Office of Road Inquiry to the
Federal Highway Administration[225]*

General Roy Stone	(1893-1899)	Frank C. Turner	(1969–1972)
Martin Dodge	(1899–1905)	Norbert Tiemann	(1973–1977)
Logan Waller Page	(1905–1918)	William M. Cox	(1977–1978)
Thomas H. MacDonald	(1919–1953)	Karl S. Bowers	(1978–1980)
Francis V. du Pont	(1953–1955)	John S. Hassell, Jr.	(1980–1981)
Charles D. Curtis	(1956)	Ray A. Barnhart	(1981–1987)
John A. Volpe	(1956–1957)	Robert E. Farris	(1987–1989)
Bertram D. Tallamy	(1957–1961)	Thomas D. Larson	(1989–1993)
Rex Whitton	(1961–1966)	Rodney E. Slater	(1993–1997)
Lowell K. Bridwell	(1966–1969)	Kenneth R. Wykle	(1997)

The Interstate Era
(1970-2000)

By 1970, as the interstate system slowly neared completion, a new era of limits was slowly becoming evident for the automobile in America. By 1970, auto insurance companies refused to insure certain models of high-performance muscle cars due to high accident rates. Detroit responded by reducing engine size and detuning the new models for less horsepower. The year 1973 was a major turning point for the American highway. Prices for petroleum products, including gasoline and diesel, were at historic lows. Cheap oil had discouraged domestic producers from exploring for further reserves, either in the United States or elsewhere. By the early 1970s, a third or more of the nation's oil was imported. The price of gasoline ranged between 20 and 30 cents a gallon, the same price as it was in the 1940s. Even after adjusting for inflation and higher state and federal taxes, motor fuel prices were at historic lows in the early 1970s. Cutthroat competition between service stations caused occasional "gas wars" to break out, driving prices below 20 cents per gallon. In October 1973 the Organization of Petroleum Exporting Countries (OPEC), a little-known group of nations with high oil exporting capacity, met and doubled the price of crude oil from a ridiculously-low $2.50 per barrel (55 gallons) to $5.00 per barrel. In response to the Israeli victory in the Yom Kippur War in the Mideast, Saudi Arabia and other OPEC states also cut off shipments of crude oil to the United States and its allies. The effect was immediate. Within weeks, filling stations across the country started running short of gas and many were forced to close, some permanently. When stations closed, those that remained open were deluged by desperate customers. The infamous gas lines of the 1970s formed.

A crisis atmosphere gripped the nation's capital as the oil shortage started to affect industry. Would the country make it through the winter? If the embargo were prolonged, would national security be at risk? What about the farm sector? The country was in a vulnerable position since it would take years for find new oil reserves. The only short-term answer was to curtail energy usage. Within weeks of the oil cut-off, President Nixon and the Congress passed a series of measures to get the nation on the road to energy independence. The Energy Petroleum Allocation Act of 1973 and the Emergency Daylight Savings Time Conservation Act of 1973 were America's early attempts to save energy in the brave new world of petroleum politics.

On January 2, 1974, President Nixon signed into law the Emergency Highway Energy Conservation Act, which instituted the mandatory nationwide 55 mile per hour speed limit on all state and interstate highways. The FHWA released testing data in November 1973 showing that reducing

Erecting the double-nickels on an interstate freeway. The 1960s came to an official end in the fall of 1973, when the Arab oil embargo quadrupled oil prices from $3 to $12 a barrel, doubling pump prices and causing shortages that disrupted commerce. Americans curtailed their driving habits and the travel industry suffered a minor recession as all unnecessary travel was avoided to save fuel. Many conservation efforts were instituted, some more symbolic than helpful, such as turning off alternating freeway lighting and turning thermostats down a few degrees. On January 2, 1974, President Richard Nixon signed the Emergency Highway Energy Conservation Act, which limited speeds on all roads and highways to 55 miles per hour. Here a highway crew is replacing a 70 mph sign with the new "double nickels" (courtesy, U.S. DOT/FHWA, FHWA by *Day*).

speeds from 70 to 50 miles per hour produced a 30 percent savings in fuel costs. From October 1973 until mid–1974, when OPEC finally resumed oil exports to the United States, America and other high energy consuming countries had learned a hard lesson on the dangers of oil dependency. The 1973–74 Arab oil embargo and the doubling of pump prices to over 50 cents per gallon caused a temporary dip in auto travel and a new national awareness of the need for fuel conservation. Gas lines were a wake-up call to a nation brought up on the idea of limitless resources. Government-sponsored ads exhorted the public and industry to save energy. The almost warlike national zeal was faintly reminiscent of the World War II rationing days. Home thermostats in winter were to be turned down to 68 degrees Fahrenheit (66 at night), municipalities turned off alternating freeway lights and numerous other small steps were taken to reduce energy consumption.

There were other changes for the American automobile following the gas shortages. Congressional legislation in 1973 required that automobile bumpers had to absorb at least a five-mile-per-hour impact. In 1975, Congress forced Detroit to start building cars with average fleet fuel mileage that increased annually, up to 27.5 miles per gallon by a target date of 1985, plus meeting new air emissions standards. The result was the downsizing of models and the disappearance of others, such as Roadrunner and Challenger. Some sporty cars, such as the Corvette, Mustang and Camaro Z-28, were reduced to shadows of their predecessors. Not everyone was in favor of these trends. The "double nickel" speed limit cut into truckers' profits, inviting speeding. The advent of radar detectors and citizen-band radios to warn drivers of highway patrols were some motorists' answer to the 55-mph speed limit. However, one consequence of the oil embargo was a sharp 16 percent drop in traffic fatalities from 1973 to 1974, and a gradual decrease in accident rates through the present day.

Although the 41,000-mile interstate system was slated for completion by 1970 under the 1956 Highway Act, only 28,000 miles were finished by the end of the 1960s. By the early 1970s, the majority of the nation's long-distance auto and truck traffic plied the interstates and the old U.S. system became limited to local use. As sections of interstates were opened throughout the country, residents adjacent to the new freeways witnessed an odd transformation. Previously jammed thoroughfares became ghostly quiet the very day they were bypassed by a new piece of interstate. In 1974, I-35 was mostly completed from Duluth, Minnesota, to the Mexico border at Laredo, Texas, except for an a 26-mile section northeast of Kansas City between Bethany and Winston, Missouri. Heavy freeway traffic on I-35 was suddenly funneled onto U.S. 69, creating a slow bumper-to-bumper caravan of cars and trucks. Passing was out of the question and drivers needed every bit of concentration to steer through the numerous narrow bridges while avoiding vehicles on the left. As the single-file columns of cars and trucks approached the beginning of old U.S. 69, a local billboard warned drivers of this dangerous stretch of highway, claiming that "many have died on the road ahead." When this section of I-35 was completed the following year, U.S. 69, like other federal-aid highways, went into quiet retirement.

The interstates and growth of auto travel was the death knell for train travel. By the 1970s, even federally-subsidized Amtrak had few profitable routes. The interstates' standard green-and-white-lettered signs directing motorists to the nearest gas, food, or lodging made travel easy. Driving was almost as effortless as watching television from your living room sofa. Nearly every creature comfort could be found just a short distance off the nearest interchange. Today's new highway oasis is the freeway interchange, clustered with today's national franchises of mega-stations, quick food, and convenient sleeping quarters.

The transition from the old two-lane U.S. system to the modern interstate was not without its detours. Local opposition, especially in urban areas, slowed construction, and delays increased the cost of freeway projects. The new interstates were not having much impact on the climbing fatality rate in the late 1960s and early 1970s. From 1970 to 1973, the death rate averaged 26.5 per 100,000, and total fatalities reached a disturbing 55,000 per year. Average freeway speeds peaked at a record 64 miles per hour.[226] But with some interstates posting speeds at 75 mph in some western states, who could blame the driver for taking some liberties with Detroit's four-barrel land cruisers? An endless modern highway designed for high speeds and gas at 1940s prices were a prescription for death on the open highway. The future of America's car culture seemed limitless.

The shock caused by the oil embargo and jump in pump prices caused motorists to curtail their driving habits for a short period. During the past 100 years, the number of vehicles on the road and miles driven have been increasing steadily. Annual vehicle mileage, likewise, continues to climb, except for only three periods: 1932–33, 1942–45, and 1973–74. Suddenly, highway travel took on a more serious tone during the 1970s.[227]

Today's interstate highway system has taken on a very standardized, homogenized appearance. Some would call it the "Blanding of America," while to others, it's merely "progress." The late Charles Kuralt of "On the Road" fame, reflecting on interstate travel, remarked that you can drive from coast to coast on the interstates and still not see a thing. The basic function of interstate travel is to get from Point A to Point B in as short a time as possible, with scenery a secondary consideration. The gasoline filling station had turned into giant self-serve operations. The experience of the roadside meal is now mainly fast food, dominated by the national chains. Competition has always been keen between the industry leader, McDonald's, and the Burger Kings, Arby's, and others, and the push to increase sales per restaurant led to the drive-thru concept. In 1972, McDonald's demolished all of its original "Golden Arches" restaurants to make way

Opposite Top: **Gasoline Prices, 1940–Present. Source:** *Statistical Abstract of the United States* **(author's collection).**

Opposite Bottom: **Motor Vehicle Speeds, 1945–Present. Source:** *Statistical Abstract of the United States* **(author's collection).**

Gasoline Price per Gallon

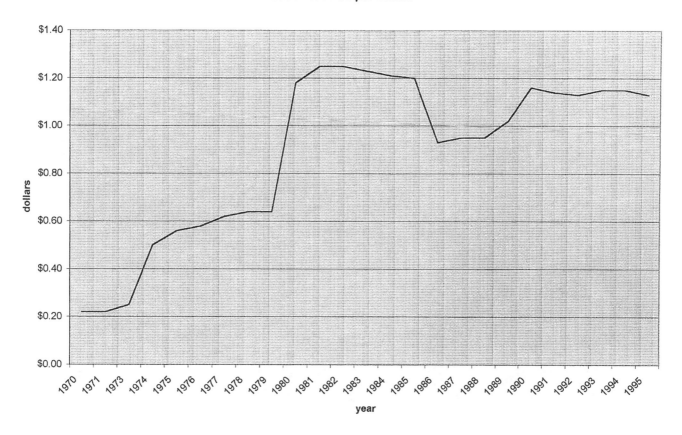

Average Motor Vehicle Speeds

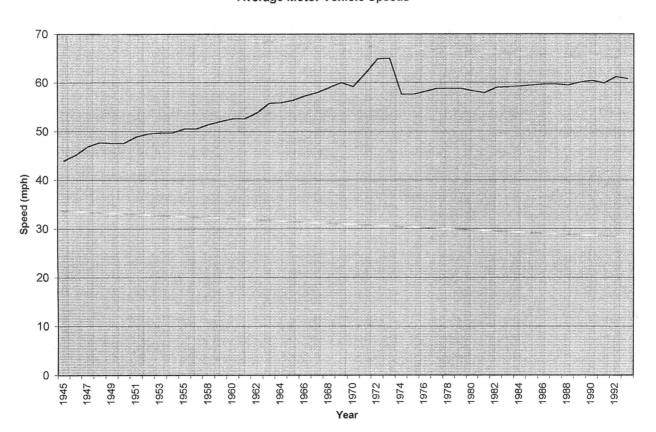

State and Federal Gasoline Taxes

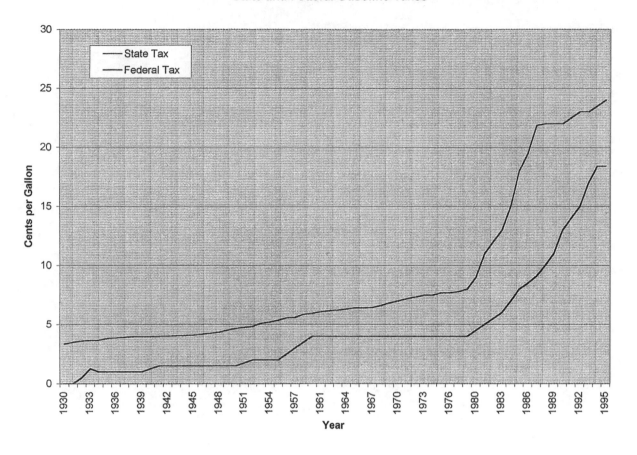

Number of Filling Stations in the U.S.

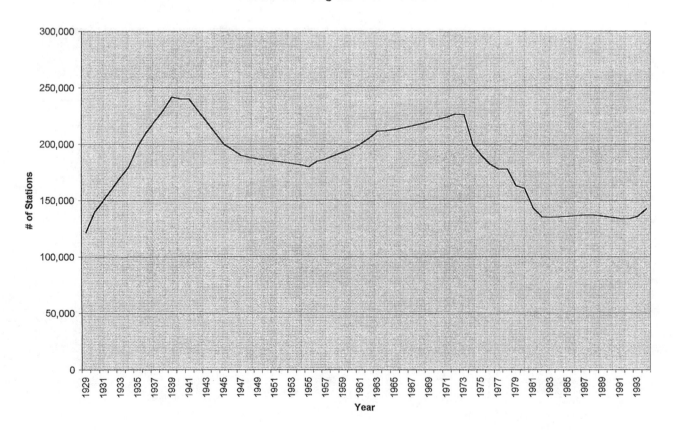

for the first drive-thru design of the current style with the sloping wooden mansard roofing popular in the 1970s. Drive-thru sales now have become an indispensable portion of today's fast food chains' profits. Only a few original McDonald's have survived, such as one in Downey, California, which was spared thanks to persistent efforts by local residents and historical preservationists. In addition to food, finding a place to stay for the night is now just a short jump off the freeway.

The increase in gasoline and diesel prices following the oil embargo had repercussions through the remainder of the 20th century. The profit margin for fuel sales being slim, labor costs were kept to a minimum by gas stations converting to self service. Today, only a few isolated stations offer full service. Most consumers seem willing to save time and money pumping their own gas. The oil companies discontinued the decades-old practice of giving away complimentary highway maps, while many also stopped producing their own maps, relying instead on popular cartographers such as Rand McNally. The modern era of consumer empowerment has made the gas station stop an efficient but more impersonal experience. Thus, the 1970s brought to an end to the era of the friendly service station attendant.

Many filling stations from 1970 to the present discontinued auto towing and garage services, focusing mainly on high-volume gas sales at cut-rate prices, along with miscellaneous auto-related products. The gas station in the last several decades copied the success of the convenience stores such as 7-Eleven that started sweeping the country in the late 1960s. Today's filling station most likely resembles a small store selling marked-up food and other items. The number of filling station outlets in the United States will never again reach its pinnacle of 1973, as competition forced the closure of the least efficient stations. Current gas station design has no "design" per se; today's models are bland buildings with the typical oversized canopy to protect the customer from the elements. The independent mom and pop stations were the first to be forced out of business. After peaking at 226,000

gasoline stations in 1972, approximately 80,000 units closed for good, many soon after the 1973–74 oil embargo. By the mid–1990s, approximately 140,000 filling stations remained.[228] The trend toward fewer and larger filling stations reflects a national economic phenomenon, as family farms are absorbed by agribusiness and mergers and acquisitions continue. National franchising in the restaurant and lodging industry likewise has resulted in more uniform, reliable service, but fewer choices. But, such is the price of progress.

Several more positive trends will be shaping the highways in the years to come. At the urging of preservationists and others interested in highway aesthetics, the U.S. Department of Transportation and state and local transportation officials are working to preserve important vintage roads and bridges. The National Park Service has designated some streets and roads as National Historical Landmarks. Roads under historical protection, such as Bellevue Avenue in Newport, Rhode Island, are being recognized as important to the nation's history and are being repaired instead of replaced. Bricks streets, old concrete bridges and other rare relics of the transportation past are being restored to original condition. Connecticut's Merritt Parkway underwent a renovation in the early 1990s as the parkway celebrated its 50th anniversary. Under the direction of the Connecticut DOT, the Parkway's character was preserved and its ornamented stone bridges restored to original condition.

The latest trend in new highway construction, particularly bridge design, is the retro look. The American public's infatuation with modern, sleek jet age designs in the 1950s and 1960s, from architecture to autos, has been replaced with a more earthbound flavor that is a throwback to earlier times. By the early 1970s, architecture was the first to change, as homes, even McDonald's restaurants, sported the wood shingle look, and home interior, appliances and other furnishings adopting "natural" earth tone colors like "avocado" and "harvest gold." Today, the colors may be different (plum and hunter green) but the emphasis is definitely away

Opposite Top: **Federal and State Gasoline Taxes, 1930–Present. Source:** *Statistical Abstract of the United States* **(author's collection).**

Opposite Bottom: **Number of Gasoline Filling Stations, 1929–1990. Source:** *Statistical Abstract of the U.S.* **(author's collection).**

Top: Motel 6, Portland, Oregon. A latecomer to the lodging business, Motel 6 opened its first location in Santa Barbara, California, in 1962. It was the start of a second wave of new motel chains, all striving to gain a piece of the burgeoning tourism industry during the 1960s and 1970s. The company chose the name "Motel 6" since their original room rates were only $6 a night. As this book goes into publication, the Motel 6 chain (headquartered in Dallas, Texas) now claims 800 locations in 48 continental states (author's collection).

Bottom: McDonald's restaurant with post–1972 architecture. In 1972, McDonald's made a major decision to expand its restaurants' capacity by adding drive-thru service. This McDonald's, with its mansard-style roof popular in the 1970s, was located just off of I-35 in southern Iowa and is shown as it appeared in July 1976 (author's collection).

from the cold, stark look of populuxe style. Building materials of wood, stone and brick are replacing steel, glass and plastic. The look of future cities suggested in General Motors' visions of the city of 1960 and the year 2000 never came to pass (at least not yet).

It appears that today's "style" has come full circle to 1900. The Victorian era's elaborate ornamentation in architecture, clothing, and virtually every manufactured good is seeing a bit of a resurgence. Architecture of the last several decades has moved away from utilitarian, featureless construction. Some building designs have copied the streamlining–art deco motifs of 50 years ago, with a modern twist. Highway planners have been influenced by the current trends and are designing new bridges, highways and land adjacent to roadways. Modern bridges of the past 30 years are plain, slab-sided concrete types, which are perhaps safer than past designs, but lack beauty or aesthetic imagination. In most instances, when crossing a scenic river or ravine, cement guard rails on "jersey barrier" bridges block the view of motorists. Some of the Federal Highway Administration's latest bridges, however, are made of wood, metal, stonework, or some combination, with openings in the bridge's railing so that passing motorists can enjoy the scenery. New bridges in many urban areas are concrete but are faced with stonework, resembling those of the first urban parkways of the 1920s and 1930s.

Federal and state highway engineers and planners have created a vast network of highways that, despite its critics, occasionally scores a few artistic points. The American Society of Civil Engineers (ASCE) named the Dwight D. Eisenhower System of Interstate and Defense Highways one of the "Seven Wonders of the United States," which also include the Panama Canal, Hoover Dam, and the Golden Gate Bridge. Bridges have long been granted honors for design. As far back as the 1930s, organizations such as the American Institute of Steel Construction (AISC) have bestowed awards to bridges noted for beauty, innovation and unique style. In 1936, AISC gave top honors to New York City's Triborough Bridge as the most beautiful bridge in the category of "monumental size," with the hurricane deck bridge over Sage Arm of Lake of the Ozarks winning the medium size class, and the Astoria Boulevard Bridge over Grand Central Parkway in Long Island, New York, taking the small span class. De-

Stuckey's Restaurant, 1970s. This photo shows a typical Stuckey's with its distinctive green roofing. In 1964, Pet, Inc., bought out the Stuckey's chain and kept some of the Stuckey family on as employees. Pet, Inc., lost interest in the restaurants, particularly after Bill Stuckey, Sr., passed away in 1977. The chain's fortunes hit a low point, with many locations closing. However, Bill Stuckey, Jr., and a group of investors bought the Stuckey's name back from Pet in 1985 and resurrected the franchise. Today, Stuckey's has over 100 locations that are still selling the same pecan rolls and other treats on which the company's reputation was built (courtesy, Stuckey's Corporation).

spite the Great Depression, 1936 was a banner year for new bridge openings. The 1,380-foot Tribor-

Modern Mobil station with Flying Red Horse. An example of what some would call "bland" service station architecture. The modern gas station is mainly self-service, although you can still get full service in rare cases. The oil shortages of 1973–74 and 1979–80 increased competition between gas stations, further reducing the profit margin on fuel sales. Many national brands forced owner-operators to abandon auto servicing as a portion of their business, and many stations have been closed and demolished. Some locations have been replaced by a smaller building housing a convenience store (photo by author).

The last several decades have seen increasing public concern among preservationists and others over freeway noise and the destruction of neighborhoods and open land by highway construction. The Federal Highway Administration has responded with freeway designs that result in minimal disruption to urban neighborhoods, while in rural areas today's interstates are built to complement the surrounding terrain and preserve natural habitat whenever possible. A recent urban freeway project in Phoenix is one example of the FHWA's new emphasis on reducing the adverse impact of highways on people. The Papago Freeway (I-10) through Phoenix, completed in 1990, features a depressed roadway with 19 cross-bridges which allows as much traffic as possible to pass over the freeway. The use of multiple overpasses reduces traffic congestion on city streets, especially during rush hour. The series of bridges on Phoenix's north side also forms a large park, and a beautiful arch bridge carries motorists and pedestrians over the freeway on Central Avenue, the city's historic main thoroughfare. A four-level omni-directional I-10/I-17 interchange moves traffic effortlessly, using 12 ramps and 347 support piers. Often referred to as "The Stack," the interchange is Arizona's first fully-directional interchange.[231]

In St. Paul, Minnesota, the last five-mile link of I-35 through the city was halted for nearly two decades by a lawsuit started by a local group calling itself "RIP 35-E." Residents of historic Summit Avenue/Crocus Hill objected to the added noise and pollution a freeway would bring as the proposed freeway passed by their neighborhoods. In the late 1980s, a compromise was reached with the state's DOT. The revised plan was a four-lane, 45 mile-per-hour parkway limited to vehicles weighing under 9,000 pounds gross weight. The roadway is depressed as it passes historic neighborhoods and paved with asphalt instead of concrete to minimize road noise. The freeway uses sound barriers along other portions of the route and extensive landscaping in the median and shoulder areas, with a varied mixture of trees and shrubs, some varieties chosen for their beautiful autumn colors.[232]

ough Bridge had some formidable competition, such as the Henry Hudson Bridge over the Harlem River (an 800-foot hingeless arch design), the West Bay crossing of the San Francisco–Oakland Bay Bridge, and the Fore River Bridge in Massachusetts, a 219-foot double bascule.[229] The Federal Highway Administration currently gives annual awards for bridge design.

Bridges of yesterday such as the Triborough Bridge appear antique by modern design standards. Today's bridges of monumental size support huge bridge decks designed to carry more and heavier vehicles, while spanning longer distances. In 1980, when a freighter struck one of the piers on Tampa, Florida's I-275 bridge across Tampa Bay, builders simply replaced it with an engineering work of art. The new bridge was the first cable-stayed bridge in the Western Hemisphere. The bridge's suspension design had a broad bridge deck supported by parallel cables suspended from two mammoth towers. Opened in 1987, the "Sunshine Skyway Bridge" has been praised for its graceful beauty. Louisiana's Hale Boggs Bridge, opened in 1983, is another fine example of cable-stayed bridges.[230]

Many examples of the FHWA's new policy to improve highway aesthetics are found in the western states. In areas where interstate freeways need to cross vast gorges and mountain ranges, the latest designs minimize the highway's grade, a big help for autos and loaded-down campers and, particularly, trucks. The amount of earth and rock removed during the history of the construction of the interstate system must be a mind-boggling figure. When the state of Maryland built I-68 to bypass U.S. 40 and the Old National Road, over 3.5 million cubic yards of rock were blasted to make a spectacular cut through Sideling Hill. Colorado's I-70 through the heart of the Rocky Mountains crosses some of the most formidable terrain in the country. Engineers built the Eisenhower Memorial Tunnel (longest in the interstate system) to bypass old U.S. 6 as it crosses the continental divide at 11,992-foot Loveland Pass. Further to the west, I-70 through Glenwood Canyon follows the Eagle River without altering the topography of this scenic area. Other excellent examples of environmentally-sensitive highways are I-15 through the Virgin River Gorge in northwestern Arizona and I-70 through eastern Utah over the San Rafael Swell.[233]

Modern highway designers are taking greater care in designing roads to protect wildlife. Several interstates already built were designed to allow wildlife to cross under the roadway to avoid collisions with vehicles. Florida's Everglades Parkway was a two-lane toll road that cut through the Everglades with little regard to the environment. When the road became part of I-75 and widened to four lanes to conform to inter-

"Environmentally sensitive" freeway through Glenwood Canyon, Colorado. The planners for interstate freeways were skilled at designing the safest and fastest highway system to date. However, leveling the area around freeways to provide for the minimum 660-foot right-of way makes for dull scenery. After several decades of using interstate freeways, the public noticed that freeway construction sometimes damaged the natural environment and rendered the adjacent landscape unattractive for travelers. The Federal Highway Administration now considers environmental and aesthetic factors in current freeway planning. A good example of the FHWA's present policy is the 11-mile segment of I-70 through the Glenwood Canyon in Colorado. Planners for the Colorado DOT and FHWA designed the freeway to follow the contours of Glenwood Canyon and not disrupt the area's natural drainage. Notice that the upper lanes are elevated and run above the lower segment in some places to avoid additional removal of rock from the canyon (courtesy, U.S. DOT/FHWA).

Hawaii's H-3, 1997. For decades, Hawaii needed a freeway to connect Honolulu and Pearl Harbor to the Kaneohe Marine Corps Air Station and the towns of Kaneohe and Kailua. However, the Koolau Mountains were a huge obstacle, and the only way across them was a hairpin two-lane highway. The Statehood Act of 1960 authorized a highway of interstate specifications with funding from the FHWA. Designated H-3 (Hawaii's own numbering system for interstate freeways), the project is a textbook case on how government regulations greatly add to freeway construction costs. A federally-mandated environmental impact statement alone took 20 years. The new freeway had to avoid the Marine Omega radar station, long sections had to be elevated, and an expensive state-of-the-art tunnel had to be built. When H-3 finally opened on December 12, 1997, 37 years and $1.3 billion later, the result was a masterfully built freeway that will last for generations, as well as being sensitive to the 50th state's natural beauty (courtesy, U.S. DOT/FHWA).

Some interstate highways have actually added to their natural surroundings. When I-80 was built along the Platte River in Nebraska in the 1960s, planners excavated sand and other materials adjacent to the right-of-way for fill and other uses. The pits left behind gradually filled with water, forming a string of over 50 lakes along the freeway. In a state with few lakes, these man-made lakes are a mecca for fishing, boating, swimming, and other outdoor recreation. In North Dakota, local conservationists convinced highway planners of I-94 west of Bismarck to design the freeway as part of Sweet Briar and Crown Butte dams. The result is two large lakes which are an important oasis for waterfowl in the state's drier western region.

The Federal Highway Administration, in recognition of the vital role that tourism plays in many areas, started a program designating certain highways of historic or scenic significance as "National Scenic Byways" in the 1980s. Since the federal government owns approximately 30 percent of the land area of the United States, the U.S. Department of Transportation has looked beyond adding to and maintaining highways and to focusing on ways the FHWA can aid individuals and businesses who rely on the highway system for their livelihoods. Surveys show that the tourism and travel industry constitutes the largest employers in 11 states, and the second or third highest employer in no less than 34 states. In 1994, the U.S. DOT started a new

state standards, planners designed tunnels and underpasses so that the endangered Florida panther and other animals can migrate under the freeway unharmed. The new "Alligator Alley" also allows natural water drainage, a major problem in south Florida as many roads and other manmade development have disrupted natural water drainage.[234]

scenic highway program in response to public interest in preserving some of the nation's older highways. That year, Transportation Secretary Federico Pena presented the DOT's "Scenic Byways Advisory Committee Report" to Congress. The report proposed designating a few chosen routes (usually

U.S. federal-aid highways) for preservation. Among the routes protected under the plan is Oatman Road, a lonely stretch of Route 66 between Kingman, Arizona, and Needles, California. Across the country, the FHWA has started posting road signs to mark these routes for travelers. Examples of some highways designated as National Scenic Byways include the Blue Ridge Parkway (Virginia, North Carolina), Natchez Trace Parkway (Mississippi, Tennessee), Going-to-the-Sun Highway (Montana), Clara Barton Parkway (Maryland), and Grand Tetons Road (Wyoming). The program has been expanded to other agencies. The Bureau of Land Management has named over 60 "Back Country Byways" covering over 3,000 miles of beautiful scenery. The National Park Service has approximately 3,000 miles of roads that meet the criteria to become "All American Roads" and "National Scenic Byways." The U.S. Forest Service has also set aside 7,000 miles of highways in 34 states as "National Forest Scenic Byways." Even the Bureau of Indian Affairs has a program and is in the process of reviewing over 5,000 miles of highways that may be preserved for future generations of travelers.[235]

Another change that will be noticed on future highways may be the conversion of road signs from the current English system to the International System of Measurements (i.e., metric). The federal government and the Congress have been working on metric conversion since the 1970s when legislation required the states and all federal agencies to convert by 1980. To acclimate the public to the metric system, the Federal Highway Administration posted speed limit and mileage signs on the interstates in both English and metric units and all newly-manufactured motor vehicles were required to add kilometers per hour on speedometers. The effort stalled, however, due to resistance from the public and industry, and the program was temporarily abandoned. A few years later, Congress resurrected its metric conversion program, including a provision in the 1988 Omnibus Trade and Comprehensiveness Act. The 1988 Act hoped that combined federal and state conversion would encourage industry to change to metric. In 1991, President Bush issued an executive order requiring all federal agencies to develop a conversion plan with a specific target date for compliance.[236]

The main argument in favor of metric conversion is that it will increase U.S. trade competitiveness in foreign markets. The trend toward glob-alization of trade and communication has made foreign exports an increasingly important segment of any country's economy. Proponents cite statistics showing an increasing proportion of international trade being conducted using the metric system as reasons for the U.S. to follow the rest of the world. Also, if domestic industry continues to use dual units of measurements, conversion between the two adds costs in terms of time and errors. The advantages to the transportation system, particularly highways, are not so clear, except that domestic suppliers of cement and other road construction materials, highway planners, and others in the transportation field could communicate and compete more effectively with their counterparts overseas. The Federal Highway Administration's metric conversion plan was approved on October 31, 1991, with a target date of September 30, 1996. The National Highway Designation Act of 1995 extended the date of completion for FHWA's conversion program to October 1, 2000. The Transportation Equity Act for the 21st Century, passed in 1998, made state DOT compliance voluntary. However, 42 states had already "substantially completed" their metric programs, so the FHWA believes it will be able to meet its target date.[237]

The Federal Highway Administration's current metric plan prohibits the agency from forcing the states to change its road signs to metric units. Recalling the U.S. government's ill-fated attempt two decades earlier, the FHWA recognizes that there is still not enough public support for nationally-mandated metric conversion. The states may still convert to metric, or use dual units on everything from printed brochures to road signs. Already, metric is being used in many highway construction projects and the experience thus far has been positive, with few errors. The FHWA and AASHTO are concerned that errors in translation between inch-pound and the international system will increase in states that continue to use the English system. The AASHTO's Metric Task Force has developed a program to educate industry and others and to encourage adoption of the metric system. Whether the state DOT's follow the federal lead remains to be seen. Much will depend on public support of metric, and opposition may delay and eventually reverse metric conversion. Since most of the world uses the international system, the momentum appears to be against the United States keeping its old system. Some day, the familiar "Speed Limit 55" sign might read "Speed Limit 89."[238]

The Federal Highway Administration continues research at its new Turner-Fairbank Highway Research Center in Lanham, Maryland, and at test sites throughout the country. In addition, the U.S. DOT and FHWA subsidize test facilities across the country in cooperation with state DOTs. Several projects are in progress using experimental road tracks or existing highways. The SHRP FHWA Long-Term Pavement Performance Program is a 20-year survey of approximately 2,200 test sections throughout the United States and Canada using conventional traffic to test different pavements, soils, bases and subbases. Ohio's state DOT started a SHRP program in partnership with the FHWA at a site 40 miles north of Columbus using a three-mile, four-lane test track using 38 different cement sections. The Minnesota Road Research Test Project (Mn/Road), also started in 1994, located northeast of the Twin Cities parallel to I-94, is a 3.5-mile track on which MnDOT is also studying various soil and pave-

ment types. Approximately 40 test pavements lined with 4,572 computer sensors monitor such factors as road stress. MnDOT has conducted dozens of experiments, and the indigenous climate's wide temperature range have produced valuable data for other state DOTs. One of the newest test facilities is the FHWA's "WesTrack" in western Nevada. Opened in March 1996, WesTrack is a 1.8-mile, two-lane oval track designed primarily for testing heavy trucks. The roadway consists of only one material, currently using "Superpave," a new privately–developed asphalt, to measure road wear under varying speeds and loads. Trucks are guided along the track by remote control.[239]

Revolutionary new materials for roadways and bridges are currently being tested. The use of "high performance concrete" (HPC) extends the life span of roadways and bridges. HPC is primarily ordinary concrete designed for increased durability. The idea is not new. The first use of HPC was Philadelphia's Walnut Lane Bridge, built in 1949, using HPC beams. The Walnut Lane Bridge was the first prestressed, post-tensioned concrete bridge in North America. Just recently, the historic bridge was refurbished. The technology advanced over the next several decades in the U.S., Canada, Europe and Japan. High performance concrete is also being used in tall buildings, such as Dallas' Interfirst Plaza Building, constructed in 1983 using HPC. Engineers for the Interfirst Plaza project estimate that HPC has six times the "stiffness" of conventional steel frame construction. The Federal Highway Administration data show that typical concrete bridges have a life expectancy of approximately 42 years, while bridges using high performance concrete are projected to last for 75 to 100 years. Besides longer life, HPC gives engineers greater freedom in designing new bridges, allowing a longer spans and requiring fewer beams, saving both material and labor costs. Since 1996, numerous HPC bridge projects have been

Turner-Fairbank Highway Research Center. In 1938, Congress acquired 581 acres of land in McLean, Virginia, for a highway research facility for the Bureau of Public Roads. In 1950, the BPR occupied its new building, called the Fairbank Highway Research Station, named for former Deputy Commissioner Herbert S. Fairbank. In 1983, an additional building was completed to meet the growing need for highway research, and was dedicated to Francis C. Turner, the first FHWA administrator. The site was renamed the Turner-Fairbank Highway Research Center and currently employs approximately 130 federal employees, 80 contract employees, and 40 graduate research fellows, with over 40 indoor and outdoor laboratories and support facilities (courtesy, U.S. DOT/FHWA).

Top: Minnesota DOT test facility. Most state DOTs routinely perform their own road testing to research improved paving materials. In 1994, the Minnesota Department of Transportation started its Minnesota Road Research Project to test for effects of climate and loads on varying road surfaces. The facility uses a 3.4-mile mainline test road and a 2.5-mile low-volume loop road to study the performance of 40 different pavement types under temperature extremes experienced in northern states. The facility is located along I-94 near Otsego, northwest of the Minneapolis-St. Paul metropolitan area (courtesy, Minnesota DOT and Neil Kveberg).

Bottom: Computer-guided truck on Westrak testing facility, Nevada. Since the 1920s, the FHWA and its predecessors have constructed road testing facilities as part of a continuing effort to develop improved highways for safety and longer life. In October 1995, the FHWA unveiled its latest program, the WesTrack test facility in western Nevada. Driverless trucks guided by control are navigated by computer on an 1.8-mile oval track. The system employs a guidance antenna mounted on the front bumper of the vehicle that receives messages from wires embedded in the pavement. A computer placed in the vehicle operates the steering, braking, and speed. The two-year study was completed in 1999 and studied varying loads on trucks to test endurance of a new hot-mix asphalt paving material (courtesy, U.S. DOT/FHWA).

started in states such as Nebraska, Virginia, and New Hampshire.[240]

The Federal Highway Administration has recently turned its attention to improving asphalt for surfacing roads. The FHWA's Office of Engineering Research and Development is conducting testing on chemically-modified asphalt. New asphalt types have been discovered by Drs. Brian Chollar and Mohammed Memon and are being subjected to extensive tests at the Turner-Fairbank Highway Research Center. The three types developed are Compatibilized Crumb Rubber Asphalt, Chemically-modified Crumb Rubber Asphalt, and Furfural-modified Asphalt. The FHWA's tests are measuring road wear, particularly "rutting," over a wide temperature range. One of these new paving materials may be eventually selected for nationwide use in the coming decades.[241]

The U.S. Department of Transportation and the Federal Highway Administration are revamping its bridge construction and repair programs to meet modern expectations in terms of safety, design and aesthetics. In the area of safety, more attention is being placed on designing earthquake-proof bridges. Although earthquakes may be perceived as primarily a West Coast problem, virtually every state has had at least one recorded earthquake in the past two centuries. Two major earthquakes have occurred in the eastern United States: the 1811 New Madrid, Missouri, quake and another in Charleston, South Carolina, in 1886. The recent San Francisco Bay area quake of 1989 and the disastrous collapse of the Cypress Elevated Freeway in Oakland have renewed safety concerns. Approximately 60 percent of the nation's 575,000 bridges were built prior to 1970. Widespread damage to freeways in Los Angeles' San Fernando Valley during the 1971 earthquake spurred new bridge designs to minimize quake damage. The AASHTO began studying seismic factors for future bridge designs and new specifications, and by 1983, proposed six new bridge configurations that are resistance to earthquakes. The AASHTO's test results are available to state transportation officials for use in state and local highway projects.[242]

The U.S. Department of Transportation and the Federal Highway Administration have conducted studies to gauge the current fairness and effectiveness of highway user fees paid by different classes of vehicles. The last such study was done by the DOT and FHWA in 1982. The new DOT report, entitled "The 1997 Federal Highway Cost Allocation Study," looked at user fees paid to the Federal Highway Trust Fund and compared the data to the amount of use by each class of vehicle and the impact on premature replacing of roads and bridges. The overall purpose of the study is to suggest changes to current user fees, particularly for diesel fuel taxes, heavy-vehicle taxes for trucks weighing over 55,000 pounds, excise taxes on the sale of heavy trucks, a progressive tax on tires weighing in excess of 40 pounds, plus two distance-to-weight tax proposals. Historically, surveys have shown that heavy trucks cause a disproportionate amount of road damage as compared to lighter vehicles. Data collected by the U.S. DOT in its 1997 "Comprehensive Truck Size and Weight Study" were useful in deciding which vehicles should pay the most taxes. The DOT's statistics showed that passenger vehicles account for 92.6 percent of all motor vehicles in the United States, with trucks making up the remaining 7.4 percent. Automobiles comprise two-thirds of all vehicles on the road (67.5 percent), with pickups and vans coming in second (24.8 percent); busses are a minuscule 0.2 percent. A comparison of vehicle types using passenger miles shows roughly the same rankings: passenger vehicles, 96.7 percent; and trucks only 3.3 percent. Based of the survey, the U.S. DOT has concluded that most vehicles are currently paying their proportionate share of highway costs.[243]

The results of surveys such as these will allow the U.S. DOT to allocate transportation funds efficiently. Under DOT's current plan for highway and other infrastructure expenditures, road repair will get the biggest slice (42.3 percent), followed by new roads (21.0 percent), with system enhancement allotted 15.4 percent, the mass transit account getting 12.4 percent, and the remaining 8.9 percent going to miscellaneous costs. "System enhancement" is technical jargon for upgrading infrastructure systems, such as work on safety projects, ITS projects, mass transit improvements, environmental costs, and pedestrian and bicycle facilities.[244]

The interstate system reached a total of 45,530 miles by 1990, with a few small projects remaining. The U.S. Department of Transportation continues to add to the system, mainly in isolated locales which have special needs. In Hawaii, the expensive H-3 project (Hawaii uses an "H" instead of "I" designation for its interstate highways) is a 15-mile engineering marvel, cutting across the Koolau Range on the island of Oahu.

Whether traveling the interstates or the old two-lane federal-aid highways, the disappearance of roadside businesses and other highway artifacts are making highway sightseeing a bit less interesting. Old age and progress have claimed most of the old barns, cafes, filling stations, and other landmarks. Highway "beautification" removed most pre–1965 highway billboards decades ago. Numerous towns and businesses along bypassed U.S. highways have faded into obscurity. Even many old two-lanes themselves are vanishing, victims of bypassing and weeds. The federal government has turned over responsibility of some of less frequently traveled routes to state and local authorities, and the U.S. federal-aid system numbering is being replaced with a state highway designation in some areas. The American Association of State Highway and Transportation Officials has "decommissioned" several federal-aid highways which parallel interstate freeways and have fallen into disuse. For example, AASHTO decommissioned U.S. Route 66 in 1985 because I-55, I-40, I-15, and I-10 have bypassed the famous road. A similar tale can be told of other remnants of the first U.S. highway system.

In 1990, President George Bush signed into law a bill designating the interstate system as the "Dwight D. Eisenhower System of Interstate and Defense Highways" in honor of Ike's role in the development of the interstate system. A few years later, the U.S. Department of Transportation added most multi-lane federal-aid highways to the Eisenhower System. The official sign for the system, a

John Eisenhower and "Eisenhower Interstate System" symbol. In honor of his contribution to the interstate freeway system, President George Bush signed a bill in 1990 naming the interstate system the "Dwight D. Eisenhower System of Interstate and Defense Highways." On July 23, 1993, the official symbol was unveiled, with Ike's son John Eisenhower present, shown above. New signs with this logo of five stars in a circular pattern symbolizing General Eisenhower's military rank are being posted on our interstate highways (courtesy, U.S. DOT/FHWA).

circle of five stars signifying General Eisenhower's military rank, was dedicated on July 29, 1993, with Ike's son John Eisenhower on hand for the dedication ceremony. By the end of the 1990s, the Eisenhower system measured over 54,700 miles. Although the project was completed long after its original 1970 target date, delays gave the U.S. DOT an opportunity to improve on early mistakes in design and construction methods. The result is safer highways that must be the envy of the world.[245]

The Future

The challenges facing the American highway system in the next century will likely be a repeat of the 20th century experience. The Federal Highway Administration, with the aid of state and local officials, continues to experiment with new construction methods and materials, as well as improved highway designs to meet ever-increasing traffic volume. To its credit, the 42,795-mile interstate system today carries 21 percent of the nation's traffic, while constituting only 1 percent of the country's total street and highway mileage. Past concerns, such as safety and highway aesthetics, will no doubt continue to be debated. Some citizens have raised concerns over the recent proliferation of newer and larger highway billboards, particularly along interstate highways, which can still be seen beyond the minimum distances from the right-of-way established under the 1965 Highway Beautification Act. One early account to curb outdoor billboards can be traced as far back as 1865, when New York City tried to ban advertising signs from being placed on everything from rocks to trees.[246] Like weeds, highway billboards have been proven to be difficult to completely eradicate and they will probably survive into the foreseeable future. Besides, they sometimes provide a mild form of entertainment for travelers along many dreary stretches of open highway.

Other activists decry the increasing size of trucks on the road. Since 1946, the average truck has increased in length from 35 feet to 77 feet. In addition, double- and triple-tandem trailers are becoming more common, although they are prohibited by some states. Statistics gathered by the U.S. Department of Transportation in 1995 show that while trucks make up only 3 percent of all registered motor vehicles, they account for 20 percent of traffic deaths. Such data are used by those advocating increased regulation of motor carriers.[247]

The safety issue will always be an ongoing debate among transportation experts and there is no end to possible innovations to improve safety. After requiring that all new cars include air safety bags, we'll add side-mounted air bags, then safer air bags, etc. Highway planners and amateur futurists of the past 50 years have speculated on the ultimate, safest highway for future generations. Articles in popular magazines have envisioned remote-controlled cars whose speed and steering are guided by a centralized control. Ford Motor Company's bold 1957 "World of the Future" projected a utopian society in the next millennium. By then, even Disneyland had displayed prefab future homes and monorail systems. General Motors' exhibit at the 1964–65 New York World's Fair unveiled its "Autoline Automatic Highway Concept." Under GM's model, all cars would be equipped with an automatic speed control device which the driver engaged when entering the expressway. The vehicle would be automatically guided safely into position at the end of the first available group of vehicles. To exit the system, the driver would signal his/her intention to leave the expressway and the vehicle would resume manual control. The system utilized three lanes: an outer lane for entering and exiting, an inner lane for through traffic, and a center lane for transitioning between the other two lanes.

Not willing to be outdone by General Motors, the Ford Motor Company went a step further with its own "out-of-this-world" exhibit at the 1964–65 World's Fair. Ford countered with an impressive thrill ride at its "Ford World Rotunda." Visitors first viewed a film featuring the earth's prehistoric past, with animation by Walt Disney and WD Enterprises. Next, fairgoers climbed into Ford's latest 1964 and 1965 convertible models that traveled on a Magic Skyway through "time tunnels" through a seven-story structure containing an eye-dazzling "Space City."

However, futurists may not have long to wait for science fiction to enter the transportation scene. The computer age is finally beginning to make an impact on surface transportation for the 21st century. Highway planners of the past have used highway design to efficiently manage traffic. It now appears that shaping the physical environment to alleviate urban congestion has reached its limits. If the past 100 years have been any guide, the United States will see an ever-growing army of vehicles crowding our streets and highways. The U.S. population, along with total number of vehicles, annual vehicle miles, and other measurements, shows no sign of leveling off.

This places transportation planning on a continuous treadmill. To keep up with increasing volume of traffic, the FHWA and state and local governments continue to add new highways and widen existing thoroughfares. Stop signs are replaced by semifours and they in turn are replaced by cloverleafs. Blacktop and cement are gradually enveloping urban areas, as highways gobble up land area, making larger smog-ridden swaths through our cities. A century of road building has proven that even continual road construction projects cannot keep pace with the uniquely American obsession with getting behind the wheel, preferably alone. Vintage photographs of early traffic snarls look familiar to today's urban commuter stopped in rush hour traffic.

Today's motor vehicles increasingly rely on computer-driven components for efficiency and diagnostics, and domestic auto makers have shown off a few concept cars at major auto shows with onboard visual displays. The Buck Rogers versions of freeways of the future popularized by General Mo-

Top: "Our Interstate Just Turned 40." A billboard paid for by a highway construction industry group warns of an approaching "mid-life crisis" for an aging interstate system. Under ISTEA and the Transportation Equity Act for the 21st Century (passed by the Congress in May 1998), the United States is on the road to meeting the highway and other transportation issues projected for the coming century. The 1998 legislation (called TEA-21) appropriated a record $162 billion in federal funding for highway, mass transit, and other ISTEA projects for the next six years. The law prevents any Highway Trust Fund money from being used for defense or other programs, and it is expected that a total of $200 billion will be available for transportation spending (photo by author).

Bottom: Scale model of future city with freeway system, New York World's Fair, 1964–65. Some 25 years after its prophetic Futurama exhibit at the 1939 World's Fair, the General Motors Corporation provided another fast-forward look at transportation possibilities in the coming decades. The motor giant's latest fair exhibit featured a future city with an "Autoline Automatic Highway Concept," where vehicles are guided by a remote control as they enter the expressway. Copyright, General Motors Corporation (used with permission).

tors' 1939–40 and 1964–65 World's Fair exhibits will eventually become reality. Can the wacky world

Close-up view of "Autoline Automatic Highway Concept" at General Motors' exhibit. Futurologists usually conceive of the future in utopian terms and seek to remedy current global problems with larger-than-life architecture and social planning. Poverty, overpopulation, traffic problems, pollution, and other societal ills were uppermost in the minds of 1960s America, and designers at GM thought they had the answer to the a projected transportation crisis in the future. In GM's model vehicles travel on a wide, automated expressway using its Autoline system. The left lane is reserved for through-traffic; the right for entering and exiting the system; and the center for transitioning between the left and right lanes. The concept was designed to alleviate traffic congestion. Copyright, General Motors Corporation (used with permission).

of flying commuter spacecraft of *The Jetsons* cartoons be far away?

The Federal Highway Administration and transportation officials in western Europe and Japan have been looking at traffic management concepts since the 1960s. The United States, with its large land area and relatively low density population compared to much of the industrialized world, has had the luxury of postponing major changes in traffic control. Countries like Japan, with 12 times the population density as the United States, have been slightly ahead in development. Japan currently has 14,000 traffic fatalities annually, and like the U.S., faces ever-multiplying vehicles. Japanese research in the 1970s led to a second phase of its program in 1984 to develop a communication and navigation system. However, the idea was still slightly ahead of its time. In 1989, Japanese cars offered optional in-dash visual systems, but with no central computerized navigational control, relegating these early systems to little more than expensive electronic road maps directing drivers to the easiest routes. An American project entitled "Electronic Route Guidance System" (ERGS) has been involved in similar research, as is a similar West German program.[248]

In the 1990s, major advances in microprocessors and other computer technology allowed development of computerized traffic control systems

Ford's "Space City" New York World's Fair exhibit, 1964. The Ford Motor Company had its own vision of the future at the Ford Rotunda at the 1964–65 World's Fair. Inside a seven-story building was a thrill ride through "time tunnels" where fairgoers sat in new Ford convertibles moving along skyways from prehistoric times to a future "Space City." Oddly, the 1964 Fords didn't seem to fit the 21st century scene, but the public's fascination with science fiction made the ride extremely popular (from the Collections of Henry Ford Museum and Greenfield Village).

to move forward. Japan coordinated all government agencies dealing with transportation, creating a single system regulating all public and private transportation, giving motorists up to the minute traffic information and collecting tolls electronically. The European Economic Community and European car makers collaborated in its own venture under the wordy heading "Program for a European Traffic System with Higher Efficiency and Unprecedented Safety" (PROMETHEUS) and "Dedicated Road Infrastructure for Vehicle Safety" (DRIVES).[249]

The United States Congress has already taken a giant step toward the future in transportation management when it passed the Inter-modal Surface Transportation Efficiency Act of 1991 (ITSEA).

"Dream Highways for Dream Cars." Scientific advances and futurism have been the major subject in *Popular Science* magazine for decades. The magazine has reported on all sorts of inventions and any manmade creations that have had practical applications. Occasionally, some ideas featured actually have made it into the marketplace. In 1946, one issue featured the Tucker automobile and a radar cooking oven, long before microwave ovens came into use. This May 1956 *Popular Science* shows a family traveling by remote control in a futuristic vehicle on an automated freeway of the 21st century (courtesy, *Popular Science* magazine).

The ISTEA is probably the most important legislation affecting America's highways since the creation of the interstate system by the Federal-Aid Highway Act of 1956. The Act's policy declaration states that its purpose is to "develop a National Inter-modal Transportation System that is economically efficient and environmentally sound, provides the foundation for the Nation to compete in the global economy, and will move people and goods in an energy efficient manner." The ISTEA seeks to integrate all sectors of the nation's transportation systems in a "unified, interconnected manner." The National Inter-modal System includes a "National Highway System" (consisting of the National System of Interstate and Defense Highways), not to exceed 155,000 miles unless changed by the secretary of DOT. Public transportation, ports and airports are included in the program. The ISTEA requires that all future transportation systems be designed to reduce pollution and be energy efficient whenever necessary. The Act establishes the "Intelligent Vehicle Highway Systems" program (IVHS) to "enhance the capacity, efficiency, and safety of the federal–aid highway system and to serve as an alternative to additional physical capacity of the federal-aid highway system." Social benefits, such as reduced traffic congestion, air pollution, and other aspects of the nation's quality of life are cited as goals of ISTEA.[250]

Under ISTEA, the U.S. Department of Transportation and the Federal Highway Administration have six objectives in development of IVHS technology (renamed "Intelligent Transportation System", or ITS):

To research ITS systems for compatibility with human factors to develop "user friendly" transportation systems.

To advance urban transportation for traffic management and improved public transportation.

To advance rural transportation for improved safety and service to more isolated areas.

To improve ITS technology to increase efficiency for fleet operators and motor carriers through better safety inspections and regulations.

To develop technology for vehicle safety systems to reduce accidents and warn drivers of hazardous conditions.

To develop an "Automated Highway System" (AHS), including "smart vehicles" equipped with crash-avoidance technology.[251]

Under ISTEA, the U.S. Congress appropriated the final federal funding for completion of the Dwight D. Eisenhower National System of Interstate and Defense Highways, extending the final date of completion to 1996. The Congress granted $645 million for ITS various research projects through fiscal year 1997. The U.S. DOT conducted studies in dozens of test areas throughout the country. Out of 83 test sites, the field was narrowed to four "ITS Project Corridors" which would benefit from ITS technology. The four Priority Corridors selected are: I-95 from Washington, D.C., to Connecticut; the Gary-Chicago-Milwaukee metro area; Houston, Texas; and I-5 San Diego to Los Angeles, including I-10. Some of the DOT's research to date has already been incorporated into some state highway systems, such as Boston's "SmarTraveler," which provides real-time travel information to motorists.[252]

As the number of vehicles on U.S. highways continues on its historical upward trend, the U.S. Department of Transportation is striving to update the nation's transportation system to meet the needs of the next century. By the late 1990s, traffic fatalities averaged slightly over 40,000 annually. Many states have been using high-occupancy vehicle (HOV) lanes reserved for passenger capacity of two or more persons to encourage car pooling for two decades. In 1982 Congress required states to use HOV lanes (California started using "diamond lanes" on urban freeways in 1977). However, many areas have experienced driver resistance to such programs, and many HOV lanes go largely unused, prompting law enforcement to ticket drivers who improperly use HOV lanes. Although mass transit and commuter rail systems continue to be promoted as the only real solution to 21st century traffic problems, the global experience has been mixed. While the French bullet trains have been an economic success, others, such as Japan's high-speed commuter trains, operate in the red. In the U.S., new mass transit systems are an expensive alternative to autos and busses, and usually lose money. Mass transit rail systems continue to be the darling of the futurists (and some anti-auto activists), but one day may become as commonplace as the street car once was.

An automated highway system remarkably similar to General Motors' Autoline Automated Highway Concept has already been tested by the U.S. Department of Transportation and the National Automated Highway System Consortium

(NAHSC), a group of auto manufacturers, infrastructure contractors, and local transportation agencies. The proposed Automated Highway System would guide vehicles by remote control and use center lanes for thru-traffic. The AHS is most exciting of the federal projects under ITSEA and the DOT and FHWA expect to have an operational system ready by the year 2015. Upon completion, the system will feature "smart cars" equipped with radar and computers that will allow the vehicle to be driven hands-free. Other ideas include a system in which cars "talk" to each other and relay information back to the traffic control center. Under the plan, vehicles are guided by sensors placed along the roadway and a central computer. All three components of the system (vehicle, sensors, and central computer) would be linked by satellite. Already the Global Positioning System, involving communication between satellites and ground reception systems, is coming into widespread use.[253]

The DOT demonstrated the AHS concept in the first phase of its ITS program in the fall of 1997 to prove the viability of ITS technology. The DOT used an HOV lane on I-15 in San Diego on a 7.5-mile route lined with sensors and linked by a central computer. Various unmanned trucks and autos were driven along the route by remote control. In later tests, vehicles traveling at speeds of up to 35 miles per hour successfully maneuvered through an obstacle course. In 1996, Japan started a similar ITS system and is currently placing computer sensors along freeways in Tokyo and the main expressway between Tokyo and Osaka for its own ITS project.[254]

Another of ISTEA's six objectives is the development of computer intelligent vehicles that

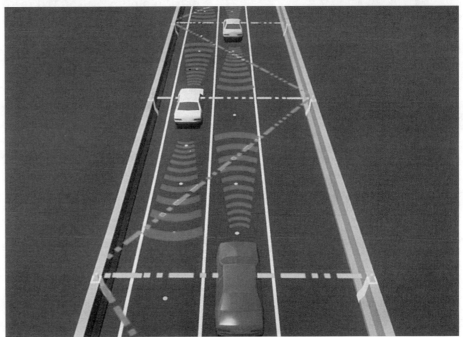

Drawings of Automated Highway System (AHS) concept. The U. S. Congress took a bold step toward a comprehensive plan to meet the nation's transportation needs for the next century when its passed the Inter-modal Surface Transportation Efficiency Act of 1991 (ISTEA). The ISTEA seeks to coordinate all aspects of transportation, whether by highways, rail, water or air. The act appropriates funds to test, design, and construct the highways of the future and will use computer and aerospace technology to manage surface and other transportation as population continues to increase. One of the first such projects started under ISTEA was the formation of the National Automated Highway System Consortium (NAHSC), which designed an automated highway similar to General Motors' Autoline Automatic Highway concept featured at the 1964 New York World's Fair. The top drawing shows dedicated center lanes for through-traffic and vehicles safely spaced after entering the system through the "check in" sign. The bottom drawing shows vehicles passing sensors at the edge of the roadway which link the vehicle and a central control to regulate traffic (courtesy, U.S. DOT/FHWA).

Test vehicle during NAHSC demonstration, San Diego, 1997. In August 1997, NAHSC finally got the opportunity to test its technology during a real-world test on a 7.5-mile portion of I-5 outside of San Diego. Test vehicles of varying sizes, equipped with on-board computers, were driven without human drivers on a roadway embedded with sensors for this first-of-a-kind experiment. Although the NAHSC was disbanded in 1998 after the conclusion of its field tests, valuable data from the project are being used for continued ITS research (courtesy, U.S. DOT/FHWA).

account for so-called "human factors." With the General Accounting Office (GAO) reporting an estimated 300 to 400 percent increase in traffic congestion by 2010, effective traffic management is essential to the survival of the entire system. The National Highway Transportation Safety Administration has estimated that ITS technologies could prevent 17 percent of the nation's 6.4 million annual collisions. The NHTSA's research has determined that three-fourths of all accidents are caused by inattentive drivers and that ITS would save approximately 17,500 lives and an estimated $26 billion in property damage per year. Currently, several urban busses and large fleet companies are already using tracking systems to locate vehicles and communicate with drivers. The DOT has several prototype vehicles with on-board information and navigation systems using in-dash liquid crystal displays (LCDs) to help drivers avoid collisions and wrong turns. A DOT test in Florida in 1992 demonstrated how vehicles equipped with route navigation systems made one-third fewer wrong turns and reduced travel time by 20 percent.[255]

Congress passed its final highway-related legislation for the 20th century when it enacted the "Transportation Equity Act for the 21st Century" (TEA-21) in May 1998. The TEA-21 initiative continues the programs started under ISTEA, and Congress appropriated a record $162 billion for federal-aid highways over a six-year period. The Act restores the fiscal integrity of the Highway Trust Fund by requiring that all future revenues in the Trust Fund's highway account be spent only for transportation purposes. Previously, Congress had been diverting revenues from the Trust Fund for defense and other domestic programs. The new law guarantees that the Trust Fund will be used for only transportation projects, which should result in more funds made available for new highway construction and improving existing highways and bridge replacement. These changes will raise the total funding for federal aid projects under the TEA-21 from $162 billion to at least $200 billion over the six-year period under the Act. Proponents of TEA-21 believe that improved roads will save an estimated 4,000 lives a year and yield other indirect savings for motorists and the economy.[256]

Engineers at the FHWA's state-of-the-art Turner-Fairbank Highway Research Center continue to experiment on human-centered vehicles of the next century. The new focus of highway research is now on the driver, since highway improvements alone cannot reduce accidents. With an aging population, future drivers need easy-to-read signage and dashboard displays. On-board visual displays must be designed to be read quickly, especially for older drivers whose reaction times are slowed. Too much electronic gimmickry would probably distract drivers, so future developments in ITS will need to find a compromise that will be user-friendly to all motorists.

The National Automated Highway System Consortium was disbanded in early 1998 after completing its San Diego road tests. However, private industry is now beginning to follow the government's lead in ITS technology. Delco Electronics demonstrated a concept car in 1996 equipped with two dozen security, safety, and communication features. When safety air bags are deployed in a front-end collision, the vehicle automatically sends a message to emergency services for assistance. Microsoft and Intel have developed computer software called "Connected Car-PC" and "Auto-PC" with some radical new features. The new software package enables driver and vehicle to become a mobile office-communication center, with traffic and weather information, e-mail, a fax/pager, and cellular telephone. The system could also be voice-activated and automatically call for police or emergency services in the event of accidents. Computer technology is making the possibilities in future transportation almost limitless.[257]

States that are using ITS technology today are reporting considerable savings in commuter time, accidents and costs to both drivers and transportation systems. Electronic toll collection systems using prepaid debit cards have been in use in several major cities for the past several years. Introduced in 1993, the New York Thruway's E-Z Pass, an electronic toll collection system, is reducing slowdowns at toll stops, particularly during rush hour. The Thruway Authority reports that 1,000 vehicles per hour now pass through its Tappan Zee Bridge toll gates, where previously only 350–400 vehicles per hour moved through the bridge under its old manual system. The Thruway Authority has also introduced movable concrete barriers on the bridge, to increase the number of lanes for rush hour traffic. Currently, a more advanced system using "toll transponders" mounted on the car's dashboard automatically debits the driver's pre-paid card as the vehicle passes the toll gate, reducing stopping time at toll booths. In Oklahoma City, such a system saves $160,000 per year per toll booth.[258]

Traffic management systems based on ITS technology are also cutting transportation costs for state and local governments. Some are modest improvements, such as installing remote cameras along freeways which are monitored by a traffic control center to spot accidents and other conditions. Traffic control centers can send messages to electronic display signs placed on bridge overpasses to warn drivers of traffic congestion and other hazards. Morning and late-afternoon rush-hour traffic entering freeways are regulated by metered entrance ramps in Minneapolis-St. Paul, Detroit, Seattle, and other locations. Cities using rush-hour metered ramps report improved traffic flow using a combination of such systems.

City bus companies have also been using ITS to cut costs. Both Baltimore and Kansas City found savings in 1995 studies of their new vehicle location systems. Such systems have improved reliability and increased rider satisfaction. Kansas City claims that ITS has saved its bus system approximately $500,000. In 1996, the U.S. DOT's ITS program chose four cities which already have invested in ITS for developing model systems for possible national application: New York City, Seattle, Phoenix, and San Antonio. The New York pro-

E-Z Pass electronic toll collection on New York Thruway. New York became the first state to implement an electronic toll collection system that shortened the time for paying tolls. The first location was at the Spring Valley toll plaza, opened on August 2, 1993. Drivers can purchase a credit card–size tag that is placed near the windshield to be read by computer scanners at toll plazas. The toll is then subtracted from the tag-holder's account. The system allows motorists to pay tolls without stopping, thereby easing traffic jams (courtesy, New York Thruway Authority).

ject encompasses a vast network of freeways which includes New Jersey and Connecticut. Although commuters were able to get local traffic reports by radio, the information was useless when crossing state lines. In response, Connecticut, New York and New Jersey created TransCom, an agency which coordinates information for the entire metropolitan area. The Phoenix, Arizona, bus system allows riders to pay fares with a prepaid Bus Card Plus or credit cards. Another proposal in Phoenix that is

Left: Movable concrete barriers on Tappan Zee Bridge, New York Thruway. In 1993, the New York Thruway Authority introduced an innovative system to alter the number of lanes on freeways for better traffic management during times of peak usage. The concept uses two transfer vehicles to shift a movable concrete barrier, creating additional lanes on the Tappan Zee Bridge over the Hudson River, depending on the time of day. The seven-lane bridge experiences daily traffic backups as commuter traffic bottlenecks while crossing the bridge. The movable barriers create four lanes for east-bound traffic headed for New York City in the morning, then reverts to four lanes for west-bound travel for the late afternoon rush hour (courtesy, New York Thruway Authority).

Right: Morning rush hour on the John F. Kennedy Expressway, Chicago. Built in the late 1960s, the John F. Kennedy Expressway (designated as I-90/I-94) is one of the nation's busiest roadways, carrying up to 300,000 vehicles per day between the northwest suburbs to downtown Chicago. This view of the 16-lane JFK demonstrates how interstate freeways can consume large tracts of urban real estate, cutting off and often destroying entire neighborhoods. However, the photo also shows the heavy volume of traffic on this congested corridor which would be forced onto city streets if not for the foresight of the planners of our interstate highways (courtesy, U.S. DOT/FHWA, from "Public Roads" magazine, March/April 1998).

sure to be welcomed by drivers would combine the suburbs into a single system that would change the timing of stop lights depending on traffic conditions, thus reducing stops and decreasing travel time for commuters heading home.[259]

For now, we will have to settle for the status quo. The automated highway of the future is still a decade or two away. Will it take away the driver's freedom, or make urban driving better, safer, and more pleasurable? We should not despair yet, be-

cause there is still much to be seen on the nation's two-lanes roads, whether they are old U.S. highways or state or local roads. An active highway preservation movement is currently working to save old manmade landmarks and even some historic highways. Organizations such as the Society for Commercial Archeology and boosters of particular routes such as the Lincoln Highway and U.S. 66 and others are making a small impact on highway preservation. Ordinary citizens are help-

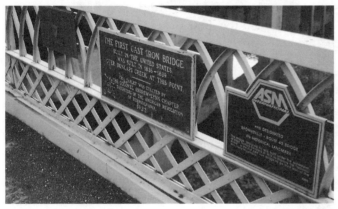

Top Left: Bridge plaque, Port Allegheny, Pennsylvania (1944). As the first generation of highways slowly deteriorate with time, roads and bridges are being replaced. Old, narrow bridges built for Model T's present a safety hazard for today's larger vehicles and heavier traffic. Fortunately, a few vintage bridges have survived. Many old bridges (as well as modern ones) memorialize the date of completion with a metal plaque mounted in a conspicuous location. Plaques such as this one on a cement bridge in Port Allegheny, Pennsylvania, on U.S. 6., are commonly found on many old bridges in the Keystone State constructed from the 1920s through the 1940s (photo by author).

Top Right: Santa Fe Trail marker, Dover, Missouri. Serious road buffs in search of roadside history are rewarded when discovering an occasional historical marker on back roads off the interstates. This monument is located on U.S. 24 west of Dover, Missouri, and marks the location where Kit Carson and other pioneers passed on the Santa Fe Trail as they traveled west to New Mexico. Hundreds of historic markers and plaques can be found on obscure roads to remind us of historic places and events from the nation's past (photo by author).

Bottom Left: Dunlaps Creek Bridge, Brownsville, Maryland. Brownsville, Maryland, is home to several interesting and historic bridges, including this antique iron bridge on U.S. 40 (the National Pike), built in 1839. Three plaques commemorate this rare bridge, the one in center being placed by the Daughters of the American Revolution in 1923. Preservationists are active designating and saving historic places, including highways and bridges, and state and federal highway officials are finding new ways to renovate bridges of architectural or historic significance (photo by author).

Bottom Right: Searights Toll House, U.S. Route 40 (National Pike). This is one of three remaining original toll houses on the Cumberland Road, also known as the Great National Turnpike and the National Pike. The Searights toll house dates to 1835, and collected tolls from thousands of settlers and immigrants headed for new lands in the Midwest. This toll house is near the town of Searights in southwestern Pennsylvania (photo by author).

ing improving highway scenery by forming "Adopt-a-Highway" groups to clear roadsides of litter. Alongside of almost every interstate freeway is an old federal-aid highway in driveable condition. These old roads serve as a reminder of America's golden age of highway travel and they are waiting to be explored just beyond the nearest freeway exit. After leaving the crowded, noisy "Big Slab," you immediately enter another realm. A local resident may occasionally pass by and the overall scene is one of an eerie calm. Standing on the faded center-line of these old roads, you scarcely encounter any traffic. One can picture how different it may have looked years ago when cars and trucks were locked in bumper-to-bumper competition. Today, you can still find aging gas stations, truck stops and other weathered roadside businesses, some amazingly still in operation. Every so often you might discover a vintage filling station manned by an old proprietor who is eager to recount the good old days of motoring, or maybe share a tale or two of past adventures on the American Highway.

A casual drive on any of our highways which make up the 40,000-mile U.S. federal-aid system and many state routes can be experienced by anyone with a car and a road map. Fortunately, the old federal aid system is too large to be completely destroyed through modernization and most are still necessary for local and other traffic, since the interstates only link major metropolitan areas. Original bridges on U.S. highways, both large and small, are gradually being replaced with plain slab-sided designs. The smaller bridges built in the early part of the century were often simple metal struc-

Left: Mileage marker on Old National Road. Construction of the National Pike took nearly 50 years, and the route was extended into Ohio by the 1820s. Benjamin Franklin's method of placing stone markers for every mile on postal roads for travelers was commonly used in the post-colonial period. Markers on the Cumberland Road used dual mileage for the nearest cities for east or west bound travelers. This marker is near Brownsville, Ohio, on a road marked "Old National Road," which runs parallel to U.S. 40 and I-70 (photo by author).

Right: Historic Highways: U.S. 30, (Lincoln Highway) near Elkhorn, Nebraska. Although the interstates have now completely bypassed the old federal-aid system, most U.S. highways are still in driveable condition. A brick section of the original alignment for the Lincoln Highway still exists, just off of U.S. 6, west of Omaha, Nebraska. A cement Lincoln Highway marker stands along the roadside of this rare piece of highway history. Proceeding slowly on this mile-long brick road, one can imagine what traveling must have felt like in 1920 in a vintage automobile (photo by author).

Top Left: Historic Highways: U.S. 66 (Will Rogers Highway), Kingman, Arizona. The Bureau of Land Management and other federal agencies have recognized the need to preserve our older highways having historic significance or passing through scenic areas. The BLM has designated U.S. 66 between Kingman, Arizona, and Needles, California, as a "Back Country Byway." Seasoned travelers heading west towards Los Angeles recall this treacherous stretch of highway. Upon leaving Kingman, the first obstacle was the Black Mountain range, crossed only by a narrow gravel road that somehow passed for a legitimate U.S. federal-aid highway. The climb up Gold Hill was too much for many vehicles. After passing the Gold Hill summit, the motorist faced an even more formidable challenge: the deadly Mohave Desert (photo by author).

Top Right: Old highway billboard, U.S. 6 near Minden, Nebraska. During the final years of the U. S. federal-aid highway system, billboard proliferation had become a public nuisance. Billboard regulation, however, has a long history. One early effort occurred in New York where an 1869 state law banned advertising on everything from rocks to buildings. The Highway Beautification Act of 1965, promoted by Lady Bird Johnson, resulted in the removal of over 600,000 billboards. This old sign on U.S. 6 west of Minden, Nebraska, somehow survived. (photo by author).

Bottom: Super America station, 1998. Countering today's trend toward large and impersonal-looking filling stations are more traditional designs which appeal to consumers tired of bland, utilitarian architecture. Some companies, such as Super America, a regional brand found in the Midwest, are now building brick-faced structures with varied floor plans to project a friendlier image. As the nation continues to discover and appreciate its rich heritage, it appears that the American highway has again come full circle (photo by author).

tures spanning a creek, sometimes improved later by cement bridges. If you inspect these vintage bridges, you may find a metal plaque commemorating the date the bridge was completed. Many remaining bridges date back to the 1920s and even earlier. One can appreciate the historic significance of the American highway, which started with earth paths and Indian trails, while discovering one of these old relics of an earlier time.

The American highway is a 20th century product of social, political and economic factors and continues to evolve to accommodate the ever-changing needs and tastes of the traveling public. Whether vacationing or driving to earn a living, consumer attitudes are a major force shaping our highways. The gasoline service station will undergo further transformation in the coming years as electrical vehicles and alternative fuels come into widespread usage. The sights and smells of the gasoline filling station will someday be just a memory to those of us who have experienced 20th century travel. The highways of the future will also change with the times, as innovations in technology such as intelligent vehicles and automated highways affect driving habits and highway design. Exciting new discoveries in our roadside culture—new roadside fuel stops, eating and lodging—await us. As our current century draws to a close, we start a new chapter in highway history. Let the post–2000 American highway begin!

Notes

A Brief History of Roads

1. *Highways and Highway Transport, Chatham, Cromwell Co.*, 1923.
2. *The Andean Republic*, William Weber Johnson and *LIFE*, 1965.
3. *The Story of America's Bridges*, Ray Spangenburg, Diane K. Moser, Facts on File, Inc., 1991.
4. *The Village in England*, Nicholson, Fawcett Press, 1988.
5. *Highways into History*, Fleming, St. Martin's Press, 1971.
6. *Ibid.*
7. *Ibid.*
8. *Dictionary of American History*, Charles Scribners' Sons, 1976.
9. *FHWA by Day*, U. S. Department of Transportation (USDOT) and Federal Highway Administration (FHWA), 1995.
10. *Ibid.*
11. *Ibid.*
12. *The Automobile—How It Came, Grew and Has Changed Our Lives*, Frank Ernest Hill, Dodd, Meade and Company, 1967.
13. *Trains—The History of Railroads*, David Jefferis, Franklin Watts, Inc., 1991.
14. *The Automobile—How It Came, Grew and Has Changed Our Lives*, Frank Ernest Hill, Dodd, Mead and Company, 1967.
15. *Ibid.*
16. *Ibid.*
17. *Ibid.*
18. *Ibid.*
19. *Ibid.*
20. *Ibid.*
21. *Ibid.*

The Early Days (1900–1919)

22. *The Automobile—How It Came, Grew and Has Changed Our Lives*, Frank Ernest Hill, Dodd, Mead and Company, 1967.
23. *Ibid.*
24. *Ibid.*
25. *Public Roads*, Thomas J. Pasko, Jr., USDOT/FHWA, July/August 1998.
26. *Ibid.*
27. *Public Roads*, Richard F. Weingroff, USDOT/FHWA, Summer 1996.
28. *Ibid.*
29. *Ibid.*
30. *FHWA by Day*, USDOT/FHWA, 1995.
31. *Ibid.*
32. *Public Roads*, Richard F. Weingroff, USDOT/FHWA, Summer 1996.
33. *Ibid.*
34. *New Visions, New Directions*, AAA Association Communication, 1997.
35. *Public Roads*, Richard F. Weingroff, USDOT/FHWA, Summer 1996.
36. *Ibid.*
37. *Society for Commercial Archeology News-Journal*, Martha Carver, Fall 1994.
38. *Ibid.*
39. *Society for Commercial Archeology News-Journal*, Spring 1996.
40. *Society for Commercial Archeology News-Journal*, Martha Carver, Fall 1994.
41. *Ibid.*
42. *Lodging News*, John D. Lesure, American Hotel and Motel Association, June 1985.
43. *The American Republic*, Richard Hofstadter, Prentice Hall, 1959.

44. *Gas Station Memories*, Michael Karl Witzel, Motorbooks International, 1994.

45. *Ibid.*

46. *Ibid.*

47. *The First 100 Years*, Chevron Corporation, 1979.

48. *Ibid.*

49. *Why 66? and The Story of Performance: The Phillips Petroleum Company*, Phillips Petroleum Company.

50. *Ibid.*

51. *A Brief History of Mobil*, Mobil Corporation, 1979.

52. *Ibid.*

53. *Ibid.*

54. *Ibid.*

55. *A Story of Achievement*, Shell Oil Company, 1984.

56. *Ibid.*

57. *Ibid.*

58. *Ibid.*

59. *A Brief History of Texaco*, Texaco, Inc., 1996.

60. *Ibid.*

61. *Public Roads*, Richard F. Weingroff, USDOT/FHWA, Summer 1996.

62. *Ibid.*

63. *Ibid.*

64. *FHWA by Day*, USDOT/FHWA, 1995.

65. *Public Roads*, Richard F. Weingroff, USDOT/FHWA, Summer 1996.

66. *Ibid.*

The First Generation (1919–1945)

67. *Statistical Abstract of the United States*, Department of Commerce, Bureau of the Census.

68. *The Automobile—How It Came, Grew and Has Changed Our Lives*, Frank Ernest Hill, Dodd, Mead and Company, 1967.

69. *Ibid.*

70. Greyhound Lines, Inc. 1989.

71. *Ibid.*

72. *Ibid.*

73. *AASHTO Quarterly*, Richard F. Weingroff, AASHTO, Spring 1997.

74. *Statistical Abstract of the United States*, Department of Commerce, Bureau of the Census.

75. *AASHTO Quarterly*, Richard F. Weingroff, Spring 1997.

76. *Ibid.*

77. *Ibid.*

78. *Ibid.*

79. *Ibid.*

80. *Ibid.*

81. *Ibid.*

82. *Ibid.*

83. *Ibid.*

84. *Ibid.*

85. *Facts About the Ethyl Corporation*, Ethyl Corporation, 1996.

86. *Main Street to Miracle Mile*, Chester H. Liebs, Little, Brown and Company. 1985.

87. *Ibid.*

88. *Ibid.*

89. *Selling Sixty-Six*, Phillips Petroleum Company, 1996.

90. *Society for Commercial Archeology News-Journal*, Tania Werbizky, August 1992.

91. *Bob Davis, Apple Farms, and Home Away from Home*, John Margolies, Little, Brown and Company, 1996.

92. *Ibid.*

93. *Colonel Sanders: From Corbin to the World*, KFC Corporation, 1980.

94. *Ibid.*

95. *Ibid.*

96. *A History of A & W Restaurants*, A & W Restaurants, Inc.

97. *Ibid.*

98. *Ibid.*

99. *A Story of Sweet Success*, Dairy Queen International, 1991.

100. *Ibid.*

101. *Ibid.*

102. *Ibid.*

103. "Stuckey's Is Back—Here Today, Here Tomorrow, Stuckey's Corporation, and Highway Icon Goes Express," Robin Earl, *Convenience Store News*, February 8, 1990.

104. *Ibid.*

105. *Ibid.*

106. *Ibid.*

107. *The Verse by the Side of the Road*, Frank Rowsome, Jr., Penguin Putnam, Inc. 1965.; Phillip Morris Corporation; American Safety Razor Company.

108. *Ibid.*

109. *Wall and Water*, Guideposts Associates, Inc., 1982, and Ted Hustead, Jr. and Bill Hustead, 1998.

110. *Ibid.*

111. *Rock City—The Story*, Rock City, Inc.

112. *Ibid.*

113. *The Legacy of a Caveman*, H. Dwight Weaver and Paul Johnson.

114. *Ibid.*

115. Meramec Caverns travel pamphlet, Courtesy, Meramec Caverns.

116. *Society for Commercial Archeology News-Journal*, Janet Murray Spring/Summer 1993.

117. *Statistical Abstract of the United States*, Department of Commerce, Bureau of the Census.

118. *Accident Facts*, National Safety Council, 1991.

119. *Anxious Decades—America in Prosperity and Depression, 1920–1941*, Michael E. Parrish, W. W. Morton and Company, 1992.

120. *Ibid.*

121. *Ibid.*

122. *Ibid.*

123. *Ibid.*

124. *Ibid.*

125. *Ibid.*

126. *Public Roads*, Thomas J. Pasko, Jr., USDOT/FHWA, July/August 1998.

127. *Ibid.*

128. *The Story of America's Bridges*, Ray Spangenburg, Diane K. Moser, Facts on File, Inc., 1991.

129. *Ibid.*

130. *Ibid.*

131. *Ibid.*

132. *Ibid.*

133. *Accident Facts*, National Safety Council, 1991.

134. *Engineering News-Record*, McGraw Hill, December 21, 1939.

135. *Engineering News-Record*, C. A. B. Halvorson, McGraw Hill, October 21, 1937.

136. *Engineering News-Record*, Paul Wooton, McGraw Hill, July 22, 1937.

137. *Ibid.*

138. *Ibid.*

139. *Public Roads*, Richard F. Weingroff, USDOT/FHWA, Summer 1996.

140. *Engineering News-Record*, Paul Wooton, McGraw Hill, July 22, 1937.

141. *Engineering News-Record*, Frank T. Sheets, McGraw Hill, June 17, 1937.

142. *Public Roads*, Richard F. Weingroff, USDOT/FHWA, Summer 1996.

143. *FHWA by Day*, USDOT/FHWA, 1995.

144. *Merritt Parkway Guidelines*, The Merritt Parkway Working Group, June 1994.

145. *Ibid.*

146. *Engineering News-Record*, McGraw Hill, July 20, 1939.

147. *Engineering News-Record*, McGraw Hill, July 29, 1937.

148. *The Pennsylvania Turnpike, A History,* Applied Arts Publishers, 1995.

149. *Ibid.*

150. *Ibid.*

151. *Ibid.*

152. *Public Roads*, Richard F. Weingroff, USDOT/FHWA, Summer 1996.

153. *Historical Statistics of the United States, Colonial Times to 1970*, Department of Commerce, Bureau of the Census, 1975.

154. *Engineering News-Record*, McGraw Hill, July 21, 1938.

155. *FHWA by Day*, USDOT/FHWA, 1995.

156. *Ibid.*

157. *Ibid.*

158. *Ibid.*

159. *Statistical Abstract of the United States*, Department of Commerce, Bureau of the Census.

The Golden Age (1946–1969)

160. *FHWA by Day*, USDOT/FHWA, 1995.

161. *Fact Book*, New York Thruway Authority, 1995.

162. *Ibid.*

163. *Ibid.*

164. *Ibid.*

165. *Ibid.*

166. *Ibid.*

167. *Ibid.*

168. *A Needed Northeast Link*, New Jersey Turnpike Authority.

169. *Pennsylvania Turnpike Commission, Chronology*, Pennsylvania Turnpike Commission.

170. *Society for Commercial Archeology News-Journal*, Tania Werbizky, Fall/Winter 1992.

171. *From the Roadside to the Information Superhighway: Best Western's Integral Role in the Changing Face of Travel*, Best Western International, Inc.

172. "Klemmons Wilson: The Inn-Side Story," Frederick A. Birmingham, *Saturday Evening Post*, Winter 1971; and *The Commercial Appeal*, Susan Adler Thorp, December 1991, Holiday Inn/Bass Resorts.

173. *Ibid.*

174. *Ibid.*

175. *Ibid.*

176. *Ibid.*

177. *Ibid.*

178. *Ibid.*

179. *Ibid.*

180. *Ibid.*

181. *Ibid.*

182. "Whatever Happened to Hojo's?" John Grossman, *Sky Magazine*, July 1997, and *50th Anniversary Biography*, 1975, Howard Johnson International, Inc.

183. *Howard Johnson International: A Business History*, Maria Cimini, Howard Johnson International, Inc.

184. *Ramada—A Business History*, Ramada Franchising Systems, Inc., 1997.

185. *Travelodge—Key Facts*, Travelodge Hotels, Inc., 1998

186. "Death of the Open Road: What's Happened to Our Highways?" Herbert Brean, *Life* magazine, May 30, 1955.

187. *Interstate—The States and the Interstates*, American Assocation of State Highway and Transportation Officials, 1991.

188. *Public Roads*, Richard F. Weingroff, USDOT/FHWA, Summer 1996.

189. "Death of the Open Road: What's Happened to Our Highways?" Herbert Brean, *Life* magazine, May 30, 1955.

190. *FHWA by Day*, USDOT/FHWA, 1995.

191. *Public Roads*, Richard F. Weingroff, USDOT/FHWA, Summer 1996.

192. "Death of the Open Road: What's Happened to Our Highways?" Herbert Brean, *Life* magazine, May 30, 1955.

193. *Ibid.*

194. *Ibid.*

195. *Ibid.*

196. *Ibid.*

197. *Public Roads*, Richard F. Weingroff, USDOT/ FHWA, Summer 1996.

198. *Ibid.*

199. *Ibid.*

200. *Ibid.*

201. *Ibid.*

202. *Ibid.*

203. Federal-Aid Highway Act of 1956, Public Law 627, 23 USC 48.

204. *Public Roads*, Richard Weingraff, USDOT/ FHWA, Summer, 1996.

205. *Ibid.*

206. *FHWA by Day*, USDOT/FHWA, 1995.

207. *Public Roads*, Richard Weingroff, USDOT/ FHWA, Summer 1996.

208. *FHWA by Day*, USDOT/FHWA, 1995.

209. *MHDT News*, Steve Miller.

210. *Public Roads*, Richard Weingroff, USDOT/ FHWA, Summer 1996.

211. *Public Roads*, Thomas J. Pasko, Jr., July/August 1998.

212. *Statistical Abstract of the United States*, Department of Commerce, Bureau of Census.

213. *Main Street to Miracle Mile*, Chester H. Liebs, Little Brown and Company, 1985.

214. *Welcome to McDonald's* and *McDonald's History Listing*, McDonald's Corporation, 1996.

215. *Ibid.*

216. "Whatever Happened to Hojo's?" John Grossman, *Sky Magazine*, July 1997.

217. *Statistical Abstract of the United States*, Department of Commerce, Bureau of the Census.

218. "The Highway as Killer," Ralph Crane, *Life* magazine, May 30, 1969.

219. *Accident Facts*, National Safety Council, 1991.

220. *Public Roads*, Richard F. Weingroff, USDOT/ FHWA, Summer, 1996.

221. *Ibid.*

222. Highway Beautification Act of 1965, Public Law 89-285.

223. *Ibid.*

224. *FHWA by Day*, USDOT/FHWA, 1995.

225. *Public Roads*, Richard F. Weingroff, USDOT/ FHWA, Autumn 1993.

The Interstate Era (1970–2000)

226. *Accident Facts*, National Safety Council, 1991.

227. *Ibid.*

228. *Statistical Abstract of the United States*, Department of Commerce, Bureau of Census.

229. *Engineering News Record*, McGraw Hill, July 8, 1937.

230. *Public Roads*, Richard F. Weingroff, USDOT/ FHWA, Summer 1996.

231. *Ibid.*

232. *Ibid.*

233. *Ibid.*

234. *Ibid.*

235. *Scenic Byways on Federal Highways*, USDOT/ FHWA, 1996.

236. *Public Roads*, Jennifer Batis, USDOT/ FHWA, September/October 1998.

237. *Ibid.*

238. *Ibid.*

239. *Public Roads*, Terry Mitchell, USDOT/ FHWA, Autumn 1996.

240. *Public Roads*, David C. Smith, USDOT/ FHWA, Autumn 1996.

241. *Public Roads*, Drs. Brian Chollar and Mohammed Memon, USDOT/FHWA, September/October 1998.

242. *Public Roads*, James W. Keeley, USDOT/ FHWA, Autumn 1996.

243. *Public Roads*, James W. March, USDOT/ FHWA, January/February 1998.

244. *Ibid.*

245. *Public Roads*, Richard F. Weingroff, USDOT/ FHWA, Summer 1996.

The Future

246. Article, Carl M. Cannon, St. Paul Pioneer Press, August 5, 1990.

247. "Should the Trucks Get Bigger?" Bernard Gavzer, *Parade Magazine*, July 20, 1997.

248. *Public Roads*, Hideo Tokuyama, USDOT/ FHWA, Autumn 1996.

249. *Ibid.*

250. *Public Roads*, Christine M. Johnson, USDOT/ FHWA, September/October 1997.

251. *Ibid.*

252. *Ibid.*

253. *Public Roads*, Nita Congress, USDOT/ FHWA, Autumn 1996.

254. *Ibid.*

255. *Public Roads*, Cheryl Little, USDOT/ FHWA, September/October 1997.

256. *Public Roads*, David Smallen, USDOT/ FHWA, September/October 1998.

257. *Public Roads*, Doug Rekenthaler, Jr., USDOT/ FHWA, January/February 1998.

258. *Fact Book, 1995* and related materials, New York Thruway Authority.

259. *Public Roads*, Maria Koklanaris, USDOT/ FHWA, September/October 1997.

Index